C. S. Lewis: Mere Christian

Books by the author

Journey Into Narnia
Light Showers (poetry)
Finding the Landlord
Dante's Inferno (annotated translation)
Light in the Shadowlands
The C. S. Lewis Hoax
Creative Writing for People Who Can't Not Write
Fakes, Frauds, and Other Malarkey
How to Grow a Young Reader
Around the Year with C. S. Lewis and His Friends
A Child's Garden of Christian Verses
The Gift of Dreams
Loving Touches
Up from Eden
Lion of Judah in Never-Never Land

C. S. Lewis

MERE CHRISTIAN

Kathryn Lindskoog

Fourth Edition

Cornerstone Press Chicago
Chicago, Illinois

Fourth edition © 1997 by Kathryn Lindskoog

Third edition © 1987 by Kathryn Lindskoog

Revised edition © 1981 by Inter-Varsity Christian Fellowship
of the United States of America under the same title

First edition © 1973 by G/L Publications under the same title

ISBN 0-940895-36-6

Published by Cornerstone Press Chicago
939 W. Wilson Ave., Chicago, IL 60640

Cover photo courtesy the Marion E. Wade Center
Layout and design by Pat Peterson
Printed in the United States of America
00 99 98   4 3

Library of Congress Cataloging-in-Publication Data

Lindskoog, Kathryn Ann.
    C. S. Lewis, mere Christian   /   Kathryn Lindskoog. — 4th ed.
        p.   cm.
    Includes bibliographical references.
    ISBN 0–940895–36–6
    1. Lewis, C. S. (Clive Staples), 1898–1963—Religion.
2. Christian literature, English—History and criticism.   I. Title.
BX5199.L53L56 1997
230 '. 092—dc21   97–9967
                                                             CIP

To John, who made this book possible;
to Jonathan and Peter, who made it highly improbable.

Contents

Appendixes

Foreword

The author of this book has long been a reader and follower of C. S. Lewis. In fact, her own life was changed and deepened by reading him. Furthermore, she has the great advantage of having actually known him personally and having had his particular and hearty approval of an earlier study which she did.

Kay Lindskoog knows the works of Lewis thoroughly, not simply the latest editions but early and late ones and periodical articles by and about him. All of this is apparent in the present book, a study which endeavors to show Lewis's views topically on some of his more important beliefs. She centers her efforts on covering as precisely as possible just what Lewis thought on these topics.

It is no easy task to pull together substantially the great number and variety of Lewis's remarks over more than a quarter century's discussion of Christian themes. Kay Lindskoog has selected and organized her work with skill and genuine insight.

I think that this book will be of real value to people wishing to know what Lewis believed.

CLYDE S. KILBY
Curator Emeritus of the
Marion E. Wade Center

Acknowledgments

Acknowledgment is made to the following for permission to reprint copyrighted material:

Scripture quotations are from the *Revised Standard Version of the Bible*, copyrighted 1946, 1952 c 1971, 1973.

Excerpts from C. S. Lewis's *The Great Divorce* (copyright 1946 by Macmillan Publishing Co., Inc., renewed 1974 by Arthur Owen Barfield and Alfred Cecil Harwood), *The Last Battle* (copyright 1956 by C. S. Lewis), *The Lion, the Witch and the Wardrobe* (copyright 1950 by Macmillan Publishing Co., Inc., renewed 1978 by Arthur Owen Barfield), *Mere Christianity* (copyright 1943, 1945, 1952 by Macmillan Publishing Co., Inc.), *Miracles* (copyright 1947 by Macmillan Publishing Co., Inc., renewed 1975 by Arthur Owen Barfield and Alfred Cecil Harwood), *The Problem of Pain* (copyright 1943), *The Screwtape Letters* (copyright 1942 by C. S. Lewis), and *The Silver Chair* (copyright 1953 by Macmillan Publishing Co., Inc.) are reprinted by permission of Macmillan Publishing Co., Inc.

Excerpts from C. S. Lewis's *The Four Loves, Letters of C. S. Lewis, Letters to Malcolm, Of Other Worlds, Poems, Surprised by Joy,* and *Till We Have Faces* are reprinted by permission of Harcourt Brace Jovanovich, Inc.; copyright 1964 by the Executors of the Estate of C. S. Lewis.

Chapter 1

Introducing
C. S. Lewis:
Sincerity Personified

*"It is the message not the
messenger that has my heart."*
The Personal Heresy [1]

Part One: The First Thirty Years

C. S. Lewis is the greatest lay champion of basic Christianity
in the twentieth century. In pictures his full, ruddy face often
looks sleepy, but in life it radiated warmth, and his eyes sparkled
with wit. His clothes were rather worn and rumpled. He was
full of surprises, contrasts and a powerful undergirding consis-
tency—a man of mirth, girth and humility. For all his personal
problems and sorrows, he was a merry man.

In 1947 a writer for *Time* magazine observed, "Having lured
his reader onto the straight highway of logic, Lewis then invei-
gles him down the garden paths of orthodox theology."[2] This
figure of speech is intentionally droll, but the question is clear.
Could such a clever man as C. S. Lewis be sincere about the
Christianity he was proclaiming?

As early as 1944 the prominent correspondent and broadcaster Alistair Cooke thought not. "We may wonder at the alarming vogue of Mr. C. S. Lewis, whose harmless fantasies about the kingdoms of Good and Evil have had a modest literary success, while multitudes of readers, and British radio listeners, succumb to the charm of his more direct treatises on Christian conduct," he complained. "But the chief danger of these homilies on behavior is their assumption of modesty. It may be assumed that the personal values of several million Britons and Americans stand in imminent danger of the befuddlement at which Mr. Lewis is so transparently adroit."[3]

The fear that Lewis's charm and supposedly false modesty would win millions of lives to Christian belief and conduct may be exaggerated, but over fifty years later his influence continues. Many indeed have succumbed to the danger of conversion or of growth in the Christian life because of C. S. Lewis.

Lewis said of his own conversion, which occurred at the midpoint of his life, "Remember, I had always wanted, above all things, not to be 'interfered with.' I had wanted (mad wish) to call my soul my own. I had been far more anxious to avoid suffering than to achieve delight."[4]

From a Soft Nest

During the first nine years of Lewis's life, in County Down of Northern Ireland, he had a sunny and sensible mother who nurtured him with "cheerful and tranquil affection" as well as with intellectual stimulation. Because of the wet weather, Clive Lewis and his older brother, Warren, spent an extraordinary amount of time indoors drawing, writing and yearning for the distant green hills on the horizon. In contrast, they also spent some dazzling sandy summer days at the beach. Lewis never lost his love for the surf. Early in this period Clive decided his name should be Jacksie, and he remained Jack to his friends and family all his life. It was a rich, happy childhood, full of books.

Before Lewis could even write, he was dictating stories.

In 1908 the boys' mother died of cancer, and they were sent to a nightmarish boarding school in England. Warren Lewis later described that experience: "With his uncanny flair for making the wrong decision, my father had given us helpless children into the hands of a madman." [5]

Jack could never communicate with his well-meaning but emotionally stormy father, who was an illogical, jocular, morose, rhetorical, larger-than-life Irish lawyer. His intense desire for his sons' total confidence coexisted with an inability to really listen to what they said. "He could never empty, or silence, his own mind to make room for an alien thought."[6] Therefore he never knew what his boys' first boarding school was like; he thought he had sent them to a fine institution.

In his autobiography Lewis wryly observed that life in such a vile boarding school is in one way a good preparation for the Christian life; it teaches one to live by hope or faith. During this time, young Jack came to serious religious belief and agonized for hours in nightly prayer, trying by will power to pray sincerely and vividly before he allowed himself to crawl into his cold bed in exhaustion. This distorted Christianity was a torture he was soon glad to abandon. At some time during this miserable period, Lewis took part in his first metaphysical argument—whether the future was like a line you can't see or like a line that is not yet drawn.

At thirteen he entered an English preparatory school where he stayed until fifteen. In this phase of his life he began smoking, acquired a strong interest in the occult, accepted atheistic thought and became unchaste. As he summed it up later, he lost his faith, his virtue and his simplicity. (He later rid himself of the unchaste behavior, the atheism and the occult, but he never could break his addiction to smoking.) A great good also happened in preparatory school; his serious education began and his imaginative inner life flourished.

At fifteen, in spite of a high fever on the day of the examination, he won a scholarship to Malvern College. This was a far less happy place than his recent preparatory school. Overgrown, clumsy, totally uninterested in the drama and gossip of homosexuality that pervaded the campus, and burdened with a heavy course of study in the classics, Lewis found the emphasis on compulsory sports and the required servitude of younger students to the ruling senior athletes a dismal and exhausting routine. He was a misfit. His solace was the library, but he rarely had a chance to get into it.

Nevertheless, his inner imaginative life was as radiant and fulfilling as his outer life was grim. He was in love with the poetry and romance of Norse mythology and, to a lesser degree, Celtic and Greek mythology. He later wondered if his near adoration of false gods in whom he did not believe was the true God's way of developing within him a keen capacity for sincere worship. Lewis taught repeatedly that God can use our errors and delays for good.

As a defense against the unpleasant school situation, Lewis took refuge in his unusual intellect and began to develop a priggish sense of superiority. Even so far as God was concerned, Lewis felt rather superior. He maintained that God did not exist. He was very angry with God for not existing, and he was equally angry with him for creating a world.

When Lewis was sixteen and the First World War began, he left Malvern to go to live in lovely Surrey with an elderly Scottish tutor and his wife. No more sports and campus life. "If you want to know how I felt, imagine your own feelings on waking one morning to find that income tax or unrequited love had somehow vanished from the world."[7] This was one of the happiest times in Lewis's entire life.

His atheistic tutor, William T. Kirkpatrick, was the essence of logical discipline. Lewis's maternal grandmother in Ireland had first impressed Lewis with that eccentric tendency.

Kirkpatrick shocked Jack by challenging every idle word he uttered for a basis in fact or logic. Jack's rational mind thrived under this stimulation; he loved it. He never got over his love of ruthless mental combat with friends. In fact, one of his oldest and closest friends has said that when Lewis wasn't arguing with his friends he was usually arguing with himself. That was his one competitive sport.

In Surrey Jack had solitude, long afternoon rambles across romantic countryside, worlds of new things to learn, and the chance to buy lots of books. The most important book he bought there was a random purchase at a bookstall—a Christian fantasy by George MacDonald, who had died about ten years before in 1905. MacDonald turned out to be the most important single influence in Lewis's life, of all his favorite writers and teachers. This Scotsman did for Lewis's imagination what "Kirk" did for his logic.

About seven years later, upon learning of old Kirkpatrick's death, Lewis wrote to his father, "It was an atmosphere of unrelenting clearness and rigid honesty of thought that one breathed from living with him—and this I shall be the better for as long as I live."[8]

Ironically, it was during this time of Kirkpatrick's influence that Lewis allowed himself to be confirmed at church in Belfast and took his first Communion in total disbelief. He did it not out of indifference or conformity, but because of the force of his father's will. No one Lewis ever knew was less interested in metaphysics than his father, and no one would be able to give more inappropriate, unanswerable reasons for an atheist son to join the church. As Warren Lewis put it, the boys had been raised on the dry husks of religion offered by semipolitical churchgoing in Ulster, and apparently their father valued those husks highly. So to avoid further alienation and useless argument, Jack lied his way into the church. Years later he repented of that act.

Kirk had once written to Lewis's father, "You may make a writer or a scholar of him, but you'll not make anything else. You may make up your mind to *that*."⁹ Thus it seemed essential that he go to Oxford. Out of hundreds who applied, Lewis was rejected by New College but was one of the few admitted to University College at Oxford. All was caught up in the war, however, and on his nineteenth birthday he arrived in the front-line trenches in France.

When he was eighteen Lewis met Paddy Moore, a fellow soldier, and became involved with Paddy's mother, Janie Moore. Paddy soon died, and Lewis took care of Mrs. Moore until she died in 1951, eventually calling her his foster mother. Lewis's early attachments were enduring.

During a brief hospitalized illness in France, he first read a book by the Christian author G. K. Chesterton and, disagreeing with the man's beliefs, was conquered by his writing. He was "charmed" by the goodness of it as a man feels the charm of a woman he has no intention of marrying. Like George MacDonald, Chesterton turned out to be one of the greatest influences in Lewis's life. As Lewis put it, "A young man who wishes to remain a sound atheist cannot be too careful of his reading."¹⁰

Lewis suffered the well-known horrors of the First World War; his dreams were haunted by it for years. He returned to England to recover from wounds, and then entered Oxford in earnest. Fortunately for him, veterans were excused from the entrance exam in mathematics which he had hopelessly failed before going to France. Otherwise, he might never have qualified for his university education. Although his motherhad been a gifted mathematician, his analytical mind was grossly inaccurate with plain numerical computation.

Lewis claimed to me that he was a poor speller as well as a poor mathematician, though I hardly believed him at the time. Indeed, his personal papers show that his spelling was less than perfect, especially when he was young. His brother's was worse: he used to keep a "dairy" instead of a diary. In neither case did a few misspelled words interfere with literary excellence.

God Closes In

At Oxford, as in the army, Lewis enjoyed some admirable friends, and eventually, with resistance, followed two of them away from real atheism. He decided that the whole universe was, in the last resort, not meaningless but mental. He switched in philosophy from materialism to absolute idealism. He did not believe in God. But he and his friends could talk religiously about the Absolute, and there was no danger of Its doing anything about them. As he put it, "It would never come 'here,' never (to be blunt) make a nuisance of Itself. . . . There was nothing to fear; better still, nothing to obey."[11]

Trying to teach philosophy forced Lewis to get more specific about his idea of the Absolute. He began to refer to It as an impersonal Spirit, still refusing to use the word *God*. One day on a now-famous bus ride, Lewis got the impression that he was shutting something out and that he could either open up or keep himself closed in. He freely chose to expose himself, for whatever that might mean.

Something strange began to happen after that. Everyone seemed to start challenging him to live his philosophy instead of playing at it intellectually. When he tried, he was shocked at the tangle of badness he found inside himself; he had never known his own spiritual inadequacy before. Of this crisis period he said, "Amiable agnostics will talk cheerfully about 'man's search for God.' To me, as I was then, they might as well have talked about the mouse's search for the cat."[12]

Lewis's account of his conversion is often quoted. "You must picture me alone in that room in Magdalen, night after night, feeling, whenever my mind lifted even for a second from my work, the steady, unrelenting approach of Him whom I so

earnestly desired not to meet. That which I greatly feared had
at last come upon me. In the Trinity [spring] Term of 1929 I
gave in, and admitted that God was God, and knelt and prayed:
perhaps, that night, the most dejected and reluctant convert in
all England."[13]

It also happened that in 1929 Lewis's father died of cancer,
and Lewis had to stay with him near the end. Since it is known
that in the throes of change people are more open to conversion, the double import of 1929 in Lewis's life could be more
than coincidence. But Lewis did not connect the two events.

At this point Lewis did not believe in Christ, only in God.
Nevertheless, he became a churchgoer, which would have
pleased his father, as a symbol of his new belief in God.
Analyzing his alternatives, he decided that Hinduism and
Christianity were the only possible choices for him. "Whatever
you could find elsewhere you could find better in one of
these."[14] Reason and history led him to choose Christianity, but
he put it off because the Incarnation would bring God near in
a new way, and Lewis never wanted God that close. He
realized, however, that his reluctance was no grounds for
evading the hard truth. Two Christian friends, J. R. R. Tolkien
and Hugo Dyson, influenced him in the final stage of his
conversion.

One sunny morning in 1931 he was riding to the Whipsnade
zoo in the sidecar of Warren's motorcycle. "When we set out I
did not believe that Jesus Christ is the Son of God, and when
we reached the zoo I did."[15] Lewis's decision was that quiet.

Part Two: A Pattern Emerges

Jack had asked Warren in a letter once, "Are you often struck,
when you become sufficiently intimate with other people to
know something of their development, how *late* their lives
begin, so to speak?"[16] Lewis had no way of knowing, but his

time on earth was just half over when, as he put it, he got out of the woods and onto the road to Jerusalem.

Looking back in his later years, Lewis observed, "I feel the whole of one's youth to be immensely important and even of immense length. The gradual *reading* of one's own life, seeing a pattern emerge, is a great illumination at our age."[17]

The second half of Lewis's life, the Christian half, mirrors the overall pattern of the first half. His first nine years had been spent blissfully in Ireland with his mother and the family; then she died. The next twenty-three years were spent mainly in England in scholarly pursuits. During those twenty-three years he had moved up from the position of a helpless child in an insane boarding school to that of a hardworking but low-paid tutor and lecturer at Magdalen College in Oxford. He had published two widely unread books of verse, and his dreams of becoming a great poet were fading.

Lewis became a Christian at thirty-two. After his conversion, his life proceeded more successfully and monotonously for another twenty-three years, and then it closed with a special nine-year final chapter full of love and loss.

At thirty-two, Lewis had already spent over ten years (with twenty more to come) caring for his "foster-mother" Mrs. Moore. She became increasingly difficult to live with as years went by. Her daughter Maureen was also part of the Lewis household for many years. Unfortunately, Mrs. Moore did not follow Lewis in his conversion to Christianity,[18] but she did follow him in his move to Headington, four miles outside Oxford, in 1930. Soon Warren Lewis, a military man with historical and literary interests, came to live with Jack permanently.

Two of Lewis's main pleasures in life were long walks in the country and merry, intellectual conversation all evening with a small group of good friends.

Success at Last

When he was thirty-five, Lewis published his first book of prose, *The Pilgrim's Regress*, in which he told by allegory the story of his feelings and beliefs, ending with his conversion. Twenty years later, he wrote to a lady: "I don't wonder that you got fogged in *Pilgrim's Regress*. It was my first religious book and I didn't then know how to make things easy. I was not even trying to very much, because in those days I never dreamed I would become a 'popular' author and hoped for no readers outside a small 'highbrow' circle."[19] The book didn't have the impact he would have liked, but it is still being bought and read and quoted. In it were the seeds of much of his later writing.

In the thirty years from *The Pilgrim's Regress* to his own death, Lewis published thirty-four other books, as well as almost three hundred shorter items such as poems, essays and letters. His big breakthrough came in 1936 when he published *The Allegory of Love*, a literary study of medieval literature that in itself would assure him permanent scholarly respect and remembrance. Another highlight in his career was the publishing of *The Screwtape Letters* in 1942. He did not consider it one of his best books (he told me he preferred *The Great Divorce*), but it made him famous with the general public and earned him a place on the cover of *Time* magazine in 1947. Three years later the first of his masterful Narnian series for children appeared.

In 1951 the oppressive Mrs. Moore died, and that year Lewis wrote to a friend, "Everything without, and many things within, are marvelously well at present."[20] During most of his thirty years at Oxford, Lewis dutifully gave of himself at home to Mrs. Moore, who once said that she considered him a good maid. At school he devoted his time to the pupils he privately tutored in his apartment. These two types of service were generally burdensome and frustrating to him; the work he enjoyed was his immensely popular lecturing and his writing. If he had had more time, he could have written more.

Lewis gave away money more gladly than time. Once he had a good income, he gave at least two-thirds of his royalties to people in need. He might have given away more than that if his friend and lawyer Owen Barfield had not organized his financial affairs. Lewis lived in a pleasant country home looking out on a lovely pond and rolling hills; he kept the house dowdily furnished, avoided new clothes as much as possible and ate plain food with lots to drink. Life was comfortable but simple. A friend called him "surely one of the most cheerful givers, according to his means, who ever lived."[21] He had a horror of poverty, but no love of wealth.

Probably the most sacrificial form of unselfishness for Lewis was his letter writing. As his fame grew, strangers as well as acquaintances wrote to him to argue or seek help and benefit of all kinds. They also wrote to express appreciation or build friendships, and Lewis never failed to answer personally. His hand grew rheumatic; his time grew shorter, and his mail increased. But C. S. Lewis doggedly answered most of his mail by hand, personally, overwhelmed by the importance of the human soul of every person who contacted him. Sometimes his brother, who served as his secretary, pecked out letters for him on the typewriter. (After Lewis's death his brother was deeply touched to learn that many people saved and treasured their letters from Lewis.) For some correspondents, Lewis became a pastoral counselor. In fact, some of his letters have been collected into books, and they are brilliant.

When I wrote to him in 1956 and asked if I might hear him lecture or see him that summer while I studied in England, he promptly invited me to four o'clock tea. My excitement bordered on terror; there was no one else in the world I so much wanted to meet. He hosted me at the Royal Oxford Hotel, talking with me jovially for a generous hour and a quarter, as if an American college girl, awkward with awe, was well worth his time and kindliness.

He asked me to pour the tea, and I was too young and embarrassed to admit that I had not yet learned to pour it as the British do. As a result, I held the teapot and milk pitcher poised over his cup for a very long time as we talked, before I finally muddled through. Later, to my chagrin, I noticed that in *Out of the Silent Planet,* the villain irritated the hero by agreeing to serve a beverage and then holding it suspended in the air while he talked instead. At the time, all I had sensed from Lewis was warmth and interest.

I was disappointed when Lewis assured me, with laughter, that he had no intention of ever coming to the United States. There went my dream of attending his lectures.

Aside from his many crossings to Ireland, Lewis's moves and travels were mainly intellectual. Mentally, he might be spending time in medieval France or on Mars, but physically he liked to stay home in his set routine. He lived thirty-three years in his house called The Kilns by an old quarry at Headington outside Oxford. Once a reporter from *Time* magazine asked him if his life was not monotonous. He replied, "Yes, indeed," because he liked monotony.

Final Changes

Things started changing in 1954 when he began the last nine years of his life, which rivaled in happiness and pain the first nine years. In 1954 he left his post at Oxford, after thirty years, for a much better position at Magdalene College, Cambridge. There, with great honor, he was made professor of Medieval and Renaissance English literature. The grinding tutorials were over. He enjoyed his new setting and company immensely and even found pleasure in his leisurely train rides home to Oxford for weekends and vacations.

In 1954 Lewis had already become friends with the American author Joy Davidman Gresham. She was an American Jew by birth. She was married to William Lindsay Gresham, a fellow writer whom she had met in the Communist party. The Greshams became Christians, largely through the influence of Lewis's books. However, their marriage was damaged by his alchoholism and involvement with other women. In 1953, she and her two sons moved to England.

Lewis had once remarked that he preferred treelike people to flowerlike people, "the staunch and knotty and storm-enduring kind to the frilly and fragrant and easily withered."[22] Joy, although attractive and seventeen years younger than Lewis, was a staunch and knotty intellectual companion for him. She was also storm-enduring.

Back in 1926 Lewis had informed his father in a letter that in spite of the wiles of the female students, he was not yet engaged to be married. Thirty years had passed. Then in April 1956, he "married" Joy in a secret civil ceremony to enable her to remain in England. Their marriage was only a legal fiction at that point; they remained neighbors. When I met Lewis in July 1956, we laughed about the silly public idea that he was a woman-hater, and he told me that some poor addled woman in the United States kept proposing to him. But, having a normal sense of privacy about his personal life, he never hinted at the existence of his good friend Joy to whom he had just dedicated *Till We Have Faces*.

Then everything changed. In the spring of 1957 a priest married the two of them in a Christian ceremony at her bedside in a hospital where she lay dying of cancer. Apparently in response to prayer and the laying on of hands, she unexpectedly rallied. They had three extremely happy years together at The Kilns. They took a brief trip to Greece together to fulfill her dream, and then she died, at forty-five.

During those six most fulfilling years, Lewis's own health had been ominously deteriorating; when he married Joy, he was no longer very well himself. His own medical facts were of no more interest to him than the facts of his financial affairs. The basic trouble was an enlarged prostate gland which caused irreparable damage to the kidneys. The bad kidneys caused complications which seriously damaged his heart. The kidney trouble was apparently also the cause of his osteoporosis, decalcification of the bones, which was painful and crippling. That was the end of his country walking. After Joy's death, Lewis went on with his work, as busy as ever. But his Joy was gone; his health was gone, and the time for work was short. In the summer of 1961 he was severely ill. He greatly needed prostate surgery, but he was too weak for it. He endured a catheter, a low protein diet, many blood transfusions, sleep problems, and the inability to walk upstairs. Worse yet, he lost his ability to write fiction; his extraordinary pictorial imagination was gone.

In the dark war year of 1940 Lewis had remarked to his brother, "What a grim business even a happy human life is when you read it rapidly through to the inevitable end."[23] In July 1963 Lewis had a flare-up of uremia and entered into a coma; he was even given extreme unction by an Anglican priest. A few hours later he unexpectedly recovered in time to ask for afternoon tea. He had never liked to miss late afternoon tea; he considered it essential.

He had to send a resignation to his beloved Cambridge. Then in October it became clear that the end was near—or, as Lewis might have put it, the beginning. He spent his last weeks with his lifetime companion, Warren.

In one of his last letters Lewis commented about death, "It is all rather fun—solemn fun—isn't it?"[24] He died on November 22, 1963, at home in his room, following late afternoon tea. Within an hour or so he was followed by John F. Kennedy, who died near midday in Dallas, Texas. Lewis was quietly buried under a yew tree in the yard of the little stone church where he was a member at Headington. His brother Warren was too grief-stricken to attend the funeral. He had the Shakespeare quotation which had been on their father's calendar the day of their mother's death, "Men must endure their going hence," inscribed on the tombstone. Ten years later Warren was buried there also, under the same stone.

Lewis's royalties were left to his wife's two sons; his thirty-seven books were left to us. Since then more than twenty-five books of Lewis materials have been published. Most of these have been edited by one of Lewis's American admirers, Walter Hooper, who met Lewis on a summer vacation in 1963, moved to England in 1964 and launched his career as Lewis's indefatigable editor and manager of the literary estate.

Shortly after C. S. Lewis died, Dr. Clyde S. Kilby of Wheaton College wrote that Lewis was "a man who had won, inside and deep, a battle against pose, evasion, expedience, and the ever-so-little lie and who wished with all his heart to honor truth in every idea passing through his mind."[25] The perspective of the passing years certainly verifies Kilby's words.

Further Reading about C. S. Lewis

"The great man, just because of his greatness, is much more intelligible than his modern commentator."[26]
Jack: A Life of C. S. Lewis by George Sayer is the most complete, authoritative, and accurate Lewis biography. Fortunately, it is also good reading.
Surprised by Joy by C. S. Lewis has become a classic in the field of spiritual autobiography. It tells the story of the first half of his life.
Letters of C. S. Lewis, edited with a memoir by W. H. Lewis, not only crowns a wide selection of Lewis's personal letters with a touching account of his life story, but includes good photos of the Lewis family. (The second edition includes an original preface by Walter Hooper introducing some unfortunate allegations and errors.)
They Stand Together, edited by Walter Hooper, is a collection of letters (1914–1963) from C. S. Lewis to his Irish friend Arthur

Greeves. (Several derogatory allegations about Warren Lewis in the introduction are wrong and should be disregarded.)

Letters to an American Lady, edited by Clyde Kilby, includes over a hundred brief letters that Lewis wrote to a troubled woman between 1950 and his death in 1963.

All My Road before Me: The Diary of C. S. Lewis, 1922–1927, edited by Walter Hooper, includes most of Lewis's erratic diary jottings during that busy pre-Christian period.

Brothers and Friends: The Diaries of Major Warren Hamilton Lewis, edited by Clyde S. Kilby and Marjorie Lamp Mead, provides a warm, intimate family view of C. S. Lewis.

C. S. Lewis: Images of His World by Douglas Gilbert and Clyde S. Kilby is a large picture album with a valuable text.

C. S. Lewis, A Biography by Roger Lancelyn Green and Walter Hooper was the first biography of Lewis. (Although it contains much valuable information, it is salted with crucial misinformation that would have upset Lewis.)

The Pilgrim's Regress by C. S. Lewis is a brilliant semiautobiographical fantasy tracing a young man's long journey back to Christian belief.

Finding the Landlord: A Guidebook to C. S. Lewis's **Pilgrim's Regress** by Kathryn Lindskoog shows how Lewis's first Christian book fit into his life as well as how his life fit into the book.

And God Came In: The Extraordinary Story of Joy Davidman by Lyle Dorsett tells the life story of C. S. Lewis's wife.

Smoke on the Mountain: An Interpretation of the Ten Commandments by Joy Davidman was written before she married C. S. Lewis, but shows his strong influence in her life and thinking.

Shadowlands: The Story of C. S. Lewis and Joy Davidman by Brian Sibley was the basis of the BBC film "Shadowlands," but the book is more inclusive and more factual than the drama.

Clive Staples Lewis, A Dramatic Life by William Griffin is a biography made up of several hundred vignettes, some factual and others only imaginative supposals. Unfortunately, readers aren't told which are which.

The Inklings by Humphrey Carpenter is a readable account of Lewis's life and the friends who were a large part of it. It is dedicated to Lewis's best friend of all, his brother Warren.

A Severe Mercy by Sheldon Vanauken shows how Lewis shared his faith as a correspondent and shared his life as a friend.

The Christian World of C. S. Lewis by Clyde S. Kilby is an early survey of the man, his writings and his themes.

Light on C. S. Lewis, edited by Jocelyn Gibb, is the earliest collection of reminiscences about C. S. Lewis by several people who knew him.

C. S. Lewis at the Breakfast Table, edited by James Como, includes reminiscences about Lewis from a variety of people including John Wain and Robert Havard.

In Search of C. S. Lewis, edited by Stephen Schofield, contains reminiscences about C. S. Lewis from a variety of people including Kenneth Tynan and Ruth Pitter.

C. S. Lewis, A Biography by A. N. Wilson is in fact a poison-pen biography of C. S. Lewis by a prominent atheist, a book remarkable for hundreds of errors and outright misrepresentations.

Light in the Shadowlands: Protecting the Real C. S. Lewis by Kathryn Lindskoog includes the previously unknown novel he began in 1927 and other revelations up to and including major developments in the 1990s.

Notes

1. C. S. Lewis and E. M. W. Tillyard, *The Personal Heresy* (London: Oxford Univ. Press, 1939), p. 103.
2. *Time*, 8 September 1947.

3. Alistair Cooke, *New Republic,* 24 April 1944.

4. C. S. Lewis, *Surprised By Joy* (New York: Harcourt Brace Jovanovich, 1955), p. 228.

5. C. S. Lewis, *Letters of C. S. Lewis* (New York: Harcourt Brace Jovanovich, 1966), pp. 3–4.

6. Lewis, *Surprised by Joy,* p. 184.

7. Ibid., p. 129.

8. Lewis, *Letters of C. S. Lewis,* p. 54.

9. Lewis, *Surprised by Joy,* p. 183.

10. Ibid., p. 191.

11. Ibid., p. 210.

12. Ibid., p. 227.

13. Ibid., p. 228.

14. Ibid., p. 235.

15. Ibid., p. 237.

16. Lewis, *Letters of C. S. Lewis,* p. 123.

17. Ibid., p. 266. Lewis wrote this to his friend Dom Bede Griffiths.

18. Ibid., p. 195.

19. Ibid., pp. 248–49.

20. Ibid., p. 232.

21. John Lawlor, "The Tutor and the Scholar," in *Light on C. S. Lewis,* ed. Jocelyn Gibb (London: Geoffrey Bles, 1965), p. 73.

22. Lewis, *Letters of C. S. Lewis,* p. 253.

23. Ibid., p. 187.

24. Ibid., p. 307.

25. Clyde S. Kilby, *The Christian World of C. S. Lewis* (Grand Rapids, Mich.: Eerdmans, 1964), p. 5.

26. C. S. Lewis, *God in the Dock* (Grand Rapids, Mich.: Eerdmans, 1970), p. 200.

Reality:
What is Life
All About?

Chapter 2

God

"When you are arguing against Him you are arguing against the very power that makes you able to argue at all."
Mere Christianity [1]

Part One: Basic Facts About God

When he was teetering on the edge of his shaky philosophy and in danger of falling down into the arms of God, C. S. Lewis wrote the following good-humored cry for help to his friend Owen Barfield:

> Terrible things are happening to me. The 'Spirit' or 'Real I' is showing an alarming tendency to become much more personal and is taking the offensive, and behaving just like God. You'd better come on Monday at the latest or I may have entered a monastery.[2]

Probably neither Owen Barfield nor anyone else could have saved C. S. Lewis from salvation at that point. He fell into grace. But instead of simply entering a monastery, he did worse. He ended up publicly explaining and openly defending his personal God to millions of listeners and readers. Such undignified behavior embarrassed the hierarchy at his college at Oxford and cost Lewis his chance of ever advancing to a higher position on the faculty there.

Lewis learned that if you speak about beauty, truth or goodness, and about God as a great spiritual force of some kind, people will remain friendly. But he found that the temperature drops when you discuss a God who gives definite commands, who does definite acts, who has definite ideas and character.

Many people mistakenly consider a personal God a crude or primitive idea. That is historically inaccurate. Primitive or not, many people simply do not want a God who does things and demands things. Lewis didn't either. But Lewis decided that God is indeed more personal than we can imagine.

Of course this presumes that there is a God in the first place. That can't be absolutely proved, Lewis admits. (Nevertheless he argues well for the existence of God in *Mere Christianity* and *The Problem of Pain*.) Arguments aside, if we fully understand *what* God is we should see that there is no question *whether* he is. He is the center of all existence, the fountain of facthood. But to some he is discoverable everywhere, and to others nowhere. "Much depends on the seeing eye."[3]

Suppose that the religion of shellfish included a hazy belief in Man. Lewis pretended that a wise, mystical limpet or barnacle, in a moment of religious vision, caught a glimpse of what Man is. In trying to explain to his followers, he reports that Man has no shell, is not attached to a rock, and is not surrounded by water. His first followers grasp something of what he means. But eventually many barnacles assume that Man is just a shapeless blob of jelly (no shell), has no location at all (no rock), and doesn't eat (no water to drift food to him). That kind of Man would certainly seem less definite and active than barnacles.

That is the very kind of mistake we often make in trying to imagine God as unchangeable, invisible, infinite and eternal. He becomes a vague blur. We are apt to miss his overwhelming life, energy, joy and concreteness, and to think of him as less definite than ourselves.

Lewis insists that God is far more personal than we are, as Man is more personal than a shellfish. Obeying him and worshiping him are the best means to realizing his concreteness and reality. Of course it is easier and less costly to think of him as a formless life-force surging through us, as Lewis had preferred. But as he put it, he found "God Himself, alive, pulling at the other end of the cord, perhaps approaching at an infinite speed, the hunter, king, husband . . ."[4]

The Christian faith begins with the local altar, the traditional feast and the treasured memories of God's judgments, promises and mercies. It moves from such concrete things as circumcision, the Passover, the Ark and the Temple to the stable at Bethlehem, the hill of Calvary and the emptied rock tomb. Today we have baptism and holy Communion. Although God is the bodiless, timeless, transcendent Ground of the whole universe, he is also the Lord who is "not far from any one of us," the utterly concrete Being (far more concrete than we) whom man can fear, love, address and "taste."[5]

Lewis claims that non-Christians who say that God is beyond personality really think of him as something impersonal, less than personal. If you want that kind of god, there are all kinds of religions to choose from. Christians, on the other hand, find God beyond personality because he is *more* than a person. If you are looking for a God who is superpersonal, more than a person, then you have no choice. The Christian idea is the only one on the market.

God Is Good

One morning in church at the outbreak of World War II, Lewis's minister asked God to "prosper our righteous cause." Lewis suggested to him afterward that it is too audacious to tell God that our cause is righteous, because God may have his own point of view on that. Lewis considered Hitler an evil genius who must be defeated, but he could only hope that God agreed. "You never know with Him," he concluded![6]

Lewis was no pantheist. He did not believe that God was present equally in Hitler and Jesus, in a cancer and in a rose. Lewis insisted above all else that God is good. He told one letter writer that there are two things one must *not* do: (a) believe that God is in any way evil—"in him is no darkness at all"; (b) throw out any Scripture passage that seems to show evil in him. Instead, we must save such passages until we understand them better.

Is it surprising that God's goodness is not simple? "It is no good asking for a simple religion. After all, real things are not simple. They look simple, but they are not."[7] If we had our choice, Lewis guesses, most of us would choose a good God who is a grandfatherly ruler, "whose plan for the universe was simply that it might be truly said at the end of each day, 'a good time was had by all.'"[8] Of course, with our own friends, lovers and children, we want more than that. We want them to develop and become all that they can be. We would rather have them suffer profitably than be happy in a self-destructive way. "If God is Love, He is, by definition, something more than mere kindness."[9]

The last two stanzas of Lewis's poem "Love's As Warm As Tears" vividly contrast certain basic kinds of good:

> Love's as fresh as spring,
>   Love is spring;
> Bird-song hung in the air,
> Cool smells in a wood,
> Whispering "Dare! Dare!"
> To sap, to blood,
> Telling "Ease, safety, rest,
> Are good; not best."

Love's as hard as nails,
  Love is nails:
Blunt, thick, hammered through
The medial nerves of One
Who, having made us, knew
The thing He had done,
Seeing (with all that is)
Our cross, and His.[10]

Sacrifice is at the heart of Lewis's strange pagan novel *Till We Have Faces*. It is written in two parts. The first part ends with the bitter old queen accusing the gods of being evil. "Why must holy places be dark places? I say, therefore, that there is no creature (toad, scorpion, or serpent) so noxious to man as the gods. Let them answer my charge if they can . . . they have no answer."[11] As she dies, she admits her error and ends the second part this way. "I ended my first book with the words *No answer*. I know now, Lord, why you utter no answer. You are yourself the answer. Before your face questions die away. . . ."[12]

There is no need, however, to worry that God's goodness could be the opposite of our idea of goodness. People in almost any society have the same basic ideas of justice and right. People know that some things are bad and meaningless. People make many mistaken judgments, of course, but God makes none, because he is wiser. If he is a good God at all, he stands for justice and right. (If we found him to be a god of hate, death, cruelty and waste, we would have no need to obey him and worship him, unless through fear.) His goodness differs from ours only in that ours is imperfect and incomplete and his is perfect and complete. We are children drawing crooked wheels; his goodness is a perfect circle.

And how can all this theoretical goodness seem real on the emotional level where we are usually living? Lewis told what it meant to the children in *The Magician's Nephew* just as they were returning from Narnia to their home in London.

> Both the children were looking up into the Lion's face as he spoke these words. And all at once (they never knew exactly how it happened) the face seemed to be a sea of tossing gold in which they were floating, and such a sweetness and power rolled about them and over them and entered into them that they felt they had never really been happy or wise or good, or even alive and awake, before. And the memory of that moment stayed with them always, so that as long as they both lived, if ever they were sad or afraid or angry, the thought of all that golden goodness, and the feeling that it was still there, quite close, just round some corner or just behind some door, would come back and make them sure, deep down inside, that all was well."[13]

Lewis believed that next to Christianity dualism was the manliest and most sensible creed. It teaches that there are two equal powers at the back of everything, one good and one bad. They fight an endless war. Both existed from eternity. One likes hatred and cruelty; the other likes love and mercy.

Christianity agrees with dualism about the war between a good power and an evil one. But Christianity teaches that the evil power is a parasite, a fallen angel, created by the good power. This war is a civil war, a rebellion, and we humans happen to inhabit enemy-occupied territory.

Wickedness is real, but it always turns out to be the pursuit of some good in the wrong way. "Goodness is, so to speak, itself; badness is only spoiled goodness."[14] You cannot have the perversion of a good thing until you first have the good thing itself. People can do an act of kindness sacrificially, simply because kindness is good. But people commit cruelty only because it is pleasant or useful to them, not simply because cruelty is bad. Cruelty is not as real as kindness; it depends on kindness. Satan was an angel created good, but he went bad.

Lewis knew that someone would ask him, "Do you really mean, at this time of day, to re-introduce our old friend, the devil—hoofs and horns and all?" He answered that he is not particular about the hoofs and horns, but that in other respects his answer is "Yes, I do."[15]

Lewis warned against thinking of Satan as an equal of God. He also warned against thinking that Satan and God are really one and the same. In the seventh and last story of Narnia, *The Last Battle,* the worship of the evil god Tash is forced upon the people of Narnia. A talking lamb objects, "Please, I can't understand. What have we to do with the Calormenes? We belong to Aslan. They belong to Tash. They have a god called Tash. They say he has four arms and the head of a vulture. They kill men on his altar. . . ."

The wicked Ape who was plotting the takeover of Narnia answered this way. "Tash is only another name for Aslan. All that old idea of us being right and the Calormenes wrong is silly. We know better now. The Calormenes use different words but we all mean the same thing. Tash and Aslan are only two different names for you know Who. That's why there can never be any quarrel between them. Get that into your heads, you stupid brutes. Tash is Aslan: Aslan is Tash."[16]

The Ape and his cohorts didn't really believe in Tash or Aslan in the beginning, but at the climax of the book and the end of Narnia, the terrible Tash came for them. He was the Anti-Aslan. Tash could not take any follower of Aslan; Aslan stood behind Tash and said, in a voice as strong and calm as the summer sea, "Begone Monster, and take your lawful prey to your own place: in the name of Aslan and Aslan's great Father, the Emperor-over-sea."[17]

Lewis was not fooling in this children's series, his science fiction books and *The Screwtape Letters* when he pitted a strong, crafty evil force against God. He was not fooling when God won in the end. God and Satan are not twins.

Lewis claimed that there is another astonishing misconception in the modern mind: that Jesus preached a simple and kindly religion which St. Paul later complicated and made cruel. In contrast, Lewis exclaims, all the most terrifying passages came from the mouth of Christ.

For example, it was Christ, not Paul, who said that a wide gate and easy way lead to destruction, and that many go that way. Few find the way that leads to life, he continued, for there the gate is narrow and the way is hard. Furthermore, many who call Christ Lord and have done mighty works in his name will be turned away with his words, "I never knew you; depart from me, you evildoers" (Mt. 7:23). "You serpents, you brood of vipers, how are you to escape being sentenced to hell?" (Mt. 23:33).

In *The Lion, the Witch and the Wardrobe*, the first of Lewis's books for children, a pair of friendly beavers are telling the four children from England about the true ruler of Narnia, Aslan.

> Mrs. Beaver explains, "If there's anyone who can appear before Aslan without their knees knocking, they're either braver than most or else just silly."
>
> "Then he isn't safe?" said Lucy.
>
> "Safe?" said Mr. Beaver. "Don't you hear what Mrs. Beaver tells you? Who said anything about safe? 'Course he isn't safe. But he's good. He's the King, I tell you."
>
> "I'm longing to see him," said Peter, "even if I do feel frightened when it comes to the point."
>
> "That's right, Son of Adam," said Mr. Beaver, bringing his paw down on the table with a crash that made all the cups and saucers rattle. "And so you shall. . . ."[18]

After the children have met Aslan and grown to love him, the two girls, Lucy and Susan, have a wild romp with him on the morning of his resurrection. He led them round and round the hilltop, diving between them, letting them almost catch his tail, bounding out of their reach, tossing them in the air with his huge velveted paws and catching them, stopping unexpectedly so that all three rolled together in a laughing heap of fur and arms and legs. Lucy could never make up her mind if it was more like playing with a thunderstorm or playing with a kitten; no one has ever had such a romp except in Narnia. Although the girls had been up all night sorrowing, they found themselves no longer tired or hungry or thirsty when the romp was over.

Then Aslan stood up to right wrongs in the land. He opened his mouth to roar, and his face became so terrible the girls did not dare to look at it. All the trees in front of him bent before the blast of his roaring like grass in the wind.

Later, after the great battle and the coronation, Aslan quietly slipped away. The Kings and Queens said nothing about it, because they had been warned by Mr. Beaver beforehand. "He'll be coming and going. One day you'll see him and another you won't. He doesn't like being tied down—and of course he has other countries to attend to. It's quite all right. He'll often drop in. Only you mustn't press him. He's wild, you know. Not like a *tame* lion."[19]

In the fourth Narnian book, *The Silver Chair*, a girl named Jill found herself transported to the land of Aslan and stranded alone in a strange forest because of her own pride and foolishness. She became extremely thirsty because of her crying, and when she found a stream she also found the Lion lying beside it. The Lion told her if she was thirsty to come and drink. The voice was not like a man's, but deeper, wilder and stronger—"a sort of heavy, golden voice."

"May I—could I—would you mind going away while I do?" said Jill.

The Lion answered this only by a look and a very low growl. And as Jill gazed at its motionless bulk, she realized that she might as well have asked the whole mountain to move aside for her convenience.

The delicious rippling noise of the stream was driving her nearly frantic.

"Will you promise not to—do anything to me, if I do come?" said Jill.

"I make no promise," said the Lion.

Jill was so thirsty now that, without noticing it, she had come a step nearer.

"*Do* you eat girls?" she said.

"I have swallowed up girls and boys, women and men, kings and emperors, cities and realms," said the Lion. It didn't say this as if it were boasting, nor as if it were sorry, nor as if it were angry. It just said it.

"I daren't come and drink," said Jill.

"Then you will die of thirst," said the Lion.

"Oh dear!" said Jill, coming another step nearer. "I suppose I must go and look for another stream then."

"There is no other stream," said the Lion.[20]

Part Two: Christian Theology

Lewis more than once likened our personal glimpses of God to our glimpse of a fringe of the ocean when we walk on the beach. Mystical or personal experiences of God are real but fragmentary, like a walk on the beach. Christian theology is different; it is like a map of the Atlantic. Reading a map is less real and less exciting than being at the beach. But one cannot cross the Atlantic without using a map, and one will not get eternal life by simply feeling the presence of God in a vague way. The map is based on the experiences of hundreds and thousands of people who have sailed the real Atlantic. Theology is based upon the experiences of hundreds and thousands of people who were really in touch with God.

Lewis thought that anyone who wants to think about God at all would like to have the clearest and most accurate ideas about him which are available. One who doesn't learn any theology will have a lot of wrong ideas about God—bad, muddled, out-of-date ideas (often considered new and novel). In fact, Lewis claimed that to carelessly believe in the popular religion of modern England is retrogression, like believing the earth is flat.

When J. A. T. Robinson came out with his book *Honest to God* in 1963, Lewis gently scalped him in a brief article entitled "Must Our Image of God Go?" He comments that there is hardly any novelty in Robinson's correct ideas about God not being geographically above us any more than he is below us. That idea is both ancient and biblical. Robinson was the Bishop of Woolwich, and in one of Lewis's last books he twitted him in passing: "Among Deists—or perhaps in Woolwich, if the laity there really think God is to be sought in the sky—one must emphasize the divine presence in my neighbour, my dog, my cabbagepatch!"[21]

Lewis felt that Robinson was unclear about the nature of God, possibly due to poor writing rather than muddy thinking. At any rate Lewis saw no reason for any excitement about the "new" ideas in this particular theological fad. What he felt most people needed was a clear, vivid presentation of the Christian creeds, not sensational debunking of supposedly traditional misconceptions.

The basic fact of Christian theology is the Trinity. That is a difficult concept indeed. As Lewis said, if we were making up Christianity we could make it easier. Invented religions are simpler, because they don't have to deal with facts. Christian theology, even more than nuclear physics, deals with fact. And so it is bound to be complex.

How could there be three persons in one? Lewis gives the example of three dimensions. If we lived in one dimension we could only envision a straight line. In two dimensions, we could draw many flat squares. But with three dimensions we can join six flat squares together and get a cube. A two-dimensional person couldn't imagine a three-dimensional object, as a paper doll couldn't understand a basketball. There are six sides to a cube, but they are part of the same cube. There are three persons in the Trinity, but it is all one God. And we do not live in such a realm that we can quite understand that now. To us, persons are all separate.

Lewis guesses that people will ask what is the use of a doctrine like that if we can't understand it. The use is to experience it.

When Christians pray, they are trying to get in touch with God. But God inside them, the Holy Spirit, is prompting them to pray. And Christ, who has taught them of God, is beside them helping them pray, praying for them.

The terms *Father* and *Son* are misleading in one way. They give the impression that the First Person of the Trinity used to be without the Second Person and then created him. Lewis tries to explain it with other terms, such as light from a fire being the expression of that fire. But such words leave out the personhood and the love. So Lewis hastens back to the words of the Bible, *Father* and *Son*. "Naturally, God knows how to describe Himself much better than we know how to describe Him. He knows that Father and Son is more like the relationship between the First and Second Persons than anything else we can think of."[22]

Lewis also defended the picture of God as a righteous king. He reacted against the idea some people have that when we do wrong we are tangling with a divine live wire rather than angering our king. "What do you suppose you have gained by substituting the image of a live wire for that of an angered majesty?" he asked. "You have shut us all up in despair, for the angry can forgive, and electricity can't."[23]

Lewis had less to say about the Third Person of the Trinity than about the first two; the Holy Spirit works quietly within us. He believed that the Holy Spirit can guide people's decisions from within when they make them with the intention of pleasing God. But the Holy Spirit also speaks through Scripture, the church, Christian friends, books and other sources.

Lewis wrote to one very excited lady who felt that something wonderful had happened to her. He urged her not to depend upon her sensations, which are merely the response of one's nervous system. He advised her, "Accept these sensations with thankfulness as birthday cards from God, but remember that they are only greetings, not the real gift. I mean that it is not the sensations that are the real thing. The real thing is the gift of the Holy Spirit which can't usually be—perhaps not ever—experienced as a sensation or emotion."[24]

As incredible as it sounds, Christians believe that the eternal, all-knowing, all-powerful God of everything entered into his creation to be born as a human being. It was the eternal Son, the Second Person, who did this.

It was a little as if the owner of some tin soldiers became a little live tin soldier himself to bring life to the rest. So it was that God became a man, but before that a baby, and before that a fetus. Lewis disgusts some readers when he tries to give them the idea by suggesting how it would seem to a man to become a slug or a crab!

In another image Lewis describes a diver stripping and diving down to the darkest depths of dirty water to recover something precious from the bottom. When he and his prize are at the bottom neither has color; when they break the surface they both shine with color again. This is a picture of the Incarnation.

In his book *Miracles,* the Incarnation is the subject of Lewis's entire chapter "The Grand Miracle." God became Man. Jesus was either what he said or a lunatic or fiend. We cannot understand how the divine Spirit lived within the human spirit of Jesus, but neither can we understand how the spirit of any person lives in his or her biological organism.

In the Narnian book *The Horse and His Boy,* Bree insists in a superior way that Aslan the great deliverer could not be a real lion. He may be as strong as a lion or as fierce as a lion. But it would be absurd and disrespectful to consider him a real lion. Then he would have four paws, a tail and *whiskers*! Just then Aslan appeared and terrified the foolish horse Bree. "Nearer still, my son," said Aslan. "Do not dare not to dare. Touch me. Smell me. Here are my paws, here is my tail, these are my whiskers. I am a true Beast." Bree was shaken and admitted he had been rather a fool. "Happy the Horse who knows that while he is still young," Aslan congratulated him dryly.[25]

Near the end of *The Last Battle,* Queen Lucy said, "In our world too, a Stable once had something inside it that was bigger than our whole world."[26] Lewis always claimed that everywhere the great enters the little, and that its power to do so almost proves its greatness.

The following sentence from *Mere Christianity,* well suited for a Christmas greeting, sums up the Incarnation: "The Son of God became a man to enable men to become sons of God."[27]

God, the Death-Slayer

The death of Christ is the point in history where something unimaginable breaks through into our world. That death has somehow put us right with God and given us a fresh start. We cannot possibly understand fully how it works. But just as man is nourished by his food without understanding how it works, so he can accept what Christ has done without knowing how it works. One has to accept Christ's sacrifice to be a Christian. Christ's death has washed out our sins and disabled death.

Lewis begs us not to argue with others about the best expression or theory of how Christ's death saves us. Some people say he paid the debt we owed or suffered the punishment we had earned. Some say he atoned for our sins. Some say we are washed in his blood. Some say he conquered death. However one states it, it was something no one less than God could do. And it hurt.

Lewis believed that Christ is the one example of what man was intended to be. His earthly career was one of poverty, misunderstanding, betrayal, injustice, torture and death. In a letter Lewis speculated, "Only he who really lived a human life (and I presume that only one did) can fully taste the horror of death."[28] But the human creature in him so closely united to the divine Son came to life again. The real, perfect man rose again.

The sacrificial death and resurrection of Aslan takes place in *The Lion, the Witch and the Wardrobe*. Edmund has betrayed his brother and sisters and all the good creatures of Narnia by joining the evil White Witch because of his foolish pride and greed. The White Witch knows she can claim all traitors as her victims, and she prepares to slay Edmund. But the great Lion Aslan offers himself in Edmund's place. The Lord of Narnia submits to a terrible and degrading death and is gloriously resurrected the next morning. Edmund becomes a loyal subject, and Aslan defeats the witch. She knew deep magic, but he knew a magic deeper still. Her knowledge went only to the dawn of time. But Aslan knew from the stillness and darkness before time dawned that when a willing victim who had committed no wrong was killed in a traitor's stead, death itself would start working backwards.

Lewis says of God, "It appears, from all the records, that though He has often rebuked us and condemned us, He has never regarded us with contempt. He has paid us the intolerable compliment of loving us, in the deepest, most tragic, most inexorable sense."[29]

The Russians smugly reported that they did not find God in outer space. Will he be found there as we probe further? Some Russians and many people in the West seem to think of God as being contained in a special place, if he exists at all. Lewis said that what would disturb Christians would be if an astronaut *did* claim to discover God out there!

If God exists, mere movement in space will never bring you any nearer to him or any farther from him than you are now. "Those who do not find Him on earth are unlikely to find Him in space. (Hang it all, we're in space already; every year we go a huge circular tour in space.) But send a saint up in a spaceship and he'll find God in space as he found God on earth."[30]

We will never discover Christ in a new way in space, but He will come to earth in a new way some day! Lewis found it impossible to retain our belief in the divinity of Christ and the truth of our Christian revelation if we abandon or even neglect the promised, and threatened, return. "If this is not an integral part of the faith once given to the saints," Lewis pronounced, "I do not know what is."[31]

Christ gave us three main teachings on the subject:

(1) That He will certainly return.

(2) That we cannot possibly find out when.

(3) And that therefore we must always be ready for Him.[32]

Many people try to figure out just when Christ will return. Lewis wondered why they believe Christ is coming at all if they disbelieve his statement that no one can know the date! Our task is not to make predictions, to be fearful or even to be excited about the Second Coming. Our task is to always be aware of it as we labor diligently in our vocations. That way we can train ourselves to ask more and more often how the things we are saying or doing or failing to do will look in the light of eternity.[33]

Further Reading about God

"For my own part, I tend to find the doctrinal books often more helpful in devotion than the devotional books, and I rather suspect that the same experience may await many others."[34]

Miracles by C. S. Lewis sets forth in chapter eleven, "Christianity and 'Religion,'" the meaning of a *personal* God.

Mere Christianity by C. S. Lewis is divided into four parts. Book One, "Right and Wrong as a Clue to the Meaning of the Universe" argues for the existence of God. Book Two, "What Christians Believe" contains the basic elements of the Christian faith. Book Four, "Beyond Personality; or First Steps in the Doctrine of the Trinity" explores the nature of God and his relationship to us.

The Lion, the Witch and the Wardrobe by C. S. Lewis presents Aslan, a clear Christ-figure, as the King and Redeemer of Narnia in this children's fantasy.

The Lion of Judah in Never-Never Land by Kathryn A. Lindskoog (now published in *Journey into Narnia*) explores the theology of C. S. Lewis expressed in his seven Narnian fantasies for children. (Although these books are commonly referred to as the *Narnia* Chronicles, Lewis wrote me in 1956 that he preferred the designation *Narnian* Chronicles.)

Reflections on the Psalms by C. S. Lewis shares with the reader what Lewis learned about God in the Psalms.

C. S. Lewis: The Shape of His Faith and Thought by Paul L. Holmer explores Lewis's theology and relates it to the thought of Søren Kierkegaard and Ludwig Wittgenstein.

Real Presence: The Holy Spirit in the Works of C. S. Lewis by Leanne Payne surveys warmly the ways in which the presence of God is manifested in Lewis's writings.

Notes

1. C. S. Lewis, *Mere Christianity* (New York: Macmillan, 1953), p. 38.
2. Lewis, *Letters of C. S. Lewis*, p. 141.
3. C. S. Lewis, *Christian Reflections* (Grand Rapids, Mich.: Eerdmans, 1967), p. 171.
4. C. S. Lewis, *Miracles* (New York: Macmillan, 1947), p. 114.
5. C. S. Lewis, *Reflections on the Psalms* (London: Geoffrey Bles, 1958), pp. 87–88.
6. Lewis, *Letters of C. S. Lewis*, p. 168.
7. Lewis, *Mere Christianity*, p. 32.

8. C. S. Lewis, *The Problem of Pain* (New York: Macmillan, 1948), p. 28.

9. Ibid., p. 29.

10. C. S. Lewis, *Poems* (New York: Harcourt Brace Jovanovich, 1964), pp. 123–24.

11. C. S. Lewis, *Till We Have Faces* (London: Geoffrey Bles, 1958), p. 259.

12. Ibid., p. 319.

13. C. S. Lewis, *The Magician's Nephew* (New York: Macmillan, 1955), p. 160.

14. Lewis, *Mere Christianity,* p. 35.

15. Ibid., p. 36.

16. C. S. Lewis, *The Last Battle* (London: The Bodley Head, 1956), pp. 37–38.

17. Ibid., p. 135.

18. C. S. Lewis, *The Lion, the Witch and the Wardrobe* (New York: Macmillan, 1950), pp. 64–65.

19. Ibid., p. 149.

20. C. S. Lewis, *The Silver Chair* (New York: Macmillan, 1953), pp. 16–17.

21. C. S. Lewis, *Letters to Malcolm: Chiefly on Prayer* (New York: Harcourt Brace Jovanovich, 1963–64), p. 74.

22. Lewis, *Mere Christianity,* p. 135.

23. Lewis, *Letters to Malcolm,* p. 96.

24. Lewis, *Letters of C. S. Lewis,* p. 243.

25. Lewis, *The Horse and His Boy* (New York: Macmillan, 1952), p. 170.

26. Lewis, *The Last Battle,* p. 143.

27. Lewis, *Mere Christianity,* p. 139.

28. Lewis, *Letters of C. S. Lewis,* p. 191.

29. Lewis, *The Problem of Pain,* p. 29.

30. Lewis, *Christian Reflections,* p. 171.

31. C. S. Lewis, *The World's Last Night and Other Essays* (New York: Harcourt Brace Jovanovich, 1960), p. 93.

32. Ibid., p. 107.

33. Ibid., pp. 107–13.

34. Lewis, *God in the Dock,* p. 205.

Chapter 3

Nature

"It is the Way in which the universe goes on, the Way in which things everlastingly emerge, stilly and tranquilly, into space and time."
The Abolition of Man[1]

Part One: What is Nature?

When Lewis was in his mid-teens he mainly cared about gods and heroes and ideal beauty, but he only believed in atoms and evolution and military service. He thought that the sciences had found that there is no world behind, or around, the material world. He looked out on "a meaningless dance of atoms" and tried hard to believe that all the apparent beauty was a trick of his own physical brain and that everything a person values is meaningless. This was a severe "faith" to follow, and it finally faltered when more data came in.[2]

Lewis eventually turned away from the drab possibility of a meaningless, entirely material universe and embraced "the real universe, the divine, magical, terrifying and ecstatic reality in which we all live."[3] And wishful thinking had no part in his decision. As he later explained it, "If the whole universe has no meaning, we should never have found out it has no meaning:

just as, if there were no light in the universe and therefore no creatures with eyes, we should never know it was dark. *Dark* would be without meaning."[4] Our looking for real meaning in the universe is one of the facts of nature that must be taken into account!

Ordinary people today may not believe in God and the supernatural, but they usually believe in the reality of their surroundings; for example the four walls of a room. People generally agree that, however they came to be, there are many concrete things that do now exist: things like flamingoes, German generals, lovers, sandwiches, pineapples, comets and kangaroos.[5] But the physicists tell us that matter, in walls or washtubs, is something totally unimaginable, describable only in mathematical terms, not at all solid, existing in curved space, charged with appalling energies.[6]

We should never ask of anything, "Is it real?" Everything in the universe is real, even a momentary dream. The question is, "A real *what*?"[7]

The scientists are always pushing further into the unexplained and revealing truths that in themselves need explanation. But no one supposes that the process could reach completion. And the final truth which science will never be able to explain is why this universe exists at all; the existence of the universe itself is as utterly unexplainable as the magic flower in a fairy tale.[8]

In his own fairy tale, *The Voyage of the "Dawn Treader,"* Lewis once commented on matter, nature and reality this way:

> "In our world," said Eustace, "a star is a huge ball of flaming gas."
> "Even in your world, my son," replied the old man, "that is not what a star is but only what it is made of."[9]

Lewis decided that the universe really exists and not just by accident. There is a power behind it that makes it what it is.

Christians believe that God invented and made the universe—space and time, heat and cold, color and tastes, animals and vegetables.[10]

Reality is always complicated, and, furthermore, it is usually odd. The apparent lack of pattern in our solar system is not what one would have expected.[11] God did not consult us when he invented sex, either. In fact, when some children are told about the curious process of reproduction, they do not believe it at first, and no wonder. It is odd. So is Christianity. We don't understand the mysteries of how food nourishes us, but we eat it and live. The material universe that God created is surprising.[12]

God even chose to make Christianity partly material, not purely spiritual. We are baptized with real water. We take communion with real bread and wine. Lewis reminds us that God invented eating. "He likes matter. He invented it."[13]

Lewis memorably retold the Christian story of creation in *The Magician's Nephew,* where he described the Lion Aslan creating the world of Narnia.

First there was nothing. Then in the darkness a deep voice began to sing an almost unbearably beautiful song without words. After awhile the blackness overhead was blazing with stars, and they joined the song with cold, tingling, silver voices. Then sunrise came—the glory and joy of a new sun and a new world. The light revealed the Singer, a huge Lion. He paced across the empty land. He sang grass and flowers and trees across the vivid bare earth, and then he sang all animals into existence from the earth. At last the Lion spoke, in the deepest, wildest voice ever heard, and he said, "Narnia. Narnia. Narnia, awake. Love. Think. Speak. Be walking trees. Be talking beasts. Be divine waters."[14]

Lewis says the fact that God created Nature and is above and outside Nature means that Nature is not divine. But that fact enables us to see natural objects as magnificent symbols of God. The clouds, the mountains, the great deep, the sun, the thunder, wind and flames are all used as descriptions of God's attributes in the Bible.

Lewis found in the Psalms a sensuous and delightful feel of weather—"weather seen with a real countryman's eyes, enjoyed almost as a vegetable might be supposed to enjoy it. 'Thou art good to the earth . . . thou waterest her furrows . . . thou makest it soft with the drops of rain . . . the little hills shall rejoice on every side . . . the valleys shall stand so thick with corn that they shall laugh and sing.'" (See Ps. 65:9–14.) From Psalm 104:16 Lewis quotes, "the great trees drink their fill."[15]

Lewis had an appreciation for the beauties of weather and landscape that was extraordinary. His personal letters and books abound with comments like, "I love the empty, silent, dewy, cobwebby hours."[16] He couldn't enjoy fiction which didn't have any particular feeling of geography and setting.

One of Lewis's short stories in *Of Other Worlds* is a fantasy called "The Shoddy Lands" in which he finds himself briefly trapped inside the head of a self-centered young woman. There he finds a few items such as women's fashions presented in vivid detail. But Nature and most of the rest of life were perceived in such a vague, drab way that that is the point of the brief story and the source of its title. Life itself seems poor and shoddy if one cannot respond to both the gentle pleasures and the resplendent glories of Nature.

Of course some people (like Lewis) have special relish for the wonder and beauty of Nature because of their early environment, their talent and their character. Lewis summed it up at the end of the creation of Narnia: "For what you see and hear depends a good deal on where you are standing; it also depends on what sort of person you are."[17]

A Good Thing Spoiled

Before Lewis was a Christian, he chewed endlessly on the problem of how Nature can be so beautiful and also so cruel, wasteful and futile.[18] If one believed that God created Nature, it would seem that God is a great artist, but also that he is quite merciless and no friend to humanity, for the universe is a very dangerous and terrifying place.[19] In fact, he would seem no friend to animals.

There is much that is bad and meaningless in the universe, and the universe contains men who know that much is bad and meaningless. The Christian answer to the problem is that this is a good world gone wrong, but with a memory of what it should have been.[20] "We find ourselves in a world of transporting pleasures, ravishing beauties, and tantalising possibilities, but all constantly being destroyed, all coming to nothing. Nature has all the air of a good thing spoiled."[21] God insists, and insists very loudly, that man should now put right again everything that he can.[22]

Since this world is spoiled and headed toward destruction, God will invade someday in force, and that will be the end of the reign of evil, ". . . you see the whole natural universe melting away like a dream and something else—something it never entered your head to conceive—come crashing in. . . . For this time it will be God without disguise; something so overwhelming that it will strike either irresistible love or irresistible horror into every creature. It will be too late then to choose your side."[23]

Most people take it for granted that time is not just the way life comes to us, but the way all things really exist. We assume that the whole universe and God himself always keep steadily moving from past to present to future just as we do, and at our rate. Theologians, philosophers and now many scientists disagree.

God's life almost certainly does *not* consist of moments following one another. "All the days are *'Now'* for Him."[24] Many people are puzzled about how God kept the whole universe going while he was a human being. When Christ was a baby or was asleep, how could he be everywhere, have all power, and know everything? The answer is that Christ's earthly life in Palestine was not a period of time taken from his life as God beyond all space and time. We wrongly think of it as a special time in the history of God's own existence. God doesn't have eras; he doesn't have history. All time is present to him. Perhaps in the next life it will be so for us.[25]

Although God is not in a time system, it is possible that he has created more than one. In *The Lion, the Witch and the Wardrobe,* the two children who had never been to Narnia were afraid that their sister Lucy, who had, was out of her mind. She claimed to have stepped through a wardrobe closet into a different world from ours. They confided her preposterous claims to the wise old professor. He indicated that they should believe her. Peter objected that when they looked in the wardrobe closet they didn't find a strange country, and if things are real, they are there all the time. "Are they?" the Professor commented.

Next, the children claimed that Lucy's story was impossible because she had only been in the wardrobe for less than a minute, and she claimed she had been in Narnia for hours.

> "That is the thing that makes her story so likely to be true," the Professor replied. "If Lucy got into another world, it is most likely it would have a separate time of its own, so that however long you stayed there it would not take up any of *our* time."

> "But do you really mean, Sir," said Peter, "that there could be other worlds—all over the place just around the corner—like that?"

> "Nothing is more probable," said the Professor.[26]

Of course these are only words in a fantasy for children. In *Miracles* Lewis explains the same idea for adults. Other natures created by God, if there are any, couldn't be in outer space, because that is part of our nature. Their space and time are unrelated to ours, or they may not even have space and time.[27] "Of course," Lewis admits mildly, "we can hardly imagine such a thing."

There are great limits upon the human imagination. We can only rearrange the elements God has provided. No one can create a new primary color, a third sex, a fourth dimension or a completely original animal. Even by writing a book, planting a garden or begetting a child, we never create anything in the strict sense; we only take part in God's creation.[28]

Part Two: What Do We Do with Nature?

C. S. Lewis sensed a great lack of appreciation for Nature among his associates at Oxford. In 1938 he mentioned a couple of cases in a letter to his old friend Owen Barfield. He had heard two undergraduates naming some pleasures which they considered pro-Nazi and leading to homosexuality. The dangerous activities were: feeling the wind in your hair, walking with bare feet on the grass, and swimming in the rain.

There had long been deer grazing silently in the grove outside Lewis's windows at Oxford, but now they were replaced by sheep, and one could hear them bleating all day long. Lewis was shocked that although all of his pupils were well acquainted with the body of fine poetry idealizing the life of shepherds, none of them regarded real sheep as anything but a nuisance. A fellow teacher at Oxford had actually been heard to ask why sheep have their wool cut off. Lewis enjoyed these ironies, but they rather alarmed him.[29]

It was clear to Lewis that indifference leads to loss, and that the powers of evil work toward the disruption and destruction of Nature. At the beginning of the adventures of Narnia, this

lovely country was ruled by an evil White Witch who kept it
perpetually winter (without Christmas) and turned unlucky
animals into stone statues. In the science fiction classic
Perelandra, a man who let himself be possessed by the devil left
a trail of torn, suffering little animals in his path. In both *The
Last Battle* and *That Hideous Strength,* the destruction of the
world began with the chopping down of sacred trees and
precious glades for the sake of commerce, expansion and
progress. In our own world, Lewis said in 1947, "The evil reality of lawless applied science (which is Magic's son and heir) is
actually reducing large tracts of Nature to disorder and sterility
at this very moment."[30]

Lewis never respected progress and development for their
own sake. In *The Voyage of the "Dawn Treader"* a wicked governor gasped to young King Caspian that social reform would be
putting the clock back. In *Mere Christianity* Lewis had already
asked, why not put the clock back, if the clock is wrong? The
governor suggested that King Caspian had no idea of progress,
of development. Caspian dryly replied that he had seen them
both in an egg when it became rotten.[31]

Years ago Lewis ruefully observed that the wonderful cross-
country walks of his youth and middle years were spoiled by the
intrusion of progress and development. In a letter he once
commented that it would be less terrible if one could attribute
the murder of beauty to any particular set of evil men. But the
truth is that from man's first and wholly legitimate attempt to
win safety and ease from Nature we move logically, step by step,
to universal suburbia.[32] Lewis never overlooked the fact that the
landscape he loved in England was thoroughly modified by
human skill and toil, and that the effect of most charming
"town-scapes" is enormously indebted to atmospheric
conditions that are not at all manmade. What he enjoyed was
simply seeing more of nature than one sees in suburbia, including the larger geological features. He was once much amused

by a railway poster which advertised Kent as "Nature's home," and he enjoyed the story of a walker who liked to be able to travel a road "untouched by the hand of man."

Although he was not unrealistically sentimental about Nature, Lewis did not thoroughly appreciate the internal combustion engine. Modern transport is said to annihilate space. Lewis says that is a true and horrible claim. Space is one of the most glorious gifts we have been given. A modern boy gets less out of traveling a hundred miles than his grandfather got from traveling ten. This is inflation which lowers the value of distance. Of course, if a man hates space, Lewis concludes, he might creep into his coffin at once; there is precious little space there.[33]

As early as 1946 Lewis began seriously to fear that men would in fact "contaminate the moon." *Out of the Silent Planet,* his own novel about men visiting Mars, was published in 1938. Lewis foresaw that a real journey to the moon would not at all satisfy the impulse which people sought to gratify with science fiction stories. The real moon, he foresaw, would in a deep and deadly sense be just like anywhere else. Cold, hunger, hardship, danger and even death among the bleached craters would be *simply* cold, hunger, hardship, danger and death like at home. "No man would find an abiding strangeness on the Moon unless he were the sort of man who could find it in his own back garden."[34]

Lewis did not live to see that "great step forward," and it is just as well. He was sure that no moonlit night would be the same to him again if, as he looked up at that pale disc, he knew that parts were claimed by America and Russia, and that it was a scene of international tension. "The immemorial Moon—the Moon of the myths, the poets, the lovers—will have been taken from us forever. Part of our mind, a huge mass of our emotional wealth, will have gone . . . he who first reaches it steals something from us all."[35]

Lewis could only hope that the very remote possibility of discovering other rational creatures in space would never occur. He pointed to the mistreatment of blacks and native Americans and the abuse of the weak here on earth. He was sure that any race technologically weaker than ourselves, no matter how innocent and friendly, would be enslaved, deceived, exploited or exterminated. At the very least we would corrupt it with our vices and infect it with our diseases. "I have wondered before now whether the vast astronomical distances may not be God's quarantine precautions."[36]

We have filled our world with massacre, torture, syphilis, famine, dust bowls, slag heaps and with all that is hideous to ear or eye. Man is not yet fit to visit other worlds.[37]

Loving Our Own World

Lewis not only felt that humans should try to preserve natural beauty and avoid the mistreatment of members of the human race, but he also taught that everything a person does to an animal is either a lawful exercise or a sacrilegious abuse, of an authority by divine right. (Man was appointed by God to have dominion over the beasts.)

Lewis was the author of an antivivisection pamphlet print-ed in New England.[38] There he observed that the very people who will most contemptuously brush aside any consideration of animal suffering if it stands in the way of "research" are the same ones who will strongly deny any radical difference between men and the other animals. He quoted Dr. Samuel Johnson's shocked description of men who practice tortures without pity and report them without shame. Since Johnson's time, says Lewis, vivisection has won. We, as well as animals, are already the victims. This is his only concession to the practice: "If on the grounds of our real, divinely ordained, superiority a Christian pathologist thinks it right to vivisect, and does so with scrupulous care to avoid the least dram or scruple of unnecessary pain, in a trembling awe at the responsibility which he assumes, and with a vivid sense of the high mode in which human life must be lived if it is to justify the sacrifices made for it, then (whether we agree with him or not) we can respect his point of view."[39]

He devoted a whole chapter in *The Problem of Pain* (and an essay in *God in the Dock*) to the nature and destiny of animals. He admitted that some of his concerns might put him "in company with all the old maids," but allowed that he thought neither virginity nor old age contemptible. Lewis recognized that if the ape could understand us, he would resent being lumped along with the oyster and the earthworm in a single class of "animals" contrasted to man. Apes and men are in many ways much more like each other than either is like a worm. He considered what pain means in animals, and the possibility of an afterlife of some kind for them.

Lewis's fiction is full of his delight in animals (including some new ones on Mars), their memorable names and descriptions, and his outrage at men who hurt and destroy them.

His letters also bring in animals sometimes, especially cats. He once described a new friend to his brother as a good man—a Christian and a cat lover. He advised one cat owner that the idea of psychological diagnosis for her cat sounded phony. He greatly respected cats, he said; they are very shrewd people and would probably see through the analyst much better than he would see through them.[40]

Just a year before his death he described his two cats:

> I can't understand the people who say cats are not affectionate. Our Siamese (my 'step-cat') is almost suffocatingly so. True, our ginger Tom (a great Don Juan and a mighty hunter before the Lord) will take no notice of *me*, but he will of others. He thinks I'm not quite socially up to his standards, and makes this

very clear. No creature can give such a crushing 'snub' as a cat! He sometimes looks at the dog—a big boxer puppy, very anxious to be friendly—in a way that makes it want to sink into the floor.[41]

Lewis admits that kindness to animals is easy when one meets them solely as pets. It is a more costly virtue for tired, hungry people who have to work with animals for a bare living or who live near dangerous wild beasts. He points out that in Psalm 104, which is devoted to Nature, the Jews praised God not only for the cattle, corn and wine, but also for creatures hurtful or irrelevant to them. The Jews had gusto, or even gratitude, which embraced things that are no use to humanity.[42] Lewis thought they were profoundly right. "I think God wants us to love Him *more*, not to love creatures (even animals) *less*. . . . No person, animal, flower, or even pebble, has ever been loved too much—i.e., more than every one of God's works deserves."[43]

The world is crowded with God, Lewis exclaimed. All ground is holy and every bush, if we could perceive it, is a burning bush.[44]

Every bush had been dull, indistinct and meaningless in the second-rate universe Lewis got caught in, in the story "The Shoddy Lands." Nature was vague and incomplete there. He was drunk with delight when he found himself free, back home from the horrible little prison of that land. "There were birds singing close to a window; there was real sunlight falling on a panel. That panel needed repainting; but I could have gone down on my knees and kissed its very shabbiness—the precious real, solid thing it was."[45]

We are not to love the supernatural at the expense of the natural. God created Nature with his love and artistry, and so it demands our reverence. "Because we love something else more than this world we love even this world better than those who know no other."[46]

Further Reading about Nature

"A book's no good to me until I've read it two or three times. . . ."[47]
The Magician's Nephew by C. S. Lewis was the sixth of the Narnian series, but it tells the origin of Narnia. It features multiple universes, the creation story and wrong uses of power.

Out of the Silent Planet by C. S. Lewis is an account of man's first adventures on Mars. It deals with the theme of scientism versus the angels.

The chapter entitled "Nature" from *Reflections on the Psalms* by C. S. Lewis beautifully expresses the psalmist's feeling about God's world.

"A Chapter Not Strictly Necessary," chapter nine of *Miracles* by C. S. Lewis, imparts Lewis's emotional response to Nature.

"Nature," the first chapter of *Studies in Words* by C. S. Lewis, gives lexical and historical insights as an aid to more accurate reading. Lewis chose eight important words to study in this book as a defense against verbicide, the murder of words.

"Likings and Loves for the Sub-human," chapter two of *The Four Loves* by C. S. Lewis, includes a delightful and penetrating analysis of the love for Nature.

Notes

1. C. S. Lewis, *The Abolition of Man* (New York: Macmillan, 1947), p. 11.
2. Lewis, *Surprised by Joy*, pp. 170–75.
3. C. S. Lewis, *George MacDonald: An Anthology* (New York: Macmillan, 1947), p. 21.
4. Lewis, *Mere Christianity*, p. 31.
5. Lewis, *Miracles*, p. 105.
6. Lewis, *Letters to Malcolm*, p. 78.
7. Ibid., p. 80.
8. Ibid., pp. 103–4.
9. C. S. Lewis, *The Voyage of the "Dawn Treader"* (New York: Macmillan, 1952), p. 175.
10. Lewis, *Mere Christianity*, pp. 30–31.
11. Ibid., pp. 32–33.
12. Ibid., pp. 43, 47.

13. Ibid., p. 50.

14. Lewis, *The Magician's Nephew,* pp. 87–103.

15. Lewis, *Reflections on the Psalms,* p. 77. In *Prince Caspian* even the trees attended a great, joyful, informal feast given by Aslan. There they were fed several courses of various rich soils and quenched their thirst with "deep draughts of mingled dew and rain, flavoured with forest flowers and the airy taste of the thinnest clouds." (C. S. Lewis, *Prince Caspian* [New York: Macmillan, 1951], pp. 177–78.)

16. C. S. Lewis, *Letters to an American Lady* (Grand Rapids, Mich.: Eerdmans, 1967), p. 76.

17. Lewis, *The Magician's Nephew,* pp. 111–12.

18, Lewis, *Surprised by Joy,* p. 170.

19. Lewis, *Mere Christianity,* p. 23.

20. Ibid., p. 33.

21. Lewis, *Miracles,* p. 147.

22. Lewis, *Mere Christianity,* p. 31.

23. Ibid., pp. 50–51.

24. Ibid., p. 133.

25. Ibid., pp. 130–33.

26. Lewis, *The Lion, the Witch and the Wardrobe,* pp. 39–40.

27. Lewis, *Miracles,* p. 20.

28. Lewis, *Letters of C. S. Lewis,* p. 203.

29. Ibid., p. 161.

30. Lewis, *Miracles,* p. 179.

31. Lewis, *The Voyage of the "Dawn Treader,"* p. 48.

32. Lewis, *Letters of C. S. Lewis,* p. 211.

33. Lewis, *Surprised by Joy,* p. 157.

34. C. S. Lewis, *Of Other Worlds: Essays and Stories* (London: Geoffrey Bles, 1966), p. 13.

35. Lewis, *Christian Reflections,* p. 173.

36. Lewis, *The World's Last Night and Other Essays,* p. 91.

37. Lewis, *Christian Reflections,* p. 173.

38. Lewis, *God in the Dock,* pp. 224–28.

39. Ibid., p. 226.

40. Lewis, *Letters to an American Lady,* p. 94.

41. Ibid., p. 105.

42. Lewis, *Reflections on the Psalms,* pp. 83–84.

43. Lewis, *Letters to an American Lady,* p. 58.

44. Lewis, *Letters to Malcolm,* p. 75.

45. Lewis, *Of Other Worlds,* p. 105.

46. Lewis, *God in the Dock,* p. 150.

47. Lewis, *Of Other Worlds,* p. 89.

Chapter 4

Humanity

"Actually it seems to me that one can hardly say anything either bad enough or good enough about life."
Letter to Dom Bede Griffiths[1]

Part One: The Dust That You Are

C. S. Lewis did not attend the coronation of Queen Elizabeth II in 1953. He could have gone, but he was not a man for crowds and best clothes, and the weather was very bad. He was deeply moved by what he heard of it, however.

He felt that the pressing of that huge, heavy crown on that small, young head was a symbol of the situation of all people. God has called humanity to be his vice-regent and high priest on earth. It is as if God said, "In my inexorable love I shall lay upon the dust that you are glories and dangers and responsibilities beyond your understanding."[2] No wonder that at the coronation there was a feeling of awe, pity, pathos, mystery. We have *all* been crowned by God already, and there is tragic splendor in the coronation.

In *Prince Caspian*, the newly crowned young king of Narnia learned to his regret of his disreputable ancestry. He expressed his wish for noble lineage.

"You come of the Lord Adam and the Lady Eve," Aslan answered. "And that is both honour enough to erect the head of the poorest beggar, and shame enough to bow the shoulders of the greatest emperor in earth. Be content."[3]

Lewis stressed that all people are "one flesh"; everyone is ultimately related to everyone else on the planet. People of noble blood are those whose families have been illustrious for so many generations that more of their genealogical background is *recorded*. But we are all of equally ancient descent. Lewis confided to a friend that he, like her, had always imagined Adam as being physically the son of the anthropoids on whom God worked after birth the miracle which made him Man.[4]

Lewis was himself of ordinary lineage—his paternal grandfather was a Welsh peasant and his maternal grandfather was an Irish clergyman. But he took hearty English pleasure in the distinction between commoners and nobility. He urged that distinctions such as those of blood, beauty, talent and fame be casually enjoyed, like tinsel crowns, but never prized above their worth. Enjoyment of the distinction of wealth, in contrast, is inevitably wrong.[5]

Lewis's enjoyment of symbolic royalty did not mean that he advocated a ruling monarchy. He was committed to democratic government. It wasn't that he believed the people of a country too good to be ruled by a king or queen; it was that no person or group is good enough to be trusted with uncontrolled power over others. Therefore, although under ideal circumstances Lewis would prefer patriarchal monarchy, in our fallen state only democracy will do. He considered figurehead royalty a good subject for public adulation, however. Deprived of that, people will idolize movie stars, football players and famous prostitutes, he said.

Believing in democracy, Lewis was greatly opposed to both theocracy, "the worst of all governments," and revolution, "the seizure of power by a small, highly disciplined group of people."[6]

He did not consider any group good enough to have such power.

Cause to Be Uneasy

In *Mere Christianity* Lewis stated that if we look at the state of the world, it is pretty plain that humanity has been making some big mistakes and seems to be on the wrong road.

God has put into the minds of all people his moral law. In spite of great cultural differences, all people have a basic core of values in common—fair play, unselfishness, courage, good faith, honesty and truthfulness. They apply these values with differing limitations, but they apply them. The moral law tells us to follow right conduct even if it is difficult, painful or dangerous. And we never measure up to it. Not even a saint ever quite succeeds.[7]

How did we get into such an uncomfortable situation? It is free will that has made evil possible for humanity. Paradoxically, the same free will is necessary for the possibility of human love, goodness and joy.

"A cow cannot be very good or very bad; a dog can be both better and worse; a child better and worse still; an ordinary man, still more so; a man of genius, still more so; a superhuman spirit best—or worst—of all."[8] Lewis points out that Satan was an archangel once with gifts as far above ours as ours are above those of a chimpanzee.[9] The Bible tells us in Isaiah 14:12–15 that Satan was not satisfied. He wanted to put himself first; he wanted the place of God.

Then Satan taught that sin to the human race. He put into the heads of our remote ancestors that they could "be like gods." They wanted to be their own masters and find happiness apart from God. *It happens that there is no such thing.* Out of that hopeless desire has come most of human history— "money, poverty, war, prostitution, classes, empires, slavery—the long terrible story of man trying to find something other than God which will make him happy."[10]

Lewis considered himself basically a historian. And he claimed that the key to history is that there is a fatal flaw in all we do. No matter how well mankind builds, something always goes wrong. Selfishness and cruelty crop up. Man seeks happiness and peace in vain; Satan has won the first round.

Biological life reaches its highest level in humanity. Man not only lives, but loves and reasons. Therefore man resembles God more than does any other known living creature. But in his natural state he, like everything he builds, comes to nothing in the end.[11]

Lewis doesn't spend time guessing how things would be for the human race if we had not rebelled against God and joined the enemy. But as it is, "the disease of temporality is incurable."[12] Lewis felt that even victory, to the natural man, leads him on to see deeper defeat. To him Communist optimism about man was out of court; the noblest position for a non-Christian was to face the futility of human endeavor and to endeavor anyway.

The natural life in each of us, temporal as it is, wants to be left to itself, to be self-centered and exploiting. It doesn't want the spiritual life to get a hold of it to kill its self-will; it is ready to fight tooth and nail to avoid that.[13] Lewis stressed the difference between the natural life in us, which like all the rest of nature runs down and decays, and spiritual life, which is eternal. He called them Bios and Zoe. Christ wants to give us Zoe.

Lewis said that through the body God showed him the whole side of his beauty which is embodied in color, sound, smell and size.[14] The animals can't appreciate it, and, most likely, neither can the angels; one lacks the intelligence, and the other, pure intelligence, probably lacks retinas and palates. "I fancy the 'beauties of nature' are a secret God has shared with us alone. That may be one of the reasons why we were made—and why the resurrection of the body is an important doctrine."[15]

Humanity has held three main views of the body, Lewis observed. The ascetic pagans and certain Christians called it the prison of the soul or a sack of dung. There are others to whom the body is simply glorious. In contrast, Lewis agreed with the third view, that of St. Francis, who called his body "Brother Ass." Lewis thought "ass" exquisitely right because no one can revere or hate a donkey. It is useful and troublesome, lovable and infuriating, pathetically and absurdly beautiful. That is how Lewis saw the body.[16]

In *Letters to Malcolm*, the last book Lewis wrote before his death (and resurrection), he said, "Bless the body. Mine has led me into many scrapes, but I've led it into far more. . . . And from how much it has saved me!"[17] He told both the fictitious Malcolm and the real American lady that if the imagination were obedient, the bodily appetites would give us little trouble and could be easily managed.

Lewis noted the same idea almost twenty years earlier in a fanciful paragraph. He had complained to his Body that it was always dragging him down.

> "Dragging *you* down!" his Body replied. "Well, I like that! Who taught me to like tobacco and alcohol? You, of course, with your idiotic adolescent idea of being grown-up. My palate loathed both at first: but you would have your way. Who put an end to all those angry and revengeful thoughts last night? Me, of course, by insisting on going to sleep. Who does his best to keep you from talking too much and eating too much by giving you dry throats and headaches and indigestion? Eh? . . . That's Soul all over; you give me orders and then blame me for carrying them out."[18]

"I have a kindly feeling for the old rattle trap,"[19] Lewis wrote to the American lady one year before his death. He had just been likening his body and hers to worn-out automobiles, because all sorts of apparently different things kept going wrong with them. The machine was running down; it wasn't meant to last forever.

God has allowed natural causes, working in a world spoiled by centuries of sin, to produce not only physical infirmities, but also damaged personalities. Some people have nastiness due to a narrow mind and jangled nerves, some are poisoned by a wretched upbringing, some are saddled by sexual perversion, and some are nagged at by inferiority complexes. Others are luckier and have much nicer personalities to manage. The big question is whether, in either case, the people will offer their natures to God. In his eyes they all need saving.

The people with very hard problems are understood by God. He knows what wretched machines they are trying to drive. Some day he will fling them away and give those people new ones; then they may astonish everyone, for they learned their driving in a hard school. Some of the last will be first and some of the first will be last.[20]

Lewis held that equality is in the same position as clothes; they are both results of the fall of man and remedies for it. The legal fiction of our equality is absolutely necessary to protect us from each other. But it would be nonsense to say that people are equally useful or beautiful or good or entertaining. And it is dangerous to say that people are all of equal value as immortal souls. God did not die for man because of some value he perceived in him. As St. Paul tells us, to have died for valuable men would have been not divine but heroic; in contrast, God died for sinners. If there is equality between people at all, it is in God's love, not in our intrinsic value.

Lewis believed that we are all fallen creatures and even the best are hard to live with. In *The Four Loves* he asks who can live even one day with those he loves best and not feel some impulse to demand much and give little. Congenital human selfishness is both normal and detestable; the name of the condition is "fallenness" or "sin." The alternatives are living alone or with all the rubs and frustrations of life, and he considered the second far better.

We are all members of one another whether we choose to recognize the fact or not. Everyone lives on others, economically, intellectually, spiritually. ("Who, after all, is *less* independent than someone with 'a private income'—every penny of which has been earned by the skill and labour of others?")[21]

Because all people are part of one organism, there are two errors along this line that Christians must avoid. They must not be totalitarians or individualists. Totalitarians want to suppress differences and make all people alike—probably like themselves. Individualists are tempted not to bother about someone else's troubles, dismissing them as if they were none of their business. These attitudes are both dead wrong. Christianity thinks of human individuals as organs in a body—different from one another and each contributing what no other could.[22]

Part Two: New People

"One has one's own dark ages," Lewis told Warren in a letter once. "But I daresay this is not so for everyone; it may be that you and I have a specially historical sense of our own lives."[23] It would be interesting to know what period Lewis then considered his dark ages. The light of his conversion had not yet broken on him.

About three months after his letter to Warren, Lewis wrote darkly to his father about a "religious revival" going on among the undergraduate students, led by a Dr. Buchman. It was not that Lewis objected to virtue and serious purpose. Indeed, he claimed that when he had arrived as a tutor at Magdalen any undergraduate who had interests beyond rowing, drinking, motoring and fornication sought his friends outside the college, and indeed kept out of the place as much as he could. It was at that time rather like a country club for idle young aristocrats instead of a center of serious study and personal growth. Lewis and one or two colleagues were trying to start a literary discussion group.

But Buchman had started groups of students meeting together to confess their sins to one another. Lewis was repulsed by it all. "Jolly, ain't it?" he complained to his father. "But what can you do? If you try to suppress it you only make martyrs."[24]

It is likely that Lewis never warmed to Buchman and the practice of public confessions. (Dr. Frank Buchman's historic Oxford Movement later became Moral Re-Armament. As the movement became less orthodox, Dr. Samuel Shoemaker broke with it and started his own Christian group movement, Faith at Work.) But Lewis's own "religious revival" was just around the corner.

Humility is one of the main themes of all of Lewis's writing about humanity. Any person in right relationship with God and other people has to recognize and admit his or her own inadequacy. Illustrations of this fact are sprinkled throughout Lewis's fiction.

For example, when Prince Caspian was to be crowned king of Narnia, Aslan asked him if he felt himself sufficient to take up the kingship.

> "I—I don't think I do, Sir," said Caspian. "I'm only a kid."
> "Good," said Aslan. "If you had felt yourself sufficient, it would have been a proof that you were not."[25]

In a later book the horse Bree confessed his inadequacy. In a shaken voice he told Aslan that he was afraid he must be rather a fool. Aslan assured him, "Happy the Horse who knows that while he is still young. Or the Human either."[26]

Humility and repentance may not be jolly and need not be public, but they are part of salvation and part of Christian liv-

ing. At the climax of *The Pilgrim's Regress,* the allegory of
Lewis's conversion, the hero came at last to Mother Kirk (the
church) and gave himself up. There he had to take off his rags
and dive into deep water. It was painful to peel off the rags so
stuck to him and frightening to fall naked, head-first into salvation.[27]

In contrast, in *The Great Divorce* a ghost who was being
invited to move from hell into heaven kept foolishly insisting
that he wanted his rights because he had led a good life. "I'm
not asking for anybody's bleeding charity," he declared. His
heavenly friend seized upon that and begged him to indeed ask
for the bleeding charity. "Everything is here for the asking and
nothing can be bought."[28]

In the novel *Till We Have Faces,* the ancient dying queen was
on her way to the gods. "Be sure," she was told, "that, whatever
else you get, you will not get justice."

> "Are the gods not just?" she asked.
> "Oh no, child. What would become of us if they were?"[29]

Lewis said that nice people, turned away from God, content
in their own niceness, looking no further, are just as desperate-
ly in need of salvation as miserable people. Of course
wholesome, integrated personalities are valued by God and
man. Redemption will improve people and in turn motivate
them to improve the world so that more people can grow up in
a healthy state. But this is not salvation. Even the nicest people
need Christ. God became man to turn creatures (nice or awful)
into sons.[30]

The big question for all people is, Will you, or will you not,
turn to him and thus fulfill the only purpose for which you were
created? As Lewis pictures it, the free will inside a person trem-
bles like the needle of a compass. God waits and watches to see
in each case if the needle will swing round and settle and point
to him.[31] God is in himself complete, and yet he chooses to love

and in some sense need us because we need to be needed.[32] God has chosen to be the wooer of his own creation; our highest activity is response to God.

In *The Silver Chair*, Aslan told Jill that he had called her out of her world into Narnia for a task. She thought he was mistaken, because she and her friend had been calling for Someone to deliver them from their pursuers. The Lion replied that they would not have called to him unless he had first been calling to them.[33]

Yet God forces no one. In *The Voyage of the "Dawn Treader"* Lucy ran to Aslan and thanked him for coming when he appeared in the doorway.

> "I have been here all the time," said he, "but you just made me visible."
>
> "Aslan," said Lucy almost a little reproachfully, "Don't make fun of me. As if anything I could do would make *you* visible!"
>
> "It did," said Aslan. "Do you think I wouldn't obey my own rules?"[34]

God has subjected himself to the free will of man.

I Became My Own

Lewis once wrote to a lady, "The writer you quote *was* very good at the stage at which you met him; now, as is plain, you've got beyond him. Poor boob—he thought his mind was his own. Never his own until he makes it Christ's; up till then, merely a result of heredity, environment, and the state of his digestion. I became my own only when I gave myself to Another."[35]

Lewis had tried to explain this at the end of *Mere Christianity*. He said that the more we let Christ take us over, the more truly ourselves we become. Christ invented all the different people that we millions were intended to be. It is as if our real selves are all waiting for us in him. The more we resist him, the more we are dominated by our heredity, upbringing, surroundings and natural desires. What we call "my wishes" are greatly determined by diet, propaganda, other people's opinions or even the suggestion of devils. We are not, in the natural state, nearly so much persons as we like to think; most of what each one calls "me" can be explained by looking at outside influences. When we give ourselves up to Christ's personality, we start to have real distinct personalities of our own.[36]

In his vivid essay "Man or Rabbit?" Lewis likens much in natural man, whether worried, conscientious and ethical, or cowardly and sensual, to a rabbit. "All right," he warns, "Christianity will do you good—a great deal more good than you ever wanted or expected."[37] That rabbit has to disappear so that he can be remade. The fur has to be pulled out bunch by bunch, accompanied by blood and squealing. But underneath we shall find a real man, strong, radiant, wise, beautiful and drenched in joy.[38]

From the Christian point of view, there isn't any crowd. No two people are alike. Everyone is special. God loves every individual as if he or she were the only creature in existence. All are different and necessary to the whole and to one another.[39]

God shows himself only to real people. In the last chapter of *Till We Have Faces* the strange title is explained. The old queen says of the gods, "How can they meet us face to face till we have faces?"[40] Real men means not simply men who are individually good, but those who are united in a body loving one another, helping one another, and showing him to one another.[41]

It is as if there is a door, behind which, according to Christians, the secret of the universe is waiting. If this is not true, it is the greatest fraud in history. It is obviously the job of every person (that is a person and not a rabbit) to try to find out if the claim is true; then to devote his life to exposing this gigantic humbug or serving this tremendous secret.[42]

Further Reading about Humanity

"Those of us who are blamed when old for reading childish books were blamed when children for reading books too old for us."[43]

Prince Caspian by C. S. Lewis is the second book of Narnia. It portrays the struggle of a defeated young man to regain his rightful throne.

Perelandra by C. S. Lewis is the second and most beautiful of his science fiction trilogy. It re-enacts the Fall of man on Venus, with a big difference.

The Abolition of Man by C. S. Lewis was a favorite of his in which he briefly described the universal moral law that he saw as uniquely threatened in our day.

Dymer by C. S. Lewis is a narrative poem over two-thousand lines long tracing a young man's adventuresome struggles against illusion. It was published before Lewis's conversion under his pen name, Clive Hamilton.

The Image of Man in C. S. Lewis by William Luther White is a comprehensive survey of Lewis and his works, in regard to the creation, Fall and redemption of humanity. It overlooks the influence of G. K. Chesterton upon Lewis, especially Chesterton's *Everlasting Man*.

Letters to an American Lady by C. S. Lewis shows how he treated an ordinary woman who turned to him for friendship.

Letters to Children, edited by Lyle Dorsett, includes all the available letters that C. S. Lewis sent to children.

Notes

1. Lewis, *Letters of C. S. Lewis*, p. 266.
2. Lewis, *Letters to an American Lady*, p. 18.
3. Lewis, *Prince Caspian*, p. 182.
4. Lewis, *Letters of C. S. Lewis*, p. 237.
5. Lewis, *Letters to an American Lady*, pp. 25, 108.
6. Lewis, *Of Other Worlds*, pp. 81–82.
7. Lewis, *Mere Christianity*, p. 24.

8. Ibid., p. 38.

9 . Ibid., p. 167.

10. Ibid., p. 39.

11. Ibid., p. 123.

12. Lewis, *Letters of C. S. Lewis,* p. 159.

13. Lewis, *Mere Christianity,* p. 139.

14. Lewis, *Letters to an American Lady,* p. 108.

15. Lewis, *Letters to Malcolm,* p. 18.

16. C. S. Lewis, *The Four Loves* (London: Geoffrey Bles, 1960), pp. 116–17.

17. Lewis, *Letters to Malcolm,* p. 17.

18. Lewis, *God in the Dock,* pp. 216–17.

19. Lewis, *Letters to an American Lady,* p. 108.

20. Lewis, *Mere Christianity,* pp. 164–67.

21. Lewis, *Letters to an American Lady,* p. 109.

22. Lewis, *Mere Christianity,* p. 145.

23. Lewis, *Letters of C. S. Lewis,* p. 123.

24. Ibid., p. 126.

25. Lewis, *Prince Caspian,* p. 173.

26. Lewis, *The Horse and His Boy,* p. 170.

27. C. S. Lewis, *The Pilgrim's Regress: An Allegorical Apology for Christianity* (London: Geoffrey Bles, 1943), pp. 169–70.

28. C. S. Lewis, *The Great Divorce* (New York: Macmillan, 1946), p. 26.

29. Lewis, *Till We Have Faces,* p. 308.

30. Lewis, *Mere Christianity,* p. 167.

31. Ibid., p. 164.

32. Lewis, *The Problem of Pain,* p. 39.

33. Lewis, *The Silver Chair,* p. 19.

34. Lewis, *The Voyage of the "Dawn Treader,"* p. 132.

35. Lewis, *Letters of C. S. Lewis,* pp. 250–51.

36. Lewis, *Mere Christianity,* p. 174.

37. Lewis, *God in the Dock,* p. 112.

38. Ibid.

39. Lewis, *Letters of C. S. Lewis,* pp. 242–43.

40. Lewis, *Till We Have Faces,* p. 305.

41. Lewis, *Mere Christianity,* p. 128.

42. Lewis, *God in the Dock,* p. 112.

43. Lewis, *Of Other Worlds,* p. 28.

Destiny:
What Will Become
of Us?

Chapter 5

Death

*"There are, aren't there, only three things we can do
about death: to desire it, to fear it, or to ignore it."*
Letters to an American Lady [1]

Part One: How Lewis Viewed Death

One April day in his twenty-fourth year, when he was a student
at Oxford, C. S. Lewis wrote in his journal, "I wish life and
death were not the only alternatives, for I don't like either." [2]

When he was exactly twice that old, he published a strange
little book called *The Great Divorce,* which describes his visit to
the edges of hell and heaven. In heaven his host was his favorite
author, George MacDonald, who taught him amazing things
about life after death. Finally MacDonald indicated that Lewis
was dreaming. Lewis replied,

> "A dream? Then—then—am I not really here, Sir?"
> "No, Son," said he kindly, taking my hand in his. "It is not so
> good as that. The bitter drink of death is still before you. Ye are
> only dreaming." [3]

Then Lewis awoke and the book ended.

But in more ways than one, Lewis always kept dreaming about the Christian meaning of death. In his first science fiction novel, *Out of the Silent Planet,* a sinless inhabitant of Mars expressed his idea of death to Ransom, his visitor from earth. He told how he had once drunk life at a certain marvelous pool and then added,

> "That was the best of drinks save one."
>
> "What one?" asked Ransom.
>
> "Death itself in the day I drink it and go to Maleldil [God]."[4]

An unfallen race on Mars would know biological death only as a good transition. In contrast, our fallen race knows death as a bitter drink, but one with great potential for good or evil. It can mean either the utter frustration or the utter fulfillment of all human values and longing.

In his first popular book, *The Screwtape Letters,* Lewis reveals the complaint of demon Screwtape that most people do not live long enough to be thoroughly worked on by his crew. From his point of view, which is not necessarily accurate, God has ordained that the majority of the human race dies in infancy and that many survivors of infancy die in youth. Only a minority of the inhabitants of heaven will have had to resist Satanic powers on earth for sixty or seventy years. His advice to demon Wormwood is to keep his "patient," a young Christian, as safe as possible.

Alas, poor Wormwood bungles and his patient is killed; his soul has slipped through their fingers into heaven. Hell is outraged.

> "Just think (and let it be the beginning of your agony) what he felt at that moment; as if a scab had fallen from an old sore, as if he were emerging from a hideous, shell-like tetter [skin disease], as if he shuffled off for good and all a defiled, wet, clinging garment. By Hell, it is misery enough to see them in their mortal days taking off dirtied and uncomfortable clothes and

splashing in hot water and giving little grunts of pleasure—stretching their eased limbs. What, then, of this final stripping, his complete cleansing?"[5]

This "stripping" idea of death reappeared in *The Voyage of the "Dawn Treader."* Eustace, an obnoxious little boy, had become an ugly dragon because of his greed. He earnestly scratched and peeled off his thick scaly skin, but there was always another layer underneath. In desperation, he submitted to the claws of the great lion Aslan. The Lion seemed to tear into his heart, he tore so deep. Then he threw the stripped dragon into the water of a miraculous well, where he became a boy again, but a new boy. This incident describes death and resurrection in either the psychological or physical sense.

At the end of the book the children were returning to our world from the land of Narnia, but they preferred to go to the high country of Aslan, which is heaven. Lucy asked Aslan how to get into his country from our world. He answered, "I will not tell you how long or short the way will be; only that it lies across a river. But do not fear that, for I am the great Bridge Builder."[6]

The old image of death as a river occurs again in *The Silver Chair*. The old king of Narnia has died. The children found themselves on the mountain of Aslan at the edge of his country. King Caspian lay under the clear water of a stream, and even Aslan wept for him. Then Aslan had Eustace pierce the great pad of his forepaw with a giant thorn, and when the red blood splashed into the stream, Caspian changed. Smooth-faced and laughing, he leaped up. "And he rushed to Aslan and flung his arms as far as they would go round the huge neck; and he gave Aslan the strong kisses of a King, and Aslan gave him the wild kisses of a lion."[7]

But when King Caspian greeted his old friends, they drew back and stammered that he was dead. "Yes," Aslan answered quietly, "He has died. Most people have, you know. Even I have. There are very few who haven't." And the new Caspian explained to them that he was not a ghost. He would be a ghost in Narnia, if he returned there. "But one can't be a ghost in one's own country."[8]

The Best Is Yet to Come

In the chapter entitled "Farewell to Shadowlands" in the final children's book, *The Last Battle*, the children were afraid of being sent away again. At Aslan's reassurance, their hearts leaped and a wild hope rose within them.

> "There *was* a real railway accident," said Aslan softly. "Your father and mother and all of you are—as you used to call it in the Shadow-lands—dead. The term is over: the holidays have begun. The dream is ended: this is the morning."
>
> And as He spoke He no longer looked to them like a lion; but the things that began to happen after that were so great and beautiful that I cannot write them. And for us this is the end of all the stories, and we can most truly say that they all lived happily ever after. But for them it was only the beginning of the real story. All their life in this world and all their adventures in Narnia have only been the cover and the title page: now at last they were beginning Chapter One of the Great Story which no one on earth has read: which goes on for ever: in which every chapter is better than the one before.[9]

This is the essence of Lewis on death. The germ of all his basic beliefs is found in the deep, rich and joyful message of his Narnian series. But even in his nonfiction, his ideas about death are vivid and pervasive.

For example, in his literary essay "Hamlet: The Prince or the Poem," he declared, "Being dead is the unknown x in our sum. Unless you ignore it or else give it a value, you can get no answer."[10]

In *Miracles* he thoroughly considered that value. There he described the two attitudes toward death which the human mind naturally adopts. First is the lofty Stoic idea that death "doesn't matter," that it is just an unavoidable part of living and should be calmly tolerated. (When his wife died, Lewis exclaimed that if death doesn't matter, neither does birth.) Second is the less philosophical idea that death is the greatest of all evils. Most people today make this latter assumption in thinking about individual survival or the survival of the human species.

Lewis dismissed both of these views and decided that death is a paradox. It is a great weapon of both Satan and God; it is a man's greatest disgrace and his only hope. It is the very thing Christ came to conquer and yet it is the means by which he conquered! At one point Lewis suggested that we could almost define the future as the period in which what is now living will be dead, and in which what order is still remaining will be diminished. But in the same book he stated that humanity must embrace death freely, submit to it with humility, drink it to the dregs, and so convert it into that mystical death which is the secret of life. Man, as originally created, was immune from death. Death is the result of human sin. Redeemed man, recalled to a new bodily life, will be immune from it again.

Because of his dramatic concept of the power and beauty of life in the resurrected body, Lewis couldn't think of the destruction of our present bodies as the greatest of evils. He thoroughly agreed with our natural distaste for both corpses and ghosts. We sense that it is somehow indecent for life to go out of our bodies; they were not originally made for death. But in a vivid figure of speech he likened our present doomed bodies to ponies given to schoolboys for them to learn on. The goal is "that some day we may ride bareback, confident and rejoicing, those greater mounts, those winged, shining and world-shaking horses which perhaps even now expect us with impatience, pawing and snorting in the King's stables. Not that the gallop would be of any value unless it were a gallop with the King; but how else—

since He has retained His own charger—should we accompany Him?"[11]

Of course the glory of our resurrected bodies will be a manifestation of our inner perfection. In *Mere Christianity* Lewis insists that Christ meant what he said when he told us to be perfect. Those of us who put ourselves in his hands will eventually become perfect as he is perfect, in love, wisdom, joy, beauty and immortality. Death comes in as an important part of the treatment that brings about the change. Some Christians will be further along toward perfection before death than others; we cannot judge.

Again in this book Lewis urges us to embrace death with confidence. We are to submit daily to the death of our ambitions and favorite wishes and in the end to the death of our whole bodies. We are to submit completely to find eternal life. We are to keep back nothing, for nothing that we have not given away will ever be really ours. Nothing in us that has not died will ever be raised from the dead. If we look for ourselves, we will find in the long run only hatred, loneliness, despair, rage, ruin and decay. But if we look for Christ we will find him, and with him everything else thrown in.

Just as we are enjoying our promises of future joy, Lewis reminds us of our present responsibilities.

> Of all men, we hope most of death; yet nothing will reconcile us to—well, its *unnaturalness*. We know that we were not made for it; we know how it crept into our destiny as an intruder; and we know Who has defeated it. Because Our Lord is risen we know that on one level it is an enemy already disarmed; but because we know that the natural level also is God's creation we cannot cease to fight against the death which mars it, as against all those other blemishes upon it, against pain and poverty, barbarism and ignorance. Because we love something else more than this world we love even this world better than those who know no other.[12]

We are especially responsible for our share in other people's destiny. In his essay "The Weight of Glory," Lewis says, "There are no *ordinary* people. You have never talked to a mere mortal. . . . But it is immortals whom we joke with, work with, marry, snub, and exploit—immortal horrors or everlasting splendours."[13]

In his essay "Membership," Lewis said that we shall be true and everlasting and really divine persons only in heaven, just as we are, even now, colored bodies only in the light. When the moment comes, it will make little difference how many years we have behind us. He believed that it is good for us always to be aware of our mortality, because all schemes of happiness that center in this world are doomed to final frustration. After all, there is bound to come a time when every culture, every institution, every nation, and the entire human race is extinct; yet every one of us is still alive. Christ did not die for society, but for humanity. Neither the natural individual nor the community can inherit eternal life; only a new creature can inherit it.

In "The World's Last Night," Lewis reminded modern Christians again that humanity, though longer-lived than individual men and women, is equally mortal. And what death is to each person, the Second Coming is to the whole human race.

In an interview in *Decision* magazine published the month before his death, Lewis's tone was rather merry about the matter:

> We have, of course, the assurance of the New Testament regarding events to come. I find it difficult to keep from laughing when I find people worrying about future destruction of one kind or other. Didn't they know they were going to die anyway? Apparently not. My wife once asked a young woman friend whether she had ever thought of death, and she replied, "By the time I reached that age science will have done something about it."

In the same interview we find Lewis's last public advice about facing death: "The world might stop in ten minutes; meanwhile, we are to go on doing our duty. The great thing is to be found at one's post as a child of God, living each day as though it were our last, but planning as though our world might last a hundred years."[14]

Part Two: How Lewis Lived Death

C. S. Lewis not only thought and wrote about death, but he experienced bereavements. His first big taste of death came when he lost his grandfather, uncle and mother all in 1908 when he was nine. He saw army friends die in World War 1. When his father was dying in 1929, Lewis had to spend some time nursing him. He felt as if his father's benign presence lingered with him for weeks after the death. Then his special friend Charles Williams died in 1945. Lewis claimed later that his view of death and his view of Williams were incompatible, and so at that point his view of death had to change.

Ultimately, the death of his wife Joy in 1960 struck him the hardest, as described in *A Grief Observed*. One night in the midst of his wrenching grief, he had a strange moment which he could not describe—rather like a friendly chuckle beside a man who believes he is alone in the dark. It made him aware in his desolation that any mortal at any time may be utterly mistaken about his true situation. He referred twice in his brief book to that impression like a chuckle in the darkness, hinting that some shattering and disarming simplicity is the real answer to our mutability and mortality.

A little later he received a brief sense of Joy's presence, which was surprisingly businesslike, with a sense of extreme and cheerful intimacy. It led him to the idea that the dead are perhaps brisk, intense, wide-awake and, above all, solid. "Utterly reliable. Firm. There is no nonsense about the dead," he speculated.[15]

In answer to a consoling friend who wrote to him about the nature of life after death, Lewis frankly stated that her words were of no help at all to him. "But don't let us trouble one another about it," he concluded. "We shall know when we are dead ourselves."[16]

Facing the Real Waking

Three years after Joy's death, Lewis was dying also. He wrote to an American woman, "Think of yourself just as a seed patiently waiting in the earth; waiting to come up a flower in the Gardener's good time, up into the *real* world, the real waking. I suppose our whole present life, looked back on from there, will seem only a drowsy half-waking. We are here in the land of dreams. But cock-crow is coming. It is nearer now than when I began this letter."[17]

Three weeks after this advice was given, Lewis went into a coma from which he unexpectedly revived. When his mind had cleared, he wrote to a friend named Sister Penelope, "Ought one to honour Lazarus rather than Stephen as the protomartyr? To be brought back and have all one's dying to do again was rather hard."[18] He had previously thought this about his wife's twice enduring her deathbed. Readers of his poetry know how skillfully he expressed this idea in what was perhaps his last poem, entitled "Stephen to Lazarus."

As his brother Warren Lewis tells it, Jack faced the prospect of his death bravely and calmly. Only once did he show any regret or reluctance. When he had to decline a certain lecture invitation that he would have enjoyed, his face grew sad; he paused, then said simply, "Send them a very polite refusal."[19]

As Lewis noted, most loves end in bereavement. In this case the longest love of his life, that between the two brothers, ended in Warren's suffering the loss. C. S. Lewis, who had often worried about his older brother's bouts with alcoholism in his later years, had the comfort of his brother's presence to the end. Furthermore, he had the promise of his wife from her own deathbed that if it was possible she would come to his deathbed to meet him. "Heaven would have a job to hold me," she promised, only partly joking, "and as for Hell, I'd break it into bits."[20] Joy was not speaking about facts, but about the will in her heart.

Lewis did not concern himself about whether or not the departed can come to those still on earth. That is an idea far more acceptable in England than in the United States. (In fact Lewis's own mother, a very matter-of-fact person, had an extraordinary mystical experience in Italy when she was young, as recorded in the Lewis family papers.) There is no way to know what Lewis, while alive, would have thought of this story, told after Lewis's death by J. B. Phillips, the famous Bible translator.

Phillips was watching television, a pastime Lewis detested, shortly after Lewis's death. Phillips describes himself as an incredulous and unsuperstitious man and says that at the time of this experience he was not thinking about Lewis. Nevertheless, he suddenly discovered Lewis, whom he had met only once in his life, sitting in a chair a few feet away. Lewis spoke to Phillips . He was ruddier in complexion than ever and glowing with health— "large as life and twice as natural." Needless to say, Phillips was puzzled.

A week later Phillips was in bed reading at night and Lewis appeared again, even more rosily radiant than before and repeated the same few words. And if Phillips's story is true, these are Lewis's final, most authoritative words to us. He came back twice to say simply, "It's not so hard as you think, you know."[21]

Further Reading about Death

"It is a good rule, after reading a new book, never to allow yourself another new one till you have read an old one in between."[22]

The World's Last Night by C. S. Lewis includes seven essays. The title essay is about the Second Coming of Christ and the end of each person as well as the whole human race.

A Grief Observed by C. S. Lewis tells with harrowing honesty the agony of bereavement when his wife died. The Bantam edition (1976) includes an afterword by Chad Walsh, personal friend of Jack and Joy Lewis.

The Ring of Truth by J. B. Phillips expresses the same strong feelings Lewis had about the defense of the gospel today and includes Phillips's account of being visited by Lewis shortly after his death.

The Silver Chair by C. S. Lewis is the fourth book of Narnia. In it the paradoxes of death are dramatically enacted.

Notes

1. Lewis, *Letters to an American Lady,* p. 81.
2. Lewis, *Letters of C. S. Lewis,* p. 73.
3. Lewis, *The Great Divorce,* p. 131.
4. C. S. Lewis, *Out of the Silent Planet* (New York: Macmillan, 1943), p. 79.
5. C. S. Lewis, *The Screwtape Letters* (New York: Macmillan, 1944), pp. 156–57.
6. Lewis, *The Voyage of the "Dawn Treader,"* p. 209.
7. Lewis, *The Silver Chair,* p. 204.
8. Ibid., p. 205.
9. Lewis, *The Last Battle,* pp. 183–84.
10. C. S. Lewis, *They Asked for a Paper: Papers and Addresses* (London: Geoffrey Bles, 1962), p. 64.
11. Lewis, *Miracles,* pp. 194–95.
12. Lewis, *God in the Dock,* p. 150.
13. Lewis, *They Asked for a Paper,* p. 210.
14. *Decision,* October 1963, p. 4.
15. C. S. Lewis, *A Grief Observed* (New York: Seabury, 1963), p. 59.
16. Lewis, *Letters of C. S. Lewis,* p. 297.
17. Lewis, *Letters to an American Lady,* p. 116.
18. Lewis, *Letters of C. S. Lewis,* p. 307.
19. Ibid., p. 25.
20. Lewis, *A Grief Observed,* p. 59.

21. J. B. Phillips, *The Ring of Truth* (New York: Macmillan, 1967), pp. 118–19.

22. Lewis, *God in the Dock,* pp. 201–2.

Chapter 6

Heaven

"Heaven is not a state of mind.
Heaven is reality itself."
The Great Divorce[1]

Part One: Further Up

In all Christendom, few adult converts have started out with
less interest in the afterlife than C. S. Lewis, and few have
ended up with a more radiantly exciting vision of heaven.

Lewis said in regard to another subject that the things he
asserted most vigorously were those he resisted long and accepted late. For about a year after his conversion to belief in God,
Lewis gave no thought at all to life after death. He later counted this early lack of interest in heaven as a great benefit. He
knew for a fact that he had never been lured into his faith by
the hope of everlasting life.

Lewis always tried to obey God simply because he was God,
not because of any threats or promises. He believed that our
obedience is due to God no matter what. If it were possible for
God to lose his power and for heaven to crumble, we would still
owe him the very allegiance and love we owe him now, because
of who he is.

Nevertheless, once a Christian accepts the idea of heaven, how can he or she keep it from the forefront of his mind or untwine it from his present existence? In his last book Lewis answered the supposed accusation that the "next world" loomed too large in his thinking. In answer, he simply asked, "How can it loom less than large if it is believed in at all?"[2]

Lewis felt that heaven is not mentioned much because Christians dislike being accused of preaching "pie in the sky." But, he reasoned, either there is pie in the sky or there is not. If there is not, then Christianity is false. Christianity entails the reality of heaven, in spite of the insistence of some theological liberals to the contrary. The doctrine of heaven is woven through the fabric of this faith. If it is true, then it must be faced like any other truth.

Once Lewis firmly believed in God, he could face the truth of heaven. But the opposite course, which some people try, will not work—no matter how tempting it is to the bereaved. Believing first in reunion with the beloved, and as a result believing in heaven, and then believing in God, is futile. It is a work of the imagination. One cannot keep believing such mental fantasy without the aid of self-hypnotism, poor quality hymns and pictures or witchcraft. In contrast, the times when Lewis's belief in heaven was strongest were times when he was thinking about God himself.[3]

Ultimately we were made for God, not for our earthly beloveds. It is usually hard for us to feel in this life that God is our true Beloved. But we can begin by believing it or trying to believe it. In heaven we will not continue in our present purely human loves as they are now. We will have turned away from God's lovable creatures to Love himself. We shall love God more than our earthly beloveds, and therefore we shall love them more than we do now.

This is not exactly the comfort sought, but it is the only comfort available. Heaven only gives heavenly comfort, not earthly comfort. "There is no earthly comfort in the long run."[4] Reunion with those we love is a second thing; we can get second things only by putting first things first.

Lewis gives short shrift to two other common misconceptions of heaven. One is the cozy, informal view. Lewis's own grandfather, an Irish minister, used to look forward to having some very interesting conversations with St. Paul when he got to heaven. Lewis suspected that his grandfather might not find himself chatting with St. Paul like two clerical gentlemen at ease in a club after all. His grandfather might instead be utterly overwhelmed by the greatness and grandeur of St. Paul in his glory.[5]

The other erroneous idea of heaven is that the scriptural descriptions are meant literally. Heaven is not really full of jewelry; heaven is indescribable. But the Bible writers, in their wisdom, used the best symbols possible. Gold is used as a symbol of timelessness (it never rusts) and of the preciousness of heaven. Crowns are mentioned to suggest that the saints in heaven share God's splendor, power and joy. Musical instruments are mentioned because music suggests ecstasy and infinity.

Of course, if a Christian takes these symbols as fact, it will do him no more harm than believing that God really has a beard. But when these symbols are ridiculed by nonbelievers who take them literally, Lewis responds that they might as well consider our biblical injunction to be like doves as a divine command to lay eggs.[6]

You Can Take It with You

Using a fanciful symbol of his own, Lewis said there may be books in heaven. But you will find that your personal library there contains only the books you gave away or lent on earth. And just as the wounds of the martyrs will have turned into marks of beauty, so the borrower's thumb marks will have turned into beautiful illuminated capitals or exquisite marginal woodcuts. Only what we give up can become truly ours.[7] "Aim at heaven and you will get earth 'thrown in': aim at earth and you will get neither."[8]

It is now as if we are on the outside of the world, on the wrong side of the door. We respond to the freshness and purity of morning, but we don't become fresh and pure thereby. We are separate from the splendors we see. "But all the leaves of the New Testament are rustling with the rumour that it will not always be so. Some day, God willing, we shall get *in*."[9]

We get a glimpse of what awaits us when we do get in, as seen through the eyes of the devil Screwtape in his letters to Wormwood. When Wormwood has let his patient slip from his reach into heaven, Screwtape writes,

> He saw not only Them; he saw Him. This animal, this thing begotten in a bed, could look on Him. What is blinding, suffocating fire to you, is now cool light to him, is clarity itself, and wears the form of a Man. . . . Pains he may still have to encounter, but they *embrace* those pains. They would not barter them for any earthly pleasure. All the delights of sense, or heart, or intellect, with which you could once have tempted him, even the delights of virtue itself, now seem to him in comparison but as the half nauseous attractions of a raddled harlot would seem to a man who hears that his true beloved whom he has loved all his life and whom he had believed to be dead is alive and even now at his door.[10]

When we get in, Scripture promises us five major conditions: we shall be with Christ; we shall be like him; we shall have "glory"; we shall be in some sense fed, feasted or entertained; and we shall have some sort of official position in the universe.[11]

Redemption always improves people in the present life, but it will later improve them to a degree we cannot now imagine.

Even now, the more we let Christ take us over, the more truly ourselves we become. This will be culminated in heaven.[12] There our natures will be expanded into the full richness of diversity which God originally intended; heaven will have far more variety than hell.[13] "Good, as it ripens, becomes continually more different not only from evil but from other good."[14]

In fact, Lewis says, it is only Christians who have any idea of how humans can be taken into the life of God and yet become very much more themselves than they were before. He illustrated this at the end of *Till We Have Faces*. Maia's lost sister, Psyche, has come to her in a vision. Psyche's hands burned Maia at the touch with a painless burning. The air from her clothes and limbs and hair was wild and sweet; it seemed to make old Maia young. Yet it was the old Psyche still—a thousand times more herself than before her death. All that one had meant most when one spoke her name was now wholly present, no longer in hints and shreds, no longer in fleeting bits. Maia felt she had never seen a real woman before.[15]

In his earlier fantasy *The Great Divorce*, Lewis described another great lady whose face had unbearable beauty. In life she had simply been a very good woman named Sarah Smith who lived at Golders Green. In heaven love shone from her face and limbs as if it were some liquid in which she had just been bathing. A procession of Bright Spirits escorted her, singing, "The Happy Trinity is her home: nothing can trouble her joy. . . . He fills her brim full with immensity: he leads her to see the world's desire."[16]

"There is no morality in Heaven," Lewis declares thankfully.[17] We won't have to pray or do loving acts there. On earth the very activities for which we were created are impeded by evil in ourselves or others. It isn't possible to practice them all spontaneously and delightfully. That is why we must live by duty, morality, the law.

But the angels have never lived by the word *ought*, and the blessed dead have gladly forgotten it. It isn't needed in heaven. Prayer and love will flow from us there like song from a lark. No evil will impede them. Duty, morality and the law will vanish in heaven. But the good results of obedience to the law will last forever.[18]

Furthermore, there is no modesty in heaven. Salvation is associated with palms, crowns, white robes, thrones and splendor like the sun and stars. The redeemed soul is going to learn at last that she has pleased him whom she was created to please. Her old inferiority complex will be healed forever, and her pride drowned. She will rejoice in what God has made of her. "Perfect humility dispenses with modesty."[19]

No one can enter heaven except as a child, and healthy-minded children take great, undisguised pleasure in being praised. There is no more humble, childlike, creaturely pleasure than the pleasure of the inferior when he pleases his superior. Lewis imagined that some people would dislike the idea of being "patted on the back" in heaven. But that dislike is an arrogant mistake, the ultimate false modesty. God will someday turn his face to each person with one of two expressions—that of divine approval or divine disappointment, conferring either glory inexpressible or incurable shame.

"To please God . . . to be a real ingredient in the divine happiness . . . to be loved by God, not merely pitied, but delighted in as an artist delights in his work or a father in a son—it seems impossible, a weight or burden of glory which our thoughts can hardly sustain. But so it is."[20]

Part Two: Further In

In a letter Lewis once reminded a lady that the character of life after death is unimaginable. He believed that the Bible never describes the otherworld except in terms of inspired parable or allegory.[21] Lewis's own descriptions of heaven were purely fantasy, with a moral. The last thing he wanted to arouse was factual curiosity about the afterworld.[22] But he knew in his heart that the human soul was made to enjoy some object that cannot be imagined, much less given, in our present mode of spatio-temporal experience. And the hunger for that object is better than any other fulness; this poverty better than all other wealth.[23]

In *The Great Divorce* busloads of unhappy passengers from hell take voluntary excursions to the edge of heaven, where they are welcome to visit and urged to stay forever. But many of them have so subjugated their natural desire for heaven to other desires that they dislike heaven despite its vivid beauty and insist upon returning to their ugly hell as soon as possible. Heaven lacks many things. For example, no one is needed there, even by his closest relatives. No one can hurt another person or manipulate others there. People have no religion there; they think only of Christ. There are no "distinguished people" there; everyone is famous, and that is one's only reputation.

The visitors from hell are all unsubstantial ghosts, human-shaped stains on the bright air, whitish or grey, transparent and fragile. The inhabitants of heaven, in contrast, have become Solid People. They all shine with love and joy, but they are all very much themselves.

An angel appears in this story, and he is, of course, the opposite of the cute, plump cherubs of popular art which Lewis loathed. He is more or less human in shape, but larger and almost too bright to took at. The heat and light radiating from him are like that of the morning sun at the beginning of a tyrannous summer day.

In this story the angel wanted to relieve a certain ghost of a powerful sexual lust which clung to his shoulder like a red lizard and was forcing him to go back to hell. The ghost feared the angel's painful operation and suggested it would be better to do it some other day. "There is no other day," the angel answered.

"All days are present now." Then the ghost offered to consult his doctor in hell first and come back the first possible moment. "This moment contains all moments," the angel decreed. The ghost submitted and was transformed into a huge, solid, radiant man.[24]

In another scene in that book a Solid Person was urging the ghost of an apostate bishop to stay in heaven. The religious ghost acknowledged his friend's interesting point of view, but hedged, "in the meantime . . . " The other answered, "There is no meantime. All that is over. . . . You have seen Hell: you are in sight of Heaven. Will you, even now repent and believe?" "I'm not sure that I've got the exact point you are trying to make," said the ghost.[25]

Lewis's own point was simply that one must ultimately submit to God or refuse him. He was not saying that there is no time at all in heaven. Just because God is above and around all time does not mean that everyone in heaven will be so. We may well be in a "thicker" time than we know here, but it will still be time that passes.

Lewis believed that in some sense heaven's door is not shut against a person when he or she dies; anyone who truly wants heaven can have it. As Lewis said in *The Problem of Pain*, it is safe to promise the pure in heart that they shall see God; they are the only ones who want to! In both his fiction and his non-fiction, Lewis expressed hope that many true seekers like Akhenaton and Plato, who never had a chance to find Christ in this lifetime, will find him in the next one. " 'Beloved,' said the Glorious One, 'unless thy desire had been for me thou wouldst not have sought so long and so truly. For all find what they truly seek.' "[26]

More Like the Real Thing

Lewis readily admitted that he did not even like to move from one house to another, much less from one world to another. He did not like psychological uprooting in this life and the feeling of having ended a chapter. He would have liked everything to be immemorial—to have the same old horizons, the same garden, the same smells and sounds always there, changeless.[27] Lewis felt the loss keenly when the lovely open countryside surrounding his childhood home was carved up into housing tracts.

He supposed that all of life's unavoidable changes should prepare us for the greater change that will come to each of us. It is best to "sit light" not only to life itself, but to all its phases. "The useless word is 'encore.' "[28]

However, Lewis's view of heaven at least took the edge off this natural sorrow for the passing of what we love on earth. In *Out of the Silent Planet*, some loving creatures sing at the funeral of their slain brother, "Open, oh coloured world, without weight, without shore. You are second and better; this was first and feeble."[29]

In the last of the Narnian series the children saw the land of Narnia die forever and freeze over in blackness before Peter locked the door against it. As they turned away to walk in Aslan's land Lucy began to cry for all that lay dead and frozen behind them. Jill said that she had hoped that Narnia, unlike our world, would go on forever. Later as they walked in the morninglike freshness they wondered why this country of Aslan seemed strangely familiar. At last they realized that they were in Narnia. Narnia was not dead after all. But now it was different, larger and more vivid, more like the real thing. It was as different as a real thing is from a shadow or as waking life is from a dream. The Narnia they had known before was a copy of the Narnia in Aslan's land just as England in our world is a copy of an inner England in the real world.[30] In the real England no good thing is ever destroyed or lost.[31]

The new Narnia was a deeper country. Every rock and flower and blade of grass looked as if it meant more. Lewis said he couldn't describe it any better than that; if you ever get there you will know what he meant.[32]

At the end of the last book that Lewis completed before his death, *Letters to Malcolm*, he stated this very idea for adults. He hoped the day was coming when he could take his friend for a walk through the long lost fields of his boyhood. The new earth will arise the same, yet not the same, as this. It will arise as a glorification of the past of redeemed mankind raised in incorruption. The hills and valleys we may experience now are like root is to flower or coal to diamond in their relationships to the hills and valleys of heaven.

Lewis did not know how soon the resurrection of the body takes place, but he sincerely believed it would. "Then the new earth and sky, the same yet not the same as these, will rise in us as we have risen in Christ. And once again, after who knows what aeons of the silence and the dark, the birds will sing and the waters flow, and lights and shadows move across the hills, and the faces of our friends laugh upon us with amazed recognition."[33]

The unicorn in Aslan's country cried, "I have come home at last! This is my real country! I belong here. This is the land I have been looking for all my life, though I never knew it till now. The reason why we loved the old Narnia is that it sometimes looked a little like this. Bree-hee-hee! Come farther up, come farther in!"[34] Farther up and farther in is the way to deep heaven.

In both *The Great Divorce* for adults and the Narnian series for children heaven was in a state of perpetual morning, and there were snowless green mountains so high that waking eyes on earth could never have seen them. On these mountains there were steep forests and green slopes, mountain cities, sweet orchards and flashing waterfalls. And the blessed ascending.

In *The Great Divorce* everyone lives only to journey further and further into the mountains. One of the Solid People urged a ghost to come with him, promising that it is a joy going to the mountains, but that there is plenty of work in it. Another Solid Person offered another ghost, "I will bring you to the land not of questions but of answers, and you shall see the face of God."[35]

New arrivals to heaven noticed how large it all seemed. Lewis said in *The Great Divorce* that he had the sense of being in a larger space or even a larger *sort* of space than ever before. In *The Last Battle* the children discovered that the farther up and the farther in you go the bigger everything gets. The inside is larger than the outside.

Lewis believed it likely that even in heaven a continually more ecstatic self-surrender will bring perpetual increase of beatitude perhaps with its own ardors and exertions but without possibility of failure.[36] Beyond nature we shall eat of the tree of life, and the whole man will drink joy from the fountain of joy. [37]

Lewis's vision of how this could be he called guesses, only guesses. "If they are not true, something better will be. For 'we know that we shall be made like Him, for we shall see Him as He is.' " [38]

Further Reading about Heaven

"I don't want my dog to bark approval of my books. Now that I come to think of it, there are some humans whose enthusiastically favorable criticism would not much gratify me."[39]

The Great Divorce by C. S. Lewis tells of Lewis's adventuresome visit to hell and heaven and the amazing things he witnessed there.

The Last Battle by C. S. Lewis is the seventh and last of the Narnian series, ending with "the beginning of the real story."

"The Weight of Glory," an essay in *The Weight of Glory*, was first given by Lewis as a lay sermon about heaven.

"Heaven," chapter ten concluding *The Problem of Pain* by C. S. Lewis, is his earliest essay about heaven.

"Hope," chapter ten of book three in *Mere Christianity* by C. S. Lewis, tells in three pages the place of heaven in our present lives.

Notes

1. Lewis, *The Great Divorce*, p. 65.
2. Lewis, *Letters to Malcolm*, p. 120.
3. Lewis, *The Four Loves*, p. 157.
4. Ibid., p. 158.
5. Lewis, *Letters to Malcolm*, p. 13.
6. Lewis, *Mere Christianity*, p. 106.
7. Lewis, *God in the Dock*, p. 216.
8. Lewis, *Mere Christianity*, p. 104.
9. C. S. Lewis, *The Weight of Glory* (Grand Rapids, Mich.: Eerdmans, 1965), p. 13.
10. Lewis, *The Screwtape Letters*, pp. 159–60.
11. Lewis, *They Asked for a Paper*, p. 203.
12. Lewis, *Mere Christianity*, pp. 167, 174.
13. Lewis, *Letters to Malcolm*, p. 10.
14. Lewis, *The Great Divorce*, p. vi.
15. Lewis, *Till We Have Faces*, p. 317.
16. Lewis, *The Great Divorce*, pp. 122–23.
17. Lewis, *Letters to Malcolm*, p. 115.
18. Ibid., pp. 115–16.
19. Lewis, *They Asked for a Paper*, p. 205.
20. Ibid., pp. 205–6.
21. Lewis, *Letters of C. S. Lewis*, p. 297.
22. Lewis, *The Great Divorce*, p. viii.
23. Lewis, *The Pilgrim's Regress*, pp. 7–8.
24. Lewis, *The Great Divorce*, pp. 101–3.
23. Ibid., p. 35.
26. Lewis, *The Last Battle*, p. 166.
27. Lewis, *Letters of C. S. Lewis*, p. 306.
28. Ibid.
29. Lewis, *Out of the Silent Planet*, p. 142.
30. Lewis, *The Last Battle*, p. 170.
31. Ibid., p. 182.
32. Ibid., p. 172.
33. Lewis, *Letters to Malcolm*, p. 124.

34. Lewis, *The Last Battle*, p. 172.
35. Lewis, *The Great Divorce*, p. 36.
36. Lewis, *Letters to Malcolm*, p. 108.
37. Lewis, *They Asked for a Paper*, p. 209.
38. Lewis, *Letters to Malcolm*, p. 124.
39. Lewis, *Reflections on the Psalms*, p. 93.

Chapter 7

Hell

*"The damned are, in one sense, successful rebels to
the end; . . . the doors of hell are locked on the inside."*
The Problem of Pain[1]

Part One: Farther Down

When Lewis was a young adult he had been far more eager to
escape pain than to achieve happiness, and he even resented the
fact that he had been created without his own permission. One
advantage of the anti-Christian materialism he clung to was its
limited danger of pain. No disaster can be infinite if death ends
all. And if this life becomes too painful, one can always commit suicide for an early escape. In contrast, the horrible thing
about Christianity is that it offers no such escape. It assures each
person that he is going to live forever. The Christian universe
has no door marked exit.[2] Perhaps a person's temper or his jealousy are getting worse so slowly that in seventy years they are
not very noticeable. But in a million years they would be hell
itself; "in fact, if Christianity is true, Hell is the precisely correct technical term for what it would be."[3]

About thirty years after Lewis's youthful enthusiasm for
materialism, he was asked in public if the devil is as real as we

think he is. He answered that it is quite possible to be a Christian without believing in the devil or devils; they are not mentioned in the Christian creeds. "I do believe such beings exist," Lewis continued, "but that is my own affair."[4] He eventually got the feeling that he and the devil were all too closely related in the public mind.[5] They even appeared together on the cover of *Time* magazine.

On the other hand, Lewis felt that a belief in hell was indeed basic. God is not safe or tame. There is that ahead which immortal spirit can desire and dread. Lewis claimed in his last book that he had never met anyone who fully disbelieved in hell and yet had a life-giving belief in heaven.[6]

There are only three eternal alternatives: to be God, to be like God, or to be miserable. That means for humans the choice of heaven or hell. How about earth? Lewis felt that a person who chooses earth instead of heaven will find that earth was, all along, just a part of hell. And the person who puts earth second to heaven will find earth to have been all along a part of heaven itself. It is no use crying for something else; God can only give us what is.[7] Those who want annihilation will find the closest thing to it in hell. But there is no exit.

Infernal Fiction

Lewis published four works of adult fiction in which damnation was a central theme. They came out between 1942 and 1946. First was *The Screwtape Letters*. It was this witty, satirical book about temptations that thrust Lewis into popularity with the general reading public.

No book was ever easier for Lewis to write than this one, and none left a worse taste in his mouth. He said it was not fun for long and almost smothered him before he was done. The state of mind he needed to write from a devil's viewpoint was all dust, grit, thirst and itch. Although he was often asked to add to these letters, it was at least seventeen years before he indulged in any more "diabolical ventriloquism"—and then it was a dinner speech by Screwtape, not a letter.

In that speech Screwtape expresses in passing the goal of hell. "The overthrow of free peoples and the multiplication of slave-states are for us a means (besides, of course, being fun); but the real end is the destruction of individuals. For only individuals can be saved or damned, can become sons of the Enemy or food for us."[8]

Screwtape advises Wormwood that jargon, not argument, can keep a man out of the Enemy's clutches. He assures him that hundreds of adult converts have been reclaimed for hell. "Keep everything hazy in his mind now, and you will have all eternity wherein to amuse yourself by producing in him the peculiar kind of clarity which Hell affords."[9] The reward for all the labors of devils is the anguish and bewilderment of a human soul; it becomes a brimful chalice of despair, horror and astonishment which a devil can drink as wine forever, according to Screwtape.

Wormwood is reminded not to reveal himself to his patient. The fact that devils are today pictured as comic figures in red tights will help keep people from believing in them until it is too late.

Although devils can make use of the comic element at times, joyful laughter is disgusting to them and a direct insult to the realism, dignity and austerity of hell. Silence and melody are also banished there. It is the kingdom of noise.

The whole philosophy of hell is one of competition. Every gain by one being in hell is loss to another. And when a soul manages to go to heaven instead of hell, everyone in hell loses. A howl of sharpened famine re-echoes all the way down to the throne itself.

A tempter has no need to produce big sins in order to win. All he needs do is edge a man away from the Light and out into the nothing. "Murder is no better than cards if cards can do the trick. Indeed the safest road to Hell is the gradual one—the gentle slope, soft underfoot, without sudden turnings, without milestones, without signposts."[10]

Screwtape has made the difference between hell and heaven clear. The devils want cattle who can finally become food; God wants servants who can become sons. The devils want to suck in; God wants to give out. And in this struggle God has limited himself; he can woo, but not ravish.[11]

Either God or Satan will eventually say "Mine" of everything that exists, and especially of every person. God now claims everything on the grounds that he made it. Satan hopes to claim it all by conquest. Man will learn that he cannot in reality claim anything for himself, according to Screwtape. "They will find out in the end, never fear, to whom their time, their souls, and their bodies really belong—certainly not to them, whatever happens."[12] In a poem directed to Satan, Lewis said, "All that seemed earth is Hell, or Heaven. God is: thou art: the rest, illusion. . . ." He concluded his overwhelming realization with a prayer to God, "Lord, open not too often my weak eyes to this."[13]

The idea of a devil possessing a human mind and body was the horror of the unforgettably beautiful space novel *Perelandra* which came out one year after *The Screwtape Letters*. In this sequel to *Out of the Silent Planet*, the evil physicist, Weston, claimed to have come into contact with his life's guiding spirit. This "Life-Force" took control of him, using him as a tool to get the newly created first woman on Venus to disobey her maker.

Ransom, God's man on Venus, soon realized that Weston had become a living corpse, a bogey, an Un-man. He was a creature who at rare moments cried out to Ransom to save him from some horrors he could hardly describe: "I'm down in the bottom of a big black hole. . . . he does all my thinking for me."[14] Superficially, the Un-man Weston seemed to be pursuing great designs against heaven which involved the fate of worlds; but deep within he seemed obsessed with a puerile lust for even tiny, stupid cruelties performed with the mentality of an imbecile or a monkey or a very nasty child.

Ransom had always pictured hell as containing lost souls that were still human; now he saw to his horror that only a ghost would be left—an everlasting unrest, a crumbling, a ruin, an odor of decay. Elsewhere Lewis called it "remains."[15] He saw that there is a confusion of persons in damnation. The question whether Satan or a person digested by Satan is acting on a specific occasion has in the long run no clear significance.

Lewis described *That Hideous Strength*, which follows *Perelandra*, as a tall story about devilry with a serious point behind it.[16] The sinister National Institute of Co-ordinated Experiments (N. I. C. E.) was quickly taking over a small university in England, under the direction of evil Masters. As this project met its destruction, its senior leader, Wither, knew with perfect clarity that he could still divorce himself from the spirits and save himself. But in his last moments before damnation he did not implore God for mercy. Seeing that endless terror was about to begin, he drifted passively into his last moments of murder and devil worship and death, losing all contact with joy and reason forever, drowsily watching the trap close upon his soul.

It was similar with his partner, Frost. Suddenly he had a chance to see that he had been on an utterly wrong course—that souls and personal responsibility existed. He hated that knowledge, rejected it, and entered eternity.

After this book was published, Lewis wrote in a personal letter that N.I.C.E. is not quite the fantastic absurdity some people think, but he had thought the part about dabbling in magic was fantasy. Only later did he learn that it was taking place. He concluded, "The trouble about writing satire is that the real world always anticipates you, and what were meant for exaggerations turn out to be nothing of the sort."[17]

Damnation is somehow sadder but less grisly in *The Great Divorce*. Lewis doesn't include devils in that portrayal of hell, but there, too, all who are in hell have chosen it.[18] (As Lewis says in *The Magician's Nephew*, "All get what they want: they do not always like it."[19])

The whole trouble with trying to understand hell is that the thing to be understood is so nearly nothing. All hell is smaller than one pebble on earth and smaller than one atom of heaven. If a butterfly in heaven swallowed all hell, hell would not be big enough to do it any harm or to even have taste. Hell seems big enough when one is in it. But if all its loneliness, angers, hatreds, envies and itchings were rolled together and weighed against the least moment of joy that is felt by the least in heaven, it would have no weight that could be registered at all. The damned soul is shrunk, shut up in itself; it is nearly nothing.[20]

Lewis wanted to arouse no curiosity about details of the afterlife. But he portrayed hell as a dismal twilight city in which people, consumed with self, moved light years away from each other. Everything there is rather shoddy and insubstantial. No one has joy, but all can have possessions galore by wishing for them. As one cynical resident put it, it's a flop, just like everything else he ever visited. He was led to expect red fire and devils and all sorts of interesting people like Henry VIII sizzling on grids, but when you get there it is just like any other town.

Ultimately, the damned will in some sense say that they were always in hell and the saved that they were always in heaven. It will be true, because both heaven and hell are retroactive. Heaven will saturate the past life with joy, and hell will poison it. Although heaven is reality itself, hell is a state of mind—the dungeon of self. Good beats upon the damned incessantly, like sound waves beating on the ears of the deaf. But they will not, then cannot, receive it.[21]

Even in his children's series, Lewis showed some of God's creatures refusing heaven. Millions of creatures streamed up from the dying land of Narnia to Aslan where he stood at a huge door. As they came right up to him they either looked into his face with love and went through the door to his right into heaven, or else they looked at his face with fear and hatred and went to his left. There they disappeared into his huge black shadow and were never seen by the others again.[22]

In that story, Lucy, being full of love, wanted no one to suffer. She found a circle of miserable, surly Dwarfs who insisted that they were in a pitch-dark, poky, smelly little hole of a stable. Lucy tried to show them the sky and trees and flowers but they insisted that it was all darkness and filthy stable litter. At last Lucy implored Aslan himself to help them.

Aslan agreed to show Lucy what he could and could not do. When he growled softly, the Dwarfs claimed that someone was trying to frighten them with a machine. When he provided them with a magnificent feast, they took it to be dirty water and hay and ended up in a brawl which destroyed the feast entirely. Then they agreed smugly that no one could take them in. "They have chosen cunning instead of belief," said Aslan. "Their prison is only in their own minds, yet they are in that prison; and so afraid of being taken in that they cannot be taken out."[23]

In *The Pilgrim's Regress* John asked his Guide if there is really "a black hole." When the Guide said yes, John asked then if God is "so kind and good."

The Guide replied that nowadays God is often accused of cruelty. To the contrary, God should be accused of taking risks. He has taken the risk of making people free. (Chesterton once said that hell is God's great compliment to humanity—it is part of the reality of man's freedom.) When man sins, God saves him from it if he can. But God doesn't save people against their will. God cannot force a man to do *freely* what a man has freely made impossible for himself. God does not make the darkness; the darkness is there already wherever sin has done its work.[24]

Only One is great enough to make himself small enough to enter hell. He did not do it just once, briefly, two thousand years ago, because God is not really in our time. Christ's descending into hell somehow includes all moments that ever were. Every spirit in prison hears him preach.[25]

What more can you ask God to do? To cancel human sins and offer miraculous help? He has done that on Calvary. To forgive them? Some will not accept forgiveness. To finally leave alone those who refuse him? Lewis says, alas, that is what he does.[26] And once a person separates himself from God, Lewis asks, what can he do but wither and die?[27]

A bad person's perdition is not simply a sentence imposed upon him or her, but the mere fact of being what he or she is.[28] "It's not a question of God 'sending' us to Hell. In each of us there is something growing up which will of itself *be hell* unless it is nipped in the bud. The matter is serious: let us put ourselves in His hands at once—this very day, this hour."[29]

Part Two: Farther Out

When Lewis was a young atheist, he embraced materialism and thought he had disposed of Christianity forever. But he learned, to his surprise, that there were some responsible adults who believed, after all, in a world behind, or around, the material world and yet were not Christians. Here were unorthodox people who dismissed the whole materialist philosophy out of hand. It was a disturbing but exciting idea. Perhaps there was "something else" after all, and perhaps it had nothing to do with Christian theology.

Young Lewis developed a ravenous desire for the occult—a mingled desire and revulsion. It had a special appeal to him because it was known to very few and scorned by many. The

fact that magic was unorthodox to both Christians and materialists made a special appeal to the rebel in him. He went on a
spiritual debauch, and if there had been an experienced dabbler
in dirt of the magical kind nearby to lead him on, in his own
view he might have become a Satanist or a maniac.

Fortunately, Lewis had no personal teacher at hand.
Fortunately, too, he experienced some strong fears from childhood which made him at least wish at night that the occult were
untrue. And, further, he came to see that even if he had the
extremely interesting experience of raising a spirit, his deeper
desires would say, "What is this to me?" His confidence in
materialism had been shaken, but he developed an absolute
antipathy to everything occult and magical which carried him
safely through future temptations of this kind. There were
future temptations, to be sure. But Lewis was set in his rejection
of the occult when he saw an acquaintance of his go mad and
die in a wretched state after pursuing it.

In his preface to *The Screwtape Letters* Lewis declares that
devils hail both materialists and magicians with equal delight.
The devils are hard put to choose between those two errors into
which men often fall: disbelief in the existence of devils or an
excessive and unhealthy interest in them.

Screwtape himself expressed hopes that eventually these two
opposite errors could be combined producing Materialist
Magicians. These would be men who retain their disbelief in
God and their allegiance to "science," while slipping into a worship of "Forces" they don't understand, which are in fact the very
devils of Christian theology.

This is exactly the extreme case that Lewis illustrated in
Perelandra and *That Hideous Strength* with the exceptional
destruction of atheists Weston, Wither and Frost. In fact, after
Weston became an Un-man, he told Ransom how hopeless and
horrible death is from the viewpoint of the damned—all darkness, worms, heat, pressure, salt, suffocation and stink. All

ghosts, he claimed, are witless, twittering, gibbering, decaying and full of hatred for the living. "Then there's Spiritualism," he continued. "I used to think it all nonsense. But it isn't. It's all true. . . . Ectoplasm—slimy films coming out of a medium's belly and making great, chaotic, tumbledown faces. Automatic writing producing reams of rubbish."[30] So much for the occult!

The End of Evil

It is obvious that few men fall prey to the devils in this atheist-Satanist way. But it is not obvious that a few men are damned. After all, Christ said, "Narrow is the way, . . . and few there be that find it." Lewis considered that the most distressing text in the Bible, although he felt that it certainly was not meant to be simply statistical.

Speaking to a minister once about the insanely cruel teacher they both had suffered under as children, Lewis said, "Well, we shan't see *him* again." "You mean we *hope* we shan't," the cleric had answered with a grim smile.[31] It was a joke, but not a joke. Lewis believed that in all discussions of hell we should have ourselves in mind, not other people.[32] Lewis did not pretend to have any information on the fate of the virtuous unbeliever. He simply assumed that in some way the result of such a life is less satisfactory than the result of a life based upon the truth. But at the same time he felt that a believer is playing for higher stakes than an unbeliever and, hence, incurring the danger of something really nasty.[33]

Some will not be saved. Lewis claimed that he would have paid any price to change that doctrine truthfully to "All will be saved." But Scripture (especially the words of our Lord), tradition and reason all support the former. It is said that hell is a detestable doctrine; of course it is.[34]

Lewis's favorite writer, George MacDonald, seemed to be a Universalist, talking in his books as if all people would finally be saved. In *The Great Divorce* Lewis boldly discusses this with

MacDonald in heaven. MacDonald tells Lewis that it is ill to talk of such questions on earth because the ultimate answers cannot be understood by people who are still in time. Surely anyone may choose eternal death, and those who choose it shall have it. In contrast, Universalism, like predestination, would seem to destroy freedom. Universalism and predestination may be true, but freedom is a deeper truth. It is useless now to try to see the shape of eternity.[35]

One of the main objections to hell is the complaint that life is so short compared to eternity; death should not deprive people of a second chance. Lewis believed that if a million chances would do any good, God would give them. But finality must come some time, and surely in each case God knows when.[36]

In *The Great Divorce* people are told on their visit to the lowlands of heaven that if they don't return to the grey town it will have been purgatory for them; if they return, it was and is hell.

Lewis frankly admitted believing in purgatory. To him it was a place for souls already saved but in need of purifying—purging. He agreed with the Protestant Reformers in tossing out the distorted idea of purgatory as a place of torture (worse yet, used as a fund-raising device for the church). There is no place of torture and punishment for the saved, only a place of cleansing.

Lewis felt that our souls *demand* purgatory. Who would want to enter heaven foul and dirty? Lewis thought of the dentist's chair. "I hope that when the tooth of life is drawn and I am 'coming round,' a voice will say, 'Rinse your mouth out with this.' *This* will be Purgatory."[37]

Is it possible for any charitable person to enter into the full joy of heaven knowing that others are lost in hell? It has to be. Otherwise hell should be able to *veto* heaven. If the makers of misery were able to infect the joy of heaven, they would destroy in others the happiness they refused for themselves. Should the loveless and self-imprisoned be allowed to blackmail the universe? The action of pity will always leap quicker than light from the highest place to the lowest to bring healing and joy, whatever the cost to itself. But there shall be no suffering of pity in heaven; "if we accept Heaven we shall not be able to retain even the smallest and most intimate souvenires of Hell."[38]

Besides, hell is in no sense *parallel* to heaven. They are not like two neighboring countries, one starving and the other flourishing simultaneously. Hell has a finality about it that heaven does not have. Hell is only the outer darkness, the outer rim where being fades away into nonentity. Those in hell enjoy forever the horrible freedom they have demanded, and they are self-enslaved. Even if hell contained pleasure instead of pain, that kind of pleasure would send any soul not already damned flying to its prayers in nightmare terror.[39]

As Lewis explained in *The Pilgrim's Regress*, if hell is a deep hole, the walls of the hole are there to enclose and limit the darkness. The walls are like a tourniquet on the wound of the lost soul to stop the flow of evil. It is God's best service to those who will let him do nothing better for them.[40]

> God in His mercy made
> The fixed pains of Hell.
> That misery might be stayed,
> God in His mercy made
> Eternal bounds and bade
> Its waves no further swell.
> God in His mercy made
> The fixed pains of Hell.[41]

Further Reading about Hell

"In all things which I have written and thought I have always stuck to traditional, dogmatic positions."[42]

The Great Divorce by C. S. Lewis tells almost as much about hell as it does about heaven. It is a book all about the great unavoidable "either-or."

The Screwtape Letters by C. S. Lewis gave Lewis his great popularity with the general public. It is a witty series of letters from a senior devil to a junior tempter. Readers should be advised that the widely distributed Spire (Revell) edition, first published in 1976 by Lord and King, is significantly altered without authorization or approval by C. S. Lewis and without mention of alterations on the cover or title page. As written by Lewis, the story is set in World War II England.

That Hideous Strength by C. S. Lewis is the final volume of Lewis's science fiction trilogy. It is a wild story about a bit of hell breaking loose on Earth.

"Hell," chapter eight of *The Problem of Pain* by C. S. Lewis, attempts to prove that this intolerable doctrine is moral, necessary and true.

Notes

1. Lewis, *The Problem of Pain*, p. 115.
2. Lewis, *Surprised by Joy*, p. 171.
3. Lewis, *Mere Christianity*, p. 59.
4. Lewis, *God in the Dock*, p. 56.
5. C. S. Lewis, *Transposition and Other Addresses* (London: Geoffrey Bles, 1949), p. 56.
6. Lewis, *Letters to Malcolm*, p. 76.
7. Lewis, *The Problem of Pain*, p. 42. Lewis, *The Great Divorce*, p. vii.
8. C. S. Lewis, *Screwtape Proposes a Toast and Other Pieces* (London: Fontana, 1966), p. 25.
9. Lewis, *The Screwtape Letters*, p. 17.
10. Ibid., p. 65.
11. Ibid., p. 46.
12. Ibid., p. 110.
13. Lewis, *The Pilgrim's Regress*, p. 177.
14. C. S. Lewis, *Perelandra* (New York: Macmillan, 1944, 1966), p. 129.
15. Lewis, *The Problem of Pain*, p. 113.
16. C. S. Lewis, *That Hideous Strength* (New York: Macmillan, 1951), p. vii.
17. Lewis, *Letters of C. S. Lewis*, p. 207.
18. Lewis, *The Great Divorce*, p. 69.
19. Lewis, *The Magician's Nephew*, p. 157.
20. Lewis, *The Great Divorce*, pp. 126–27.

21. Ibid., p. 127.

22. Lewis, *The Last Battle*, p. 154.

23. Ibid., p. 150.

24. Lewis, *The Pilgrim's Regress*, p. 181.

25. Lewis, *The Great Divorce*, p. 128.

26. Lewis, *The Problem of Pain*, p. 116.

27. Lewis, *Mere Christianity*, p. 137.

28. Lewis, *The Problem of Pain*, p. 111.

29. Lewis, *God in the Dock*, p. 155.

30. Lewis, *Perelandra*, p. 170.

31. Lewis, *Surprised by Joy*, p. 234.

32. Lewis, *The Problem of Pain*, p. 116.

33. Lewis, *Letters of C. S. Lewis*, p. 164.

34. Lewis, *The Problem of Pain*, pp. 106–7

35. Lewis, *The Great Divorce*, p. 129.

36. Lewis, *The Problem of Pain*, p. 112.

37. Lewis, *Letters to Malcolm*, p. 109.

38. Lewis, *The Great Divorce*, pp. 124–25, vi.

39. Lewis, *The Problem of Pain*, pp. 114–16.

40. Lewis, *The Pilgrim's Regress*, p. 181.

41. Ibid., p. 180.

42. Lewis, *God in the Dock*, p. 60.

Mystery:
How Can
We Believe
This Business?

Chapter 8

Miracles

*"The Christian story is precisely
the story of one grand miracle."*
"The Grand Miracle," God in the Dock[1]

Part One: The Problem of Miracles

C. S. Lewis believed that most stories about miraculous events are probably false. But so far as that goes, he believed that most stories about nonmiraculous events are false as well. He figured that lies, exaggerations, misunderstandings and hearsay make up at least half of all that is said and written in the world. So his purpose in discussing miracles was not to persuade readers to believe most miracle stories that they hear. His primary purpose was to help people who wanted to know whether the New Testament miracles could have happened. Above all, his purpose was to show whether we could without absurdity believe that Christ rose from the emptied tomb.

Lewis uses the word *miracle* to mean an interference with Nature by supernatural power. Therefore he devotes the first six chapters of his book *Miracles* to showing that there is, indeed, a Supernature. Naturalism has to be wrong. He was once criti-

cized for refuting naturalism because no one believes in it anyway. He answered that there may be no naturalists in some
circles, but that there were plenty of them where he came
from—and, presumably, in Moscow.[2]

A naturalist believes that our vast, interlocking system of
time and space is going of its own accord and that there is nothing else in existence. Nature is "the whole show." If naturalism
is true, there can be no miracles because there is nothing outside
of Nature to interfere. Events we mistake for miracles are in
reality just misunderstood natural events. Carried to its logical
conclusion, naturalism declares that people have no free will
because they, like the rest of Nature, are part of a very complex
system in which all behavior is determined in advance by the
overall pattern of physics, chemistry and biology.

Some naturalists believe in an "emergent god" of some kind
that developed within Nature and is part of Nature; no naturalist believes in a supreme God who created Nature.

Two of Lewis's main objections to naturalism are based on
what it does to human mentality and morality. If man is just a
temporary product of mindless nature, a complex biological
accident, how could the electrical patterns in his cortex really
discover truth? Naturalism cannot allow for genuine reason in
man, and so it invalidates the thoughts of those who believe in
it. Likewise, naturalism exposes all our value judgments and
morals to be simply matters of conditioned personal prefer-
ences. It leaves us no right and wrong.

Lewis seeks to demonstrate that only a supernatural source
can account for rational thought and our ideas of good and evil.
Supernaturalism means that One Thing is basic and original
and all else is derived from it. This One Thing has produced
our framework of space and time and the whole procession of
systematically connected events which fill the framework. The
Thing itself (God) is outside the system, which is Nature, and
is more important than Nature.

Thus Lewis claims that human reason and morality are proofs of the Supernatural. They do not show that Nature is invaded by the Supernatural, but they show that there is a possible invader. God created Nature, he maintains her existence, and perhaps he does *other* things to her. Those other things are called miracles.[3]

To Lewis's immense chagrin, one part of his argument against naturalism was effectively challenged by G. E. M. Anscombe in 1948. She presented her criticism of the third chapter of *Miracles* at a meeting of the Socratic Club in Oxford, and it is said that Lewis was, for once in his life, unable to come out on top in an informal debate. As a result, he changed the third chapter. (Anscombe, a Roman Catholic, later became a professor of philosophy at Cambridge.)

Ten years later Lewis easily rebuffed an attack on his teaching about miracles launched by another teacher destined also to find a place as a professor at Cambridge. This opponent was Dr. W. Norman Pittenger, and the forum was *The Christian Century*.[4] Pittenger claimed that Lewis defined miracles as violations of the laws of Nature. Lewis answered in print in short order, even exclaiming, "How many times does a man need to say something before he is safe from the accusation of having said exactly the opposite?"[5]

What Lewis had actually said in the passage Pittenger referred to was "It is therefore inaccurate to define a miracle as something that breaks the laws of Nature."[6] To Lewis there was a great difference between interference and broken laws.

Observation and experiment have showed us what the norm is in parts of Nature. A miracle is an exception to the norm because it feeds new events into the established pattern and thus causes a new result.[7]

For example, if Lewis put six pennies into a drawer on Monday and six more on Tuesday, according to the laws of mathematics he should find twelve pennies there on

Wednesday—*other things being equal*. But, if a robber stole ten pennies in the night, Lewis will find only two left. The laws of arithmetic will not have been broken—only the laws of England. If God works miracles, he does it "like a thief in the night," in that he makes other things *not* equal. He introduces supernatural force which people do not reckon on, and they get an unexpected result. That is why Lewis defines miracles as an interference with Nature by a supernatural power.

Possibility, Probability, Propriety

If we grant the existence of the Supernatural and the fact that Nature works according to regular laws, Lewis reasoned, we are then ready to question whether it is possible for the Supernatural to invade Nature. Is it possible for a thief to steal ten pennies from the drawer? Or does the character of Nature render such invasions absolutely impossible?

Many ordinary people disbelieve in the New Testament miracles because they feel that science has absolutely disproved them. For example, some people actually believe that early Christians accepted the virgin birth because, unlike us, they didn't know it was contrary to the course of nature. But any person who reads the biblical account would see that Joseph knew as well as any modern husband that women do not have babies unless they have lain with men. Joseph consciously chose to believe that his fiancée's pregnancy was due to a miracle, contrary to the known order of Nature.

The event would not have been a miracle without this interference in the regular process of Nature. That is why twentieth-century science has nothing significant to say against the virgin birth. Increasing knowledge about Nature cannot demonstrate that a unique invasion of Nature by something from outside never occurred. Surely many erroneous ideas about facts of Nature have been well disproved by scientific exploration and experiment. But it was not Nature that produced the virgin birth.

Another confused modern objection to the possibility of miracles is that the earth is very small compared to the size of the universe. This has been known since the days of Ptolemy, the second-century astronomer whose works were the standard astronomy textbooks for thirteen hundred years. Lewis could never see how the awesome size of the universe should today discredit Christianity or the possibility of miracles. It is also hard to see how the small size of man indicates that God could not be deeply involved with him.

Astronomy and modern science have in no way eliminated the possibility of miracles. If a person believes in the normal stability of Nature and the existence of the Supernatural, he must in all honesty admit the theoretical possibility of miracles. The probability or propriety of miracles is another matter.

Even after admitting the possibility of miracles, many modern people will accept the most farfetched "natural" explanations of mysterious events rather than conclude that a miracle occurred. They assume that a miracle is more improbable than collective hallucination, hypnotism of unconsenting spectators or outright lying and instant conspiracy by reputable people who have nothing to gain by it. They assume that any miracle is more improbable than the most improbable natural event.

The more improbable a story is, the more historical evidence is required for it. Since miracles cannot be reproduced in laboratory situations, it is impossible to produce the amount of historical evidence required by people who consider them the most improbable of all occurrences. History never provides that degree of evidence for any event.

As Lewis observed in the first paragraph of *Miracles*, even seeing is *not* believing. The only person Lewis ever met who claimed to have seen a ghost strongly disbelieved in life after death before her unusual experience. Therefore, right or wrong, she disbelieved in the ghost she saw. So far as she was concerned, there had to be some trick or illusion involved. So it is that miracles can't be proved by experience.

Only a person who does not consider miracles intrinsically improbable will assent to any given miracle or will find the existing evidence sufficient to prove that quite a number of miracles have occurred. Accounts of the Supernatural meet us on every side; history is full of them. And each story should be judged on its own merits, Lewis maintained.

For example, the Bible tells us that Sennacherib's invasion was stopped by angels, and another source says it was stopped by mice which ate up all the army's bowstrings one night. We know that mice do not behave that way. We do not know that angels don't exist or don't behave that way. Therefore, an open-minded person will be on the side of the angels.

Of course every miracle is improbable. But all events whatever are improbable. It was highly improbable in one sense that you, with your specific genetic complex, would ever have been born. Looking at the railroad timetable, it seems improbable in another sense that an accident will change the departure time of the 3:15 train. There are different kinds of probability and improbability. We know enough about Nature to know that some natural events are extremely improbable. We do not know enough about the Supernatural to know that miracles are in that category.

Even if miracles are possible and not infinitely improbable, would the Supernatural stoop to invading Nature and disrupting the regular flow of events? Many people think that such behavior would be unworthy of God and unsuitable to the dignity of God or Nature. They feel that after setting things in motion, God would not want to tamper with them, especially for such a small creature as man. Lewis feels that this view is a great mistake. There are rules behind the rules, he liked to say, and there is a unity deeper than uniformity. Miracles are not flaws in God's work, but expressions of its truest and deepest unity.

Is Nature mistreated by God if a miracle occurs? Miracles must of course interrupt her usual course, but they are not contradictions or outrages to her. Left to her own resources, Nature could never produce miracles. But if Nature can be modified by supernatural power, then that capability is part of her basic character.

If miracles do occur, then for God *not* to have caused them would have been the real inconsistency. If miracles occur, they are the very thing the universal story is about. Death and resurrection are the center of the plot. "If you have hitherto disbelieved in miracles, it is worth pausing a moment to consider whether this is not chiefly because you thought you had discovered what the story was really about?—that atoms, and time and space and economics and politics were the main plot?"[8] If such were the case, miracles would be an impropriety.

Over half the disbelief in the possibility of miracles is due to a mistaken sense of their *unfitness*. From the Christian point of view, the probability of miracles must be judged by our sense of fitness related to historical evidence. The possibility of a miracle is already decided by logic.

Part Two: The Meaning of Miracles

C. S. Lewis stated flatly that the accounts of the miracles in first-century Palestine are either lies, legends or history. If all or the main part of them are lies or legends, the two-thousand-year-old claim of Christianity is false. It could still have some noble sentiments or innocuous moral platitudes in it, as Greek and Norse mythology do. But it would still be just as false.

When Christianity is stripped to its bare essentials, it is still something quite unambiguously supernatural, miraculous and shocking. "We may not believe in a flat earth and a sky-palace. But we must insist from the beginning that we believe, as firmly as any savage or theosophist, in a spirit-world which can, and does, invade the natural or phenomenal universe."⁹

God became man. This is the central miracle of Christianity. All the others fit around it. The Incarnation is the grand miracle.

If the thing really happened, it is the central event in the history of Earth. It is very hard to give any historical explanation of the sayings and influence of Christ that is not harder than the Christian explanation.

The credibility of the Incarnation depends upon the extent to which it illuminates and integrates the whole mass of our knowledge. We do not need to fully comprehend the doctrine itself. We believe that the sun is overhead on a summer noon because of the way it illuminates everything else, not because we can clearly see the sun itself.

The first problem about the Incarnation that occurs to people is that of combining eternal self-existent Spirit with a natural human organism to make one person. It would seem impossible except that every human is a wholly supernatural entity united with a part of Nature. The difference is that in people a supernatural creature in union with a natural creature becomes one human being, and in Jesus the Supernatural Creator himself does so. Thus the strange composite nature of man seems to be a faint image of the divine Incarnation—the same theme in a minor key.

In the descent and reascent of God one can see one of the world's most familiar patterns. Death and rebirth, go down to go up, is a key principle of all vegetable life, animal life, and even our moral and emotional life. This pattern in nature is a transposition of the divine theme into a minor key. Nature religions had already told the story of a dying God, a Corn-King who personified the grain in its annual pattern of rebirth. But Christ came to the people who were most militantly against Nature religions, who had no such tradition. Jehovah was not a Nature

God, but the God of Nature, the inventor, maker, owner and controller. The earth was likened to his footstool, not his garment or grave. Christ is like the Corn-King only because the Corn-King is a portrait of him—an idea men drew from Nature, which Nature in turn had long ago received from her Creator.

Selectiveness is Nature's amoral method. Space is enormous but matter occupies little of it. Of all the stars, only ours is known to have planets. Here countless billions of seeds and sperm are produced; few are fertilized. Of all the species only one is rational, and only a few of its members attain excellence. God's workings have been selective to the highest degree also. When the knowledge of God had been lost, he chose one man, Abraham, that through his descendants all the nations should be blessed with the knowledge of the true God. Abraham had to go to a strange country and father the Jewish nation. This nation was pruned repeatedly, in the desert, in Babylon and elsewhere. "The process grows narrower and narrower, sharpens at last into one small bright point like the head of a spear. It is a Jewish girl at her prayers. All humanity (so far as concerns its redemption) has narrowed to that."[10]

Vicariousness, not privilege, was the lot of God's chosen people. Mary suffered the depths of a mother's anguish. The whole nation suffered through centuries that others might be healed. "The Sinless Man suffers for the sinful, and, in their degree, all good men for all bad men." Like death and rebirth and selectiveness, vicariousness is a basic characteristic of Nature. In Nature self-sufficiency is impossible. "Everything is indebted to everything else, sacrificed to everything else, dependent upon everything else."[11]

In these four areas and many others we see Nature illuminated by the Incarnation, which casts a new light upon everything. God and Nature were joined in the Person of

Christ, and there will be no divorce. God will not leave Nature again. She will be redeemed and glorified.

The miracle of the Incarnation, far from denying what we know of reality, fills in the main part which we were lacking and ties all the rest together. Its credibility does not lie in its obviousness. It works quietly in our minds explaining both our laughter and our logic, our fear of the dead and our acceptance of death. Lewis concluded that when you turn to the historical question of whether the Incarnation happened, you will not ask for the amount of evidence you would rightly demand for something intrinsically improbable. You will ask only for the amount of evidence you demand for an event that has a peculiar and compelling fitness.

In his miracles Jesus did instantly, right at hand, some of the very things that God does at other times in slower, larger ways that men do not usually notice. The miracles of Jesus are a demonstration of the power which all people who become children of God will someday have. Christ was the first man of his kind, but he will not be the last.

The first type of miracle Jesus performed was that of *fertility*. At the wedding feast in Cana he created in a moment wine from water in earthenware jars. Ordinarily God creates wine in a vegetable organism which turns water, soil and sunlight into grape juice. This miracle was a shortcut to God's usual result.

Jesus multiplied a little bread into much bread to feed a multitude. We take it for granted that every year God multiplies a little wheat into much wheat. Jesus also multiplied fish. At the beginning God commanded all species to be fruitful and multiply. He has always been multiplying fish underwater in seas, bays, lakes and rivers. Jesus did it closely and quickly in his hands.

The virgin birth itself was a fertility miracle, no less and no more surprising than the others, but for some reason harder for people to accept today. Actually, God's creative power is at work every time a woman conceives. But this one time he does it without a line of human ancestors. He created a miraculous spermatozoon in the body of a virgin. From there on the pregnancy and birth were normal.

The second type of miracle of Jesus was *healing*. Of course all who are cured are cured by God, because he put the recuperative energy into the human body. That is why every cut must heal itself if it is to be healed. But at one time Jesus quickly and visibly healed the sick people he encountered in Palestine.

The third type of miracle is that of *destruction*. Jesus withered a fig tree as a symbol of God's sentence upon all that is unproductive. This miracle, too, repeats visibly what God is doing all the time in Nature. "No tree died that year in Palestine, or any year anywhere, except because God did—or rather ceased to do—something to it."[12]

The fourth type of miracle is that of *dominion over the inorganic*. We see this when Jesus stilled the storm. But since God arranged for both storms and calm in the first place, ultimately all storms are stilled by God. Some people may fear that miraculous interference with weather would upset all of Nature. Although a miracle is not interlocked with the previous history of Nature, it is always absorbed into Nature like all other events. Miraculous bread and fish are normally digested; miraculously healed bodies live on and die as usual; a miraculously destroyed tree made ordinary wood; and a miraculously stilled storm contributed its part to the year's weather pattern.

Lewis claimed that when Christ and Peter walked briefly together on the water, this was a foretaste of the future. We had a momentary glimpse into the new Nature. It was a special kind of dominion over the inorganic. Nature was obedient to Spirit.

The Miracle of the New Life

The fifth category of miracles is *reversal*. That is what happened when the dead were raised; the process of death was reversed. Lazarus was restored to the kind of life he had before. He who will raise all people at the general resurrection here raised one man in an immediate, lesser way. As Lewis puts it, the mere restoration of Lazarus was as inferior in splendor to the glorious resurrection as five little barley loaves were to all the waving bronze and gold of a fat valley ripe for harvest.

The final category of miracles is the greatest, that of *perfecting* or *glorification*. The first of these was Christ's Transfiguration, a glimpse of something to come. The most obvious, of course, is the resurrection. This event opened a new chapter in cosmic history; the new creation began. Christ re-appeared, not as a ghost, but as a solid man who could eat boiled fish. The resurrection was not a reversal or undoing of the Incarnation. For about six weeks Christ appeared occasionally to his apostles who became the core of the church. This miracle became the core of their preaching to the rest of the world.

The necessary corollary to the resurrection is another miracle of perfecting or glorification—the Ascension. Christ was not a phantom who would just fade away. Christ's new life had its own new nature. He said that he was going to create a place for us. Lewis felt sure that Christ was going to create a whole new Nature which would provide the environment for his glorified humanity and, in him, for ours. The spectators at the site seemed to see a short vertical movement, a vague luminosity, and then nothing.

The biblical account of the Ascension would seem to place Christ on a chair in the sky next to God's throne. Lewis finds profound meaning in that imagery: imagery it is, not fact. But Lewis hastens to add that a simple person who really believes that heaven is in the sky may have a far truer and more spiritual conception of it than many logical thinkers who could quickly disprove such a foolish idea but miss the main concepts. For the deeper knowledge comes through obedience. "I must fully allow that it is of more importance for you or me today to refrain from one sneer or to extend one charitable thought to an enemy than to know all that angels and archangels know about the mysteries of the New Creation."[13]

Lewis urges his readers to develop a nose like a bloodhound for the concealed assumption that miracles are impossible, improbable or improper. The books of many modern Christian scholars and critics base their arguments against New Testament miracles upon those three hidden assumptions. Lewis warned his readers to study the New Testament itself first, and then to remember that those reading modern New Testament scholars often go among them as sheep among wolves.

Even more important, Lewis warned his readers who had not believed in miracles previously to be on guard against simply slipping back into the habit of disbelief. That tendency is no evidence at all against new ideas. It is just a natural characteristic of the human mind. New thoughts have to have time to become habitual, to become "Belief-feelings." Feeling certain that miracles can never really occur after all is not important. Many of the most basic facts of our lives feel untrue at some times.

Finally, few people see miracles done, and it is just as well. If we were heroic missionaries, apostles or martyrs it would be more likely. Only if we are at one of the special places in spiritual history are we apt to see miracles for ourselves.

In the May 7, 1980, issue of *The Christian Century*, an account of one of those miracles was published, and it involved the book *Miracles* itself. A theology student with an A average at Duke Divinity School, Thaniel Armistead wrote an essay about herself in December 1979. She was handicapped with cystic fibrosis and told how six years before she had moved from calling herself an atheist into the struggle of committed Christianity. One month after she wrote that account, called

"Tragedy and Christian Faith," she died. She had lived with much suffering to the age of twenty-two.

According to Thaniel Armistead, one night in November 1973 she began to read C. S. Lewis's book *Miracles*. Halfway through the book she was in terror that God might be real, because Lewis had demolished her favorite defenses for atheism. Then she read a section which made John 3:16, the only Bible verse she knew, perfectly clear to her. She saw that Jesus was God incarnate, that the crucifixion had overcome sin, death and evil. Furthermore, she realized that if this were true, it was the most important thing that ever happened and contained the meaning and mystery of all suffering. A living Presence came into her room and utterly changed her, overwhelming her with love and causing her to surrender herself to Jesus Christ. Thaniel told this story in vivid, moving detail in an analytical and frank style.

One of the most interesting facts of all is that she later discovered that this passage which opened her understanding and led to a life-changing encounter with the Spirit of God was never a part of Lewis's book *Miracles* after all. She later reread the book several times, and the section she read the night she became a Christian *is not there*.

All she could say was, "Draw your own conclusions."[14]

Further Reading about Miracles

"No reader worth his salt trots along in obedience to a time-table."[15] *Miracles* by C. S. Lewis equips readers to assess accounts of miracles for themselves by furnishing many Christian ideas about the possibility or probability of the miraculous. The Fontana edition (1960) includes Lewis's important revision of chapter three not otherwise available.

The Voyage of the "Dawn Treader" by C. S. Lewis, third of the Narnian series, tells of a journey full of miracles, culminating with word of the Greatest Miracle.

"Miracles" in *God in the Dock* by C. S. Lewis was originally a sermon preached in 1942 and was later largely incorporated into *Miracles*.

"The Grand Miracle" in *God in the Dock* by C. S. Lewis was originally a sermon preached in 1945 about the miracle of Christ's descending and then rising, bringing us up with him if we will.

Notes

1. Lewis, *God in the Dock*, p. 80.
2. Ibid., p. 179.
3. Lewis, *Miracles*, p. 54.
4. Lewis, *God in the Dock*, p. 177.
5. Ibid., pp. 178–79.
6. Lewis, *Miracles*, p. 72.
7. Ibid.
8. Ibid., p. 119.
9. Lewis, *God in the Dock*, p. 69.
10. Lewis, *Miracles*, p. 141.
11. Ibid., p. 143.
12. Ibid., p. 169.
13. Ibid., p. 193.
14. Armistead, Thaniel, "Tragedy and the Christian Faith," *The Christian Century* (7 May 1980), pp. 517–20.
15. Lewis, *Of Other Worlds*, p. 28.

Chapter 9

Prayer

"It may be a mystery why He should have allowed us to cause real events at all; but it is no odder that He should allow us to cause them by praying than by any other method."
"Work and Prayer" God in the Dock[1]

Part One: The Theory of Prayer

Prayer was the main thing that turned Lewis away from Christianity when he was about thirteen years old. He had known unanswered prayers for his mother's life and for delivery from his miserable boarding school, but that was not his trouble. What turned him away was the terrible burden of false duties in prayer which he had somehow set as his standard.

Young Lewis wasn't worried about God's not paying attention. He was worried about his not paying attention. Having been told as a child that one must think about what one was saying in prayer, he carried that advice to a boyish extreme. As soon as he reached the amen, his conscience accused him of not having concentrated quite well enough and made him start all over again. By the time he abandoned Christianity, every evening was cloaked in gloom because he so dreaded bedtime and the nightly struggle for supreme concentration. Prayer meant pain, defeat and much lost sleep. Was this a surprisingly serious encounter with religion for a young adolescent? Lewis thought not. He supposed that most people who think at all have done a great deal of their thinking in their first fourteen years.[2] It was with great relief that he gradually gave up prayer, and Christianity with it.

Twenty years later, shortly after his conversion to Christianity, Lewis wrote a letter to his brother, Warren, in Shanghai. Lewis admitted that he had resorted to prayer for Warren's safety during a Japanese attack and found it philosophically a rather embarrassing position. After all, Providence already knows what is best and will certainly do it. But Lewis reasoned that one could prove the uselessness of any action that way. Why do anything at all if Providence will take care of everything? Assuming that other actions are useful in spite of Providence, he decided that prayers of request may be useful and appropriate.[3]

Four years before his death, Lewis published an article in *The Atlantic Monthly*, developing this idea. Does God ever really follow people's suggestions? Of course God doesn't need to be told what is best, and he doesn't need to be urged to do it. But he doesn't need any other things people do either. He could produce food without farmers, knowledge without scholars and heathen conversions without missionaries. The fact is that, instead, he allows people, animals and all things in creation to take part in the execution of his will. God's will shall be done in the long run, but the details of how it works out depend upon the actions, including the prayers, of his creatures. We have to collaborate with him; he delegates all he can to us.[4]

> No stranger that omnipotence should choose to need
> Small helps than great—no stranger if His action lingers
> Till men have prayed, and suffers their weak prayers indeed
> To move as very muscles His delaying fingers . . . [5]

Lewis thought the question, Does prayer work? was a bad one. Prayer is not a vending machine. Prayer is a request. And the very nature of requests is that some are granted and some are refused. If Christian prayers were always granted (an obvious impossibility, since some contradict others) the result would be more like magic than Christian doctrine. The Christian picture of prayer is more like children putting requests to a very wise parent than like children controlling things with a magic wand. We are only children in our understanding.

Prayer works in that it is a personal contact between ourselves, incomplete as we are, and the one utterly concrete Person. Confession and penitence are the beginning, adoration is the main part, and enjoyment of the presence of God is the highlight. Asking for things is a correct and important part of prayer, but it is not the most important part. Prayer works when God shows himself to us—and that is not always as we expect or desire.[6]

Perhaps most believers find it natural and easy to speak to God. But for adult converts with highly analytical minds it is not always natural and easy. One can't "simply talk to God" if one realizes that one's own self-concept and one's concept of God are false and misleading.

For Lewis the moment of prayer should include a temporary awareness of rock-bottom realities, an awareness of himself as a creature of God caught in time and space, and awareness that the "real world" and his "real self" as ordinarily perceived are not very real at all. He wanted honest perspective. He wanted the real Lewis speaking to the real God. "The prayer preceding all prayers is 'May it be the real I who speaks. May it be the real Thou that I speak to.'"[7] Lewis didn't want his false idea of himself speaking to a bright blur in his own mind. In his poem "Footnote to All Prayers," he begs God to mercifully translate the false and inadequate ideas in our prayers into something acceptable to himself.

It is clear that even in his adult Christian life, Lewis's demands upon himself concerning prayer were far more difficult than those of the ordinary Christian. He was not satisfied with emotional intensity as a sign of spiritual depth. As a philosophical thinker, he was concerned about the true nature of things.

He believed that the most blessed result of prayer would be to rise from prayer thinking, "But I never knew before. I never dreamed . . ."[8]

Problems of Petition

Lewis found that worship was more noble than petitionary prayer and far easier to write about, but he concentrated more on petitionary prayer in his writing. Why? Because that is where so many problems are. The avoidance of petitionary prayer can easily spring from a lack of faith or effort rather than from spiritual superiority.[9]

At the end of his book *Miracles*, Lewis explained how he rejected the idea of "special providences" as answers to prayer. He believed in miracles and he believed in natural events. Those are the two things we ask for most in our prayers—miracles or events whose foundations were laid when God made the universe. Since God is not in time, a Christian's prayer today is just as much present at the creation of the world as it is now or will be in the future. Prayers are in eternity with God. Therefore, although all events except miracles come about by natural causes, all events are providential and all can be influenced by prayer.

It is never possible to prove whether a given nonmiraculous event was or was not an answer to prayer. It came about by natural events, but the whole chain of natural events hangs upon God's will. And even though one prays after the event has been decided, his prayer still contributes to that decision. One may effectively pray for the safety of someone who was in danger yesterday. That prayer contributes to what happened. If the man was kept safe, the prayer helped shape that safety. If the man was killed, that prayer was heard and refused. (Of course, once it was known that the man had been killed, no true prayer could be offered for his safety anymore; one must submit to God's will.) Every prayer is heard and "considered" by God. They are all answered in his providence, either yes or no.

Like many Christians, Lewis had witnessed yes answers to prayer that filled him with awe. One minor example was the time he had a compulsion to go to the barber although there was no necessity for a haircut that day, and he always considered haircuts a nuisance. The barber had needed to see him and had been praying for him to come.

A much greater example was the time a minister had laid hands on Joy Lewis as she lay dying of cancer and prayed for her healing. In the months that followed she was miraculously transformed from a helpless, suffering invalid into an active, joyful woman whose bones had rebuilt themselves. She lived for three years until she had a relapse and died.[10] Lewis hastily admitted that the granting of any such prayer of petition cannot be proved; the event, no matter how strange, might have occurred without the prayer.

On the other hand, when the answer to prayers is no, Lewis found it easy to assume that wisdom must sometimes refuse what ignorance may request with the best intentions. Since God's knowledge of our real needs and the way in which they can be satisfied infinitely exceeds our own, his operations will often appear to us far from beneficent and far from wise. Then it is our greatest wisdom to give him our confidence anyway.[11]

The granting or denial of prayer requests is a problem to some people, but not to C. S. Lewis. He saw another problem as the main one, and he sought the answer to it for years. In fact, in 1953 he gave a complete address on the subject to the ministerial group at Oxford, claiming that he had taken the problem to almost every Christian he knew, learned or simple, lay or clerical, in the Church of England or out, and had received no answer. He concluded his ten-page talk with a request for guidance. "How am I to pray this very night?"[12]

His problem was the fact that the Bible seems to instruct us to pray in two mutually exclusive ways. The first is the way of Christ in Gethsemane, the way of submission to God's will. This suited Lewis well and was his pattern. The second way is that of sure expectation. Several Bible passages clearly promise that our requests will be granted if we pray with faith that they will be granted. Lewis had always prayed that his friends' illnesses might be healed "if it was God's will." Was such praying a ghastly mistake?

Lewis believed that we must never ignore unsolved problems. He frankly acknowledged that the Bible makes lavish promises about the granting of prayers. These promises are the worst possible place to begin Christian instruction for children or pagans. These promises are truth for very advanced pupils in the faith. The most advanced saints do not receive more things they pray for than beginners; sometimes the opposite seems to be the pattern. "If we were stronger, we might be less tenderly treated."[13]

At the end of his life Lewis had concluded that for Christians no further advanced than he was, the prayer in Gethsemane is the only model. "Removing mountains can wait."[14] At the common level of faith, the main struggle is to believe that, whether he will grant them or not, God listens to our prayers and takes them into account. In fact, in bereavement and ill health it is often a struggle to go on believing that there is a Listener at all. "Are we only talking to ourselves in an empty universe? The silence is often so emphatic. And we have prayed so much already."[15]

Lewis thought about the charge that prayer is only someone speaking to himself and said, "Very well, suppose it is."

Thinking of Romans 8:26-27, he assumed that if the Holy Spirit enables one to pray, then in a sense God speaks to God. Our prayers are really his prayers.[16] Lewis put this idea into verse and warned readers not to take the last line too seriously.

> Master, they say that when I seem
>   To be in speech with you,
> Since you make no replies, it's all a dream
>   —One talker aping two.
>
> They are half right, but not as they
>   Imagine; rather, I
> Seek in myself the things I meant to say,
>   And lo! the wells are dry.
>
> Then, seeing me empty, you forsake
>   The Listener's role, and through
> My dead lips breathe and into utterance wake
>   The thoughts I never knew.
>
> And thus you neither need reply
>   Nor can; thus, while we seem
> Two talking, thou art One forever, and I
>   No dreamer, but thy dream.[17]

Part Two: The Practice of Prayer

Right in the middle of his book *Letters to Malcolm: Chiefly on Prayer*, Lewis confides to his fictitious friend Malcolm, "But however badly needed a good book on prayer is, I shall never try to write it."[18] He explains that comparing notes with a friend in private is fine, but that publishing such discussion in a book would turn it into instruction. "And for me to offer the world instruction about prayer would be impudence."[19]

One can imagine the twinkle in Lewis's eye as he disclaimed the very book he was writing. But he was serious about his own inadequacy. He remarked later in the same book that putting down a spiritual experience of his in black and white made it sound far bigger than it really was. He said he had no language weak enough to depict the weakness of his spiritual life. Trying to describe it weakly enough is like trying to turn the gas flame down a little lower, and it just goes out.[20]

Lewis refused to judge the prayer practices of others,[21] but he didn't see how anyone in his senses could save his main prayers of the day for bedtime. Any time or place, however unsuitable, seems better than one's last waking moment; sleepiness makes concentration too difficult.

The main advantage of bedtime prayer is that one can kneel then, and kneeling is often impossible at other times and places. Lewis believed that it is best if the body prays with the soul. But a seated body and a concentrating mind are far better than a kneeling body and a mind half asleep: "Kneeling does matter, but other things matter even more.[22] Because of bone disease, Lewis sometimes lost the ability to kneel in his last years.

Lewis felt silence and solitude necessary for a good prayer environment, but he could understand some people who find a moderate amount of external distraction helpful because it cuts down on inner distractions. He noted wryly that the worse one is praying, the longer it takes.[23]

Lewis kept an ever-lengthening list of people to pray for. (He found it much easier to pray for others than for himself.) He felt it is all right to remove people from one's list, but he found it very difficult to actually do it. Such a long list is burdensome; it makes it a little hard to really think about each person while praying. Lewis felt that the best approach is to keep one's mind fixed on God and let thoughts of the people come automatically.[24] Incidentally, he felt it unnecessary to pray for people by name; one may have lost or never known the name of a person who needs one's prayers. He figured God knows their names.[25]

Lewis could never accept the Roman Catholic practice of praying to saints, and he hoped the Church of England would not move in that direction because of the divisiveness of the issue. He believed that when we pray we pray *with* the saints and whole company of heaven.[26] However, he emphatically believed in praying for the dead.[27] His reasons were more emotional than theological. In his last years the majority of those he loved were dead. He believed that his prayers could somehow bless them. He felt that 1 Corinthians 15:20 and 1 Peter 3:19-20 imply this. One must remember that Lewis believed in a temporary purgatory for the blessed dead as a kind of entryway to heaven, and degrees of beatitude in heaven itself.[28]

Of course Lewis devoted most of his petitionary prayer to the living. For example, he corresponded with one American lady regularly for the last thirteen years of his life and assured her in about twenty-six of the letters that he was praying for her. Because of the rheumatism in his hands, he almost surely found the praying easier than the letter writing.[29] In *Mere Christianity* he likened Christian prayer to "dressing up as Christ" and suggested that when one prays Christ is at his side changing him. This may send a man away from his prayers to help his wife in the kitchen or a woman to her desk to write a needed letter.[30] Lewis augmented his prayers for the American lady by an arrangement with his American publisher that gave her part of his royalties. He was leery of too many prayers that leave all the work to God and other people.[31]

For many years after Lewis's conversion he never used any ready-made prayers except the Lord's prayer. But eventually the choice between ready-made prayers and his own words came to seem less important. One reason was the fact that a third form of prayer was Lewis's ideal form anyway—the prayer without words.

To pray successfully and genuinely without words one must be at his or her best physically and spiritually. Lewis would envision the people he was praying for rather than naming them and communicate his ideas to God with no words at all. But he finally came to see that the ability to pray thus was a gift—for him, at least—given at special times, not constantly.

The advantages of prayers in one's own words are obvious. These prayers specifically fit the speaker and his situation. Such prayers were Lewis's most frequent kind. However, he warned that unavoidable repetition can harden even our own prayers into a formula.

The advantages of prayers written by other people include reminders of proper theology, a sense of perspective about what to request and an element of the ceremonial that encourages reverence.[32] If we attend a church that uses written prayers in the service, these prayers are more meaningful if we have also used them at home.[33] When we use someone else's prayers, we pour into them our own meaning.[34]

Lewis's conclusion was that whether one should use written prayers, one's own words or no words at all is a matter of individual experience. His only supposition was that one should change the prayers from time to time to keep them alive.[35]

Near the end of *Mere Christianity*, Lewis suggested that anyone interested enough to read that far was probably interested enough to make a shot at saying his prayers. And, whatever else he says, he will probably say the Lord's prayer. Lewis devoted the rest of that chapter to the implications of the words "Our Father." They imply that we are to be like Christ.

Lewis referred to private overtones he put upon certain parts of the Lord's prayer as "festoonings." He didn't recommend his own additions to anyone else; they were part of his personal devotional life. But he did seem to recommend the practice.

He festooned the phrase "hallowed be thy name" with the phrase "with angels and archangels and all the company of heaven."[36] He festooned "thy kingdom come" with several ideas, mainly "in my heart." "Thy will be done" easily became "thy will be done—by me—now." "Lead us not into temptation" became "Make straight our paths. Spare us, where possible, from all crises, whether of temptation or affliction."[37]

Lewis's festooning is the opposite of the prayer paraphrase he sent his brother in 1932. There he contrasted "Our Father which art in heaven" with "the supreme being transcends space and time." He pointed out to his brother that the first really means something to those who use it; the second doesn't refer to any concrete fact at all.[38] The purpose of Lewis's festoonings was to move from the general to the particular and concrete.

The Right Attitudes

No soul ever perished for believing that God the Father really has a beard. But people who are attacking Christianity often object to the anthropomorphism in Christian prayers. They have a point. We think of meeting God in prayer almost face to face as if he were a creature like us, when all along he is above and within and below and all about us. We ask for his attention, as if it were not his attention that keeps us in existence in the first place. Lewis thought that when he called upon God, God often replied, "But you have been evading me for hours."[39] We tell him our sins as if he did not see them more clearly than we do. And God, whom we believe to be omniscient, ends up being informed or reminded of our needs.

There is reason as well as irony in this situation. First, anthropomorphic images are as necessary as abstractions for a balanced view of God. Second, prayer puts people into the position of depending on God and revealing themselves to God by choice rather than by necessity. This purposeful exposure to God is the essence of prayer. It makes the quality of the relationship.[40]

Another problem of attitude is the question of which needs or desires are important enough to be brought up in prayer. What if our present set of values is askew? It is no use talking to God about noble concerns while our heart is set upon other matters. We must open ourselves to God as we are, not as we should be. Lewis taught that the subjects of our thoughts should be the subjects of our prayers—whether in penitence or petition or a mixture of the two. We have to pray for an appropriate set of concerns, instead of faking it. Prayers about trivial matters may be good practice anyway. Lewis felt that high-minded religion tends to be a snare. "I fancy we may sometimes be deterred from small prayers by a sense of our own dignity rather than of God's."[41]

In *The Magician's Nephew* Digory was complaining because he and Polly had been sent on a long journey and no one had provided food for them. Fledge, their flying horse, was sure that Aslan would have done so if Digory had asked. Polly asked if Aslan wouldn't know they needed food without their asking. The horse answered, with his mouth full of grass, that Aslan would know, but that he seems to like to be asked.[42]

Digory had already asked Aslan for a momentous favor, a piece of magic fruit to heal his dying mother. Instead of answering yes or no, Aslan first sent him on a long, arduous journey. Digory had for a second thought of saying he would do Aslan's bidding only if Aslan would promise to help his mother. But he instantly realized that one does not bargain with Aslan.

When Digory asked for the fruit for his mother, Aslan had responded by showing him, step by step, the great evil that had entered Narnia through Digory's one foolish act of arrogance, cruelty and dishonesty. Digory saw himself for what he really was. The evil would centuries later fall heaviest upon Aslan himself. But Digory was spared the knowledge of what that meant. (Unlike the boy Lewis, Digory had his prayer answered—his mother lived.)

Lewis himself sometimes prayed not for self-knowledge in general but for just as much as he could bear and use at the moment: "the little daily dose."[43]

Near the end of *Letters to Malcolm*, Lewis said that he decided to come clean. He admitted that for most people prayer is a duty, and an irksome duty at that. He observed that we are reluctant to begin and delighted to finish. This is even true right after we have experienced comfort and exaltation in recent prayers.

There are two explanations for this. First and most commonly taught is the reason of sin. We shrink from direct contact with God because of demands he might make of us. Second is the fact that our minds find it so difficult to concentrate on anything that is neither material (like potatoes) nor abstract (like numbers). God is immaterial but concrete, and concentration on him requires painful effort.

We were created to glorify God and enjoy him forever. The few minutes we spend in prayer now are a pitiful contrast to that promise. The rich moments are all too rare. But who knows? Perhaps our most struggling, dutiful, unemotional prayers here and now are the most valuable in God's eyes. At any rate, we must do our duty now and say our prayers, knowing that some day they will no longer be a burden. It will be different in heaven—spontaneous delight.

Lewis ended his last book with five pages about heaven. Before the book was published, Lewis was dead. To him, heaven was the logical conclusion of a book about prayer. And prayer, he said, was a subject that was a good deal in his mind.[44]

Further Reading about Prayer

"An unliterary man may be defined as one who reads books once only."[45]

Letters to Malcolm: Chiefly on Prayer by C. S. Lewis is the last book Lewis completed before his death. He pretends to be comparing notes on prayer with a friend in private.

Letters to an American Lady by C. S. Lewis is an actual collection of personal letters from Lewis to a woman with many problems. It gives a glimpse of his faithful prayer life.

"On 'Special Providences,'" appendix B in *Miracles*, by C. S. Lewis considers the providential nature of all natural events and the contribution of prayer to providence.

"The Efficacy of Prayer" in *The World's Last Night and Other Essays* by C. S. Lewis is an article about answers to prayer, first published in *The Atlantic Monthly* in 1959.

"Petitionary Prayer: A Problem Without an Answer" in *Christian Reflections* by C. S. Lewis is an address Lewis gave to a group of ministers in 1953.

"Work and Prayer" in *God in the Dock* by C. S. Lewis is an article first printed in 1945 answering the commonly advanced case against prayer.

C. S. Lewis: Life at the Center by Perry Bramlett focuses most on Lewis's wisdom about prayer, Bible reading, and friendship.

Notes

1. Lewis, *God in the Dock*, p. 106.
2. Lewis, *Surprised by Joy*, p. 63.
3. Lewis, *Letters of C. S. Lewis*, p. 149.
4. Lewis, *The World's Last Night and Other Essays*, pp. 8–9.
5. Lewis, *Poems*, p. 120.
6. Lewis, *The World's Last Night and Other Essays*, pp. 4–5, 8.
7. Lewis, *Letters to Malcolm*, p. 82.
8. Lewis, Ibid.
9. Lewis, Ibid., p. 87.
10. Lewis, *The World's Last Night and Other Essays*, p. 4.
11. Ibid., pp. 24, 25.
12. Lewis, *Christian Reflections*, p. 151.
13. Lewis, *The World's Last Night and Other Essays*, p. 11.
14. Lewis, *Letters to Malcolm*, p. 60.
15. Ibid., p. 61.
16. Lewis, *Letters to an American Lady*, pp. 21–22.

17. Lewis, *Poems*, pp. 122–23; or Lewis, *Letters to Malcolm*, pp. 67–68.
18. Lewis, *Letters to Malcolm*, p. 63.
19. Ibid.
20. Ibid., p. 113.
21. Ibid., p. 15.
22. Ibid., p. 18.
23. Ibid., pp. 18, 116.
24. Ibid., p. 66.
25. Ibid.
26. Ibid., p. 15.
27. Ibid., p. 107.
28. Ibid., pp. 107–10.
29. Ibid., p. 66.
30. Lewis, *Mere Christianity*, p. 147.
31. Lewis, *Letters to Malcolm*, p. 66.
32. Ibid., p. 12.
33. Ibid., p. 100.
34. Ibid., p. 11.
35. Ibid., p. 245.
36. Ibid., pp. 15–16.
37. Ibid., pp. 24–28.
38. Lewis, *Letters of C. S. Lewis*, p. 147.
39. Lewis, *Letters to Malcolm*, p. 75.
40. Ibid., pp. 19–22.
41. Ibid., p. 23.
42. Lewis, *The Magician's Nephew*, p. 134.
43. Lewis, *Letters to Malcolm*, p. 34.
44. Ibid., p. 3.
45. Lewis, "On Stories," *Of Other Worlds*, p. 17.

Chapter 10

Pain

*"If only my toothache would stop, I could
write another chapter about Pain."*
"Myth Became Fact," God in the Dock[1]

Part One: How to Understand Suffering

C. S. Lewis was well qualified to write about pain. His entire
life was the usual succession of colds, toothaches, bereavements
and flu. Furthermore, he was wounded on the battlefield when
young and ended up with a complex of painful diseases when
old. In his life he experienced at least as much pain as the ordinary person, and, more importantly, he found pain absolutely
intolerable. He claimed to be a great coward: "If I knew any way
of escape I would crawl through sewers to find it."[2]

In 1940 Lewis wrote his first book explaining and defending
the Christian faith, *The Problem of Pain*. He felt this was a point
at which the Christian faith most needed defending. Only a
dozen years before he would have pointed to the fact of pain as
the main logical reason for his being an atheist.

Young Lewis looked at the nightmare size and age of the
universe and our tiny earth temporarily teeming with life. He

observed that all the forms of life on earth seem to prey upon each other in order to survive. All the higher forms experience pain. They cause pain at their birth, experience and inflict pain while they live, and most often die in pain.

In addition, the highest life form of all, man, suffers acute mental anguish because of his perception of this situation. Yet man also uses his extraordinary mental ability to inflict extraordinary pain on lower forms of life and fellow human beings. Human history is largely a record of crime, war, disease and terror. Furthermore, all life is ultimately doomed because the universe is running down.

Lewis's conclusion was that either there is no spirit at all behind the universe, or, far worse, that this spirit is not committed to good. Lewis the pessimist much preferred to be an atheist and let it go. But once Lewis became a Christian, he had to grapple with the problem. His brilliant friend Charles Williams claimed that on his own he would never have suspected that existence is good. Williams accepted that fact only because God has revealed it to us; he claimed that for him such belief required wholly supernatural faith.

In its simplest form the problem of pain asks why God, who is supposedly all-good and all-powerful, allows suffering.

If God is all-powerful, he can do anything and everything he wants to. All things are possible with God. Lewis agrees with that, but he quickly points out that nonsense and absolute impossibilities are not *things* in that sense. For example, so far as we know (and we must remember that our understanding is incomplete) it is nonsense to think of making red and green into the same color. No physicist could perform such an intrinsic impossibility, and neither could God. The very idea is self-contradictory and a nonentity. Everyone has heard the old question, "If God can do anything, can God make a stone too large for him to move?" God cannot carry out two mutually exclusive alternatives: "nonsense remains nonsense even when we talk it about God."[3]

Can God give humanity free will and yet protect us from all pain? Perhaps that is also nonsense. Surely people need a material world with a fixed nature of its own in which to function as free agents. And such a world is not going to always be equally comfortable to all people. We have the capacity for pain built into our nervous systems to warn us of danger. Physical pain itself is a matter of degree, and mild pains are often tolerated with pleasure, such as the "warm—beautifully hot—too hot—it stings" process which warns a person to move farther from the fire.

Given the possibility of pain, wicked people are bound to use it against one another. When people use their free wills for hostility instead of courtesy, the same fixed nature of wood which makes it useful as a beam also makes it useful to hit a man on the head. And the same permanent nature of matter usually gives victory in conflict to the group with superior weapons, skill and numbers, even if their cause is unjust and they inflict suffering. This is the nature of our world, where souls can meet and interact through matter.

Lewis did not argue about whether it would have been better if God had not created our suffering universe in the first place. Such a question was beyond his scope—or anyone's. The fact is that we exist, and we cannot tell how, if we did not exist, we would profit by not existing. The fact is that God is the only good of all creatures. "God gives what He has, not what He has not: He gives the happiness that there is, not the happiness that is not."[4]

The proper role of every creature is surrender to his Creator. Self-surrender to God is, in our present state, quite a feat. So long as things seem to be going well, the human spirit usually won't even try to surrender self-will. Man feels safe as long as he can. Error and sin are often masked evils, and their victim is unaware of his trouble with them. But pain is not masked.

Pain is the megaphone which makes evil impossible to ignore. A man knows that something is wrong when he is being hurt. First pain shatters the illusion that all is well; then pain shatters the illusion that what we have is our own and enough for us. Pain can lead an unbeliever to religion and to God; it can force a Christian to depend upon God as he should.

Lewis claimed that the fullest surrender to God, to be perfect, must be done against a person's inclination. The highest truth that pain can tell a person is that he or she is submitting to God's will although it is contrary to his nature. Of course what God commands is always intrinsically good, and the better a person is, the more he will like it. But there are painful tests and trials that people must endure, and for a person to choose painful obedience, like Abraham's, is the supreme reversal of Adam's rebellion.[5]

Needless to say, when Lewis was experiencing pain, he did not transcend it entirely by reflecting on these truths. Eleven years after he published *The Problem of Pain*, he suffered a case of the mumps. Referring to his friend and doctor R. E. Havard (who wrote the epilogue at the back of the book) as Humphrey, Lewis reported to another good friend, "Humphrey kept on quoting me bits out of *The Problem of Pain*, which I call a bit thick."

Points about Pain

Lewis made seven specific points about pain very clear. First, whether put to good use or not, pain hurts. Lewis admits that pain hurts terribly. It is said that mental pain is worse than physical pain, but Lewis doubted that easy assumption. He suspected that suffering nausea is worse than suffering moderate pain, but he supposed that nothing is worse than the most intense physical pain.

Second, suffering is not good in itself. The sufferer may benefit by submission to God, and spectators may benefit by aroused compassion and mercy. But woe to the person who caused the evil! It is true that God confronts evil and uses it for redemptive purposes, producing a complex good composed partly of accepted suffering and repented sin. But there is not the slightest question about the fact that Christians are to prevent and alleviate suffering in every way they can.

Third, we cannot believe that suffering will ever be removed from this earth by social or scientific progress. No heaven on earth is coming. We are spurred on to remove all the miseries we can without false hopes.

Fourth, the Christian doctrine of self-surrender and obedience is purely theological. There is no political parallel to the kind and degree of obedience which a creature owes to its Creator.

Fifth, the security and happiness we crave, we can never have in this life; it would keep us from God. But he has scattered moments of fun, love and even ecstasy here to refresh us.

Sixth, we must never be concerned about the *total* suffering in the world, because there is no such thing. The maximum that a single person can suffer is a horrible amount indeed, but there is no more pain than that, for no one suffers the pain of more than one person.

Seventh, pain is the only evil that does not tend to spread, recur or reproduce itself. Errors and sins need "undoing," but pain, once over, is sterile. Its effect on normal observers is to arouse not further error, sin or pride, but pity, which is a virtue. Pain is a unique kind of evil.

The hardest pain to understand, it seemed to Lewis, is animal pain. In the first place, we don't understand animals. To some extent we understand the eternal purpose of a person or an angel, but what is the purpose of a flea or a wild dog?

A year before he died, semi-invalid Lewis was sad to hear from the American lady about a little dog's death. Right to the end, Lewis shared his own house with a loud, pesty Siamese cat named Snip, an arrogant old ginger cat named Tom, and a frisky boxer pup named Ricky. He thought it strange that God brings us into such intimate relations with creatures of whose real purpose and destiny we remain forever ignorant.

Sometimes Lewis experienced such pity and indignation over the incessant suffering of animals that every argument for the existence of a good God sounded hollow. The insect world in particular (Lewis loathed large spiders) sometimes seems to be hell itself, teeming with pain.

Some people dismiss animal pain and, in fact, tolerate cruelty to animals with the theory that animals have no souls. Lewis wondered what such a theory means. Could it mean that horses, dogs and apes are not conscious of pain? If, on the other hand, it only means that animals have no moral responsibilities or immortality, it makes animal pain even harder to justify than human pain. For then animals cannot deserve pain, profit morally from the discipline of pain, or be compensated with happiness in the next life. Pain without guilt or fruit is serious, no matter how lowly the sufferer.

There is admittedly the appearance of reckless divine cruelty in the animal kingdom. We can only guess at the reality behind the false appearance. Lewis made three guesses in answer to this problem.

First, he guessed that a great deal of apparent suffering among lower forms is very likely not suffering at all, because such animals probably lack self-consciousness. (Their nervous systems may deliver the letters A, P, N, I, but they never put it together and get PAIN.)

Second, animal pain is probably not the handiwork of God, but of Satan; it may be that one of the original functions of man was to alleviate animal suffering, since animals came first.

Third, although Satan probably originated animal pain and fallen man has perpetuated it, God may yet do something for these innocents in the new heaven and new earth to come. The higher animals may be in some sense resurrected. Of course the biblical prophecy that in that day the lion will eat hay like an ox would sound like a description of hell to a lion in his present state. But Lewis could imagine a herbivorous new leonine body expressing whatever energy, splendor and exulting power dwelt within the lion on earth—no longer dangerous, but still awful, with something like the shaking of a golden mane.

And for those wiseacres who scoff at the possibility of future bliss for animals with the question "Where will you put all the mosquitoes?" Lewis replied dryly that a heaven for mosquitoes and a hell for men could very conveniently be combined.

Part Two: How to Cope with Suffering

The pain hardest for Lewis to understand was animal pain, but the only pain that ever shook his faith was that of the loss of his wife. Lewis poured out this pain and openly protested to God in *A Grief Observed*.

If he had been alive to read it, Charles Williams would have approved of this book, because Charles Williams liked Job. Job had taken hot, impatient complaints right to God, and God had approved of him. It is true, Williams noted, that God's answer took the surprising form of inviting Job to observe the hippopotamus and the crocodile.

The weight of God's displeasure, Williams once told Lewis, was reserved for Job's comforters who tried to show that all was well: "the sort of people," he said, immeasurably dropping his lower jaw and fixing Lewis with his eyes, "who wrote books on the *Problem of Pain*."[6]

Charles Williams's very sudden death in 1945 was a cruelly sharp but clean pain for C. S. Lewis. Joy's death in 1960 was more difficult.

Joy's final illness was terrible. After her death, the exhausted and lonely widower felt for a while that his years of theorizing about pain had not stood the test of experience.

Twenty years before, Lewis had observed "The real difficulty is—isn't it?—to adapt one's steady beliefs about tribulation to this particular tribulation: for the particular, when it arrives, always seems so peculiarly intolerable."[7]

Lewis had always known that bereavements happen daily. He had never expected worldly happiness for any length of time. He expected sufferings. He had accepted the teaching "Blessed are they that mourn." He had even supposed shortly before Joy's death that bereavement compels us to try to believe what we cannot yet feel, that God is our true Beloved.[8] And yet when his own loss came he was inconsolable. He accused himself of not caring as he thought he did about the sorrows of the world; otherwise, when his own came, he would not have been so overwhelmed.

Perhaps Lewis had forgotten about his disappointment in himself in World War II when the prospect of losing all that was dearest to him in this life was more shattering than he expected. He suddenly found that his Christian progress toward detachment from this world disappeared in the face of a real threat to his friends, his books, his brains and all. However, at that time his faith was not shaken. Although he sometimes felt that he would rather die than to live through the horrors of another war, he got busy and served his country as best he could: by morale-lifting radio talks, lectures to the R.A.F., and taking in children who had been evacuated from London. He was sure that God would turn any present misery into ultimate good. After Joy's death, he did not feel so sure at times.

A couple of months after his loss, Lewis answered a friend's question about how he took sorrow. "In nearly all possible ways. Because, as you probably know, it isn't a state but a process. It keeps changing—like a winding road with quite a new landscape at each bend."[9] That is the winding road he described in *A Grief Observed*. At one point he exclaimed, "What do people mean when they say 'I am not afraid of God because I know He is good'? Have they never even been to a dentist?"[10] Elsewhere in that book he likened his loneliness to endless drilling on his teeth and again likened God to a relentless surgeon.

Lewis once wrote a poem expressing how an angel cannot understand special human love for one nation above another, one person above another. The angel wonders why men grieve at the grave for one voice and face instead of easily receiving another in its place. In his endless existence of pure joy and light, the angel has never known special love and never tasted sorrow. And in his unbroken peace he exclaims ironically and innocently, "Woe's me!"[11]

When he wrote *The Great Divorce* Lewis depicted himself asking George MacDonald if one who is not bereaved could go to a bereaved mother in her misery:

> No, no, Son, that's no office of yours. You're not a good enough man for that. When your own heart's been broken it will be time for you to think of talking. But someone must say in general what's been unsaid among you this many a year: that love, as mortals understand the word, isn't enough. Every natural love will rise again and live forever in this country: but none will rise again until it has been buried.[12]

That teaching of MacDonald is exactly what Lewis taught for years. But he had observed once that the advice we give to others we cannot give ourselves, and that truth is more effective through any lips rather than our own.[13] His own teaching was empty comfort when Joy died, especially after the torture he had watched her go through.

In the depth of his lonely grief, before *A Grief Observed* was completed, Lewis speculated that his faith would probably be restored, but that he wouldn't know if it was genuine or not until the next blow came—perhaps the diagnosis of a fatal disease in his own body.[14] Of course his faith was soon restored, and the fatal diagnosis was not far behind. His final book,

Letters to Malcolm, ended with the hope of joyful reunion in heaven, cheerfully affirmed by some of his last letters. His final months were full of fortitude, patience and faith. He had suffered the worst pain of his life and come through.

Lewis records that Charles Williams was a continual flow of gaiety, enthusiasm and high spirits, but in contrast he never forgot the evil side of life. The world is bound to be painful, but it is unbearable if we are taught that we are supposed to like it. Williams said that when young people confide in adults about their troubles and discontents, it is all wrong to tell them that they are not really unhappy. Young people usually are unhappy, and the most helpful reply we can give them would begin, "But *of course....* "[15] Lewis agreed.

Once Lewis was asked if Christians must be prepared to live a life of personal discomfort in order to qualify for heaven. He began his answer, "All people, whether Christian or not, must be prepared to live a life of discomfort."[16] At the same time, Lewis maintained that there is little practical help in the sometimes emotional idea that our sorrow is part of the world's sorrow: "the mere *fact* that lots of other people have had toothache does not make toothache less painful."[17]

Lewis more than once advised readers to imagine a set of people sharing the same building, but half of them thinking it is a grand hotel and the other half thinking it is a prison. Those who thought it a hotel might find it intolerably frustrating and disappointing, but those who thought it a place of training and correction might find it surprisingly good. Holding a pretty stern view of this world, as Charles Williams did, makes one more optimistic in the end.[18] Goodness knows how Lewis would have recovered from Joy's death if he had started out as a vulnerable optimist.

Lewis endured a "queer night" at the beginning of 1963. At about 1:30 A.M. something went wrong with him and, in some pain, he called for an ambulance in order to get to his surgeon.

That winter was an extraordinarily severe one for the area, and his six-hundred-foot driveway was full of snowdrifts. So the sick old man had to make his way out to the road in the bitter cold and wait from 2:00 until 2:20 A.M. for the ambulance to pick him up. He said the full moon on the snow was nice to look at, but his ears almost fell off from the cold. By 6:00 A.M. he was doctored, returned, and climbed back into bed.[19] No harm done, he concluded later.

Within a couple of weeks he remarked in a letter that kind actions taken for the welfare of a cat (such as temporary placement in a pet hospital) seem utterly cruel and terrifying to the cat. That comforted Lewis, because it brought to life his belief that strange, terrifying or painful things which happen to us are really for our benefit.

It was at about this time that a correspondent in America who seemed to live in a continuous stream of alarms and misfortunes informed him that she was threatened with a painful disease. Lewis responded sympathetically that at their age a dangerous disease would be easier to face than a painful disease, since pain is more distressing than impending death. He remarked that their main job now was to make a good exit. Apparently he misjudged the lady, because he immediately had to defend himself against the charge of despondency, and a couple of months later he found himself trying to alleviate her fear of death. (She outlived Lewis by quite a few years.)

He reminded her that sometimes we are afraid because we struggle. "Are you struggling, resisting? Don't you think our Lord says to you, 'Peace, child, peace. Relax. Let go. Underneath are the everlasting arms. Let go, I will catch you. Do you trust me so little?' "[20]

Exactly twenty years before, Lewis had put words about fear into the mouth of a devil. Screwtape advised Wormwood to make sure that his patient never thought of his present fear itself as his appointed cross. Resignation to present suffering, even when it consists of fear, is easier than resignation to a dozen different possible future misfortunes. Wormwood should make his patient forget that they can't *all* happen to him and let him wear himself out trying to resign himself to all of them, so that he neglects his real assignment completely—patient acceptance of present anxiety and suspense.

In *Letters to Malcolm*, Lewis struck this theme again. By this time he had gone through both World Wars, suffered the suspense of his young wife's dramatic struggle against cancer, and now was living an uncertain semi-invalid life himself. Lewis stated flatly that anxieties are afflictions, not sins.

The perfect Man endured anxiety in Gethsemane. That was the beginning of the Passion. Jesus could not have honestly prayed to the Father to be spared the cup of the Crucifixion unless his knowledge of its inevitability was withdrawn and he was suffering the torments of hope. To live in a fully predictable world is not to be a true man, and Christ was a true man. His prayer in Gethsemane, his sweat of blood, shows that the preceding anxiety is a part of human affliction which we must try to accept with some sort of submission.

The End of the Matter

Anxieties, like all afflictions, can become our share in the Passion of Christ. Any tribulations we can't avoid, if embraced for Christ's sake, we are told, become as meritorious as voluntary sufferings.[21] Lewis believed that what we suffer for others and offer to God on their behalf becomes united with Christ's sufferings and in him may help in their redemption or the redemption of other people. His main basis for that belief was Colossians 1:24 where Paul wrote about himself, "Now I rejoice in my sufferings for your sake, and in my flesh I complete what is lacking in Christ's afflictions for the sake of his body, that is, the church." In 1951 he cited that verse to a woman and said, "I wish I had known more when I wrote *The Problem of Pain*. . . ."[22]

The real problem is not why some humble, pious people suffer, Lewis said, but why some do *not*. Some old people whose state of grace we can hardly doubt seem to have got through their seventy years surprisingly easily. The sacrifice of Christ is repeated, or echoed, among his followers in greatly varying degrees, from the cruelest martyrdom to the mildest kind of submission. But martyrdom is always the supreme enactment of Christianity.

The idea of voluntarily taking on someone else's suffering is the main theme in Charles Williams's books, according to Williams, and the idea sank deep into Lewis's mind. In *The Lion, the Witch and the Wardrobe* Aslan died in Edmund's place. In *Till We Have Faces* Psyche was all but unscathed by her ordeals because Orual had borne most of the anguish. "We're all limbs and parts of one Whole," their old teacher explained, "Hence, of each other."[23]

Lewis's housekeeper felt that the effort of turning Joy's heavy, swollen body in her bed was what gave Lewis his severe bone trouble. But as Lewis saw it, when Joy was recovering from her first bout with cancer, her riddled bones were regaining needed calcium at the same rate that his were strangely losing it.[24] He believed that he had been allowed to accept Joy's pain into his legs through Christian love, in order to relieve her.[25]

Lewis had no natural curiosity about other people's private lives, and perhaps that is why so many people confided in him. In one woman whose husband was unfaithful, Lewis saw charity, submission to God's will, and the control of jealousy. He told her that these qualities were gifts from the Holy Spirit (not her own merits) to enable her to go through her tribulation "not without pain but without stain." She was forced to rely on God because of her husband's love for another woman, and Lewis claimed that the time would come when she would regard all her misery as a small price to pay for having been brought to that dependence. The trouble is that relying on God has to begin all over again, every day.[26]

Christians must not be surprised when things don't go smoothly, when illnesses, money troubles, new kinds of temptation come along. God puts us into situations where we have to be very much braver, or more patient, or more loving, than we ever dreamed of being before. His purposes are obscure to us. We have not the slightest notion of what tremendous thing he intends to make of us.[27]

In *The Great Divorce*, as a flaming angel approached, a pale ghost protested that the heat was hurting him. The angel replied, "I never said it wouldn't hurt you. I said it wouldn't kill you."[28] The angel had to wait for the ghost's permission, which at last he blurted forth in fear and dread. He let out an unearthly scream of agony and reeled backwards, gasping, thinking he was done for. Then as Lewis watched, the ghost was transformed into a huge, bright, golden man full of energy and joy. The treatment had worked.

Ultimately, heaven is the answer to the problem of pain. Lewis counted upon Romans 8:18, where Paul said, "I consider that the sufferings of this present time are not worth comparing with the glory that is to be revealed to us." In fact, Lewis added that as there may be pleasures in hell (God shield us from them) there may be something not all unlike pains in heaven (God grant us soon to taste them).[29] In the meantime, we have the sufferings of the present to endure.

In his last book, Lewis's imaginary friend Malcolm was suffering fear for his son's life at one point. Referring to his own loneliness and Malcolm's fear, Lewis said, "We are not on an untrodden path. Rather on the main-road."[30]

Yet between that book and his death, Lewis wrote one of his last letters to a stranger—a little girl in America named Ruth Broady. His advice to her could be taken as his last comment about how to cope with suffering. He told her, "If you continue to love Jesus, nothing much can go wrong with you, and I hope you may always do so."[31] In four weeks he was dead.

That last statement sends one back to the preface of *The Problem of Pain*, written over twenty-three years before. There Lewis stressed that his purpose was to solve the intellectual problem raised by pain, not the far higher purpose of teaching fortitude and patience. All he could offer his readers in that area was his conviction that when pain is to be borne, a little courage helps more than much knowledge, a little human sympathy more than much courage, and the least tincture of the love of God more than all.

Further Reading about Pain

"All arguments in justification of suffering provoke bitter resentment against the author. You would like to know how I behave when I am experiencing pain, not writing books about it."[32]

The Problem of Pain by C. S. Lewis was his first book of Christian apologetics. In it he tries to solve the intellectual problem raised by suffering.

"Vivisection" in *God in the Dock* by C. S. Lewis probes into the ethics of inflicting experimental pain and suffering on animals and people.

"The Pains of Animals" in *God in the Dock* by C. S. Lewis is C. E. M. Joad's critical response to Lewis's chapter "Animal Pain" in *The Problem of Pain*. Also included is Lewis's six-page, point-by-point reply to Joad.

Till We Have Faces by C. S. Lewis is a novel full of suffering which ends in redemption.

Notes

1. Lewis, *God in the Dock*, p. 66.
2. Lewis, *The Problem of Pain*, p. 93.
3 . Ibid., p. 16.
4. Ibid., p. 42.

5. Ibid., pp. 86-90.

6. C. S. Lewis, ed., *Essays Presented to Charles Williams* (Grand Rapids, Mich.:Eerdmans, l966) p. xiii.

7. Lewis, *Letters of C. S. Lewis*, p. 186.

8. Lewis, *The Four Loves*, pp. 158-59.

9. Lewis, *Letters to an American Lady*, p. 89.

10. Lewis, *A Grief Observed*, p. 36.

11. Lewis, *Poems*, p. 107.

12. Lewis, *The Great Divorce*, p. 98.

13. Lewis, *Letters of C. S. Lewis*, p. 195.

14. Lewis, *A Grief Observed*, pp. 32-33.

15. Lewis, *Essays Presented to Charles Williams*, p. xii.

16. Lewis, *God in the Dock*, p. 53.

17. C. S. Lewis, *Selected Literary Essays* (London: Cambridge Univ. Press, 1969), p. 300.

18. Lewis, *God in the Dock*, p. 52.

19. Lewis, *Letters to an American Lady*, p. 110.

20. Ibid., p. 114.

21. Ibid., p. 20.

22. Lewis, *Letters of C. S. Lewis*, p. 234.

23. Lewis, *Till We Have Faces*, pp. 311-12.

24. Lewis, *Letters of C. S. Lewis*, p. 280.

25. Jocelyn Gibb, ed., *Light on C. S. Lewis* (London: Geoffrey Bles, 1965), p. 63.

26. Lewis, *Letters of C. S. Lewis*, pp. 219-20.

27. Lewis, *Mere Christianity*, p. 160.

28. Lewis, *The Great Divorce*, p. 101.

29. Lewis, *The Problem of Pain*, p. 140.

30. Lewis, *Letters to Malcolm*, p. 44.

31. Unpublished letter dated Oct. 26, 1963; available in the Wade Collection.

32. Lewis, *The Problem of Pain*, p. 93.

Character:
What Does Christ
Cost Us?

Chapter 11

Love

"*The only place outside Heaven where you can be perfectly safe from all the dangers and perturbations of love is Hell.*"
The Four Loves[1]

Part One: Love Is Not God

Lewis liked the story about William Morris's poem "Love Is Enough." Someone reviewed it by saying simply, "It isn't."

Lewis agreed. He compared our natural loves to a glorious garden which must be weeded and pruned. When God planted the garden of our nature, Lewis explained, he caused flowering, fruiting loves to grow there. But they need care if they are to be tall trees instead of scrubby tangles, and sweet apples instead of crabs. Natural loves, with their splendor and vitality, still need to be controlled by our rational will if they are to flourish and stay sweet.

The humblest and most widespread of the four kinds of love is affection, known in the Greek as *storge*. Lewis claimed that Dickens and Tolstoy are the only writers who really deal with it well in fiction. Lewis figured that affection accounts for nine-tenths of whatever solid and durable happiness we find in our natural lives.

Storge originates in parenthood (imagine a mother nursing a baby, or a dog or cat with a basketful of puppies or kittens, all in a squeaking, nuzzling heap together). It extends to all kinds of situations where there is a relationship of warm comfortableness and satisfaction in being together. Affection lives with soft slippers, old clothes, the thump of a sleepy dog's tail on the kitchen floor, the sound of a sewing machine, a child's toy left on the lawn.

Affection is the least noticeable and least discriminating of our loves. No matter how unattractive, almost anyone can be the object of affection; affection ignores the barriers of age, sex, class and education. It is based on familiarity, not merit. By the time one becomes aware of affection, it has usually been going on for some time. It seeps through our lives.

And affection broadens our minds. It unites people who find themselves thrown together in the same household, neighborhood, school, or job—people who might never have chosen each other for companions. We choose our friends and lovers because of traits that attract us. But affection, when it occurs, teaches us to appreciate traits that wouldn't attract us.

Affection, however, does not always stand alone. It also serves as homespun clothing for both friendship and erotic love. Affection enters other loves and becomes the very medium in which they operate from day to day. As Lewis put it, "not all kisses between lovers are lovers' kisses," and he could imagine nothing more disagreeable than prolonged sexual love unmixed with affection.

For all its virtues, affection in itself is only a natural, not a divine, love. The Victorian novelists were all wrong when they pointed us to family affection, in contrast to worldliness, for our salvation. Affection may work for ill as well as for good!

Affection is a sincere mourner at a graveside, but it can be a demon to live with. An affectionate relative can be unbearably demanding, rude, jealous and possessive. There are those who abuse affection in every neighborhood.

It is a fact of human nature that almost anyone may be the object of affection. Yes, Lewis says, and almost everyone *expects* to be. We crave affection from others. "I was a craver," Orual realizes at the end of Lewis's novel *Till We Have Faces*. And because many people receive affection far beyond what they deserve, many others feel they have a right to expect the same treatment. This is a hideous misinterpretation of the unmerited nature of affection. Many unlovable people have a ravenous appetite for affection, and they rely upon continual demands and reproaches and self-pity instead of doing anything to deserve love. It shouldn't have to be deserved, they say. It is a wonder that the demands of the unlovable are met so often as they are.

Another abuse of affection is a distortion of its ease and informality into obnoxious rudeness. (There is a difference between old clothes and dirty clothes that smell.) Lewis himself had seen more bad manners exhibited by parents to children than by children to parents. Why are so many people rude at home? Because they have no *real* courtesy away from home and are merely copying the behavior of others in public. True affection practices subtle and sensitive courtesy at home, no matter what liberties or language it employs, because it doesn't wound, humiliate or domineer. On the other hand, when a rude family member gets on his high horse and becomes elaborately "polite" at home, this is intentionally bad manners.

Jealousy is usually thought of in terms of erotic love, but it is just as common to affection. Selfish affection hates change. It is almost as easy for a son to break his parents' hearts by turning to Christianity or science or serious music as by turning to depravity and low living. Jealous affection doesn't want one family member to flood his life with a new interest that the rest of them don't care for. This accounts for the almost fiendish rancor which an unbelieving (or worse yet, semibelieving) family often turns upon a new Christian.

"We'd rather you drank their blood than stole their hearts," Orual complained to the gods in *Till We Have Faces*. "We'd rather they were ours and dead than yours and made immortal. But to steal her love from me, to make her see things I couldn't see. . . . What should I care for some horrible, new happiness which I hadn't given her and which separated her from me? Do you think I wanted her to be happy, that way?"[2]

This sample of Orual's complaint includes another and slightly different perversion of affection. It is that of the unbridled need to be needed. Distorted parental-type affection wants the loved one to have only the good that the lover can provide (whether it is wanted or not), and wants to go on providing that good forever. "They need me no longer" should be the ultimate reward of nurturing love. But some parents shudder at those words and would rather hobble and pester people than let them lead independent lives. Lewis suggests that such oversolicitous parent figures (they are not always parents) would often profit by using a pet and pampering it constantly. He feels sorry for such pets, but he feels sorrier for human victims of a tyrannical love which often comes close to hate. The woman who works herself into an early grave for her family unnecessarily is apt to have done them a favor by her early demise.

Greed, egoism, self-deception and self-pity are common human failings. It is no wonder that they infect affection and make it go bad. In *The Great Divorce* the ghost of a doting mother was loaded with these failings. Her greeter at the edge of heaven tried to convince her that she was not *only* a mother, that she existed as the mother only because she first existed as God's creature, an older and closer relationship. She defended mother-love as the highest and holiest feeling in human nature. Her guide answered, "No natural feelings are high or low, holy or unholy, in themselves. They are all holy when God's hand is on the rein. They all go bad when they set up on their own and make themselves into false gods."[3]

Love is not enough; affection needs "common sense" (reason), "give and take" (justice) and "decency" (goodness) to keep it working. That goodness consists of patience, self-denial, humility and the "intervention of a far higher sort of love than Affection, in itself, can ever be."[4]

Friends and Lovers

"Without Eros none of us would have been begotten and without Affection none of us would have been reared; but we can live and breed without friendship."[5] Lewis points out that friendship, in the sense of the Greek word *philia*, is the least instinctive, biological and necessary of our loves. In contrast to the throaty, organic qualities of affection and eros, friendship is the luminous, tranquil, rational world of relationships freely chosen. It is not popular today.

When people ordinarily speak of their friends and friendships now, they really mean their companions and what Lewis likes to call "clubbableness." But Lewis uses the word friendship in a special sense when he explains it as the second form of love. This is the love that arises out of companionship when two or more companions discover that they share a minority insight, interest or taste. Companions do outward things together; friends also do inward things together, less easily defined. They see the same truth or care about the same truth. Their friendship is about something. That is why lovers are pictured face to face, but friends are pictured side by side looking ahead together. Lewis claimed that nothing so enriches erotic love as discovering that the beloved actually fits into the small circle of one's friends, with a common vision.

Affection wants to be needed and enjoys gratitude, but friendship has none of that trait. A perfect friend will gladly help, of course, when need arises. But true friendship, unlike affection, never seeks the loved one's dependence and gratitude. "Don't mention it" is a helpful friend's sincere response to thanks. On the other hand, eros is inquisitive, wanting to know every detail about the beloved, but friendship lacks that trait. A friend is simply what he is; background, race or income are incidental and are not learned for their own sakes. As Lewis puts it, eros asks for naked bodies and friendship for naked personalities.

Another distinction of friendship is its relative lack of jealousy. Two friends are delighted to add a third and a fourth if they truly fit in. Each person brings out different facets in each of the others and augments the joy of the entire circle. The members are apt to feel that they are lucky beyond any deserving to be in such company; they often feel humble to be included among those they admire so much. More than once Lewis stated that there is no greater pleasure in life than gathering around a fire to spend an evening with a circle of beloved, delightful old friends.

The first weakness of natural friendship is the fact that it can be either a school of virtue or a school of vice. Friendship makes good people better and bad people worse. The shared point of view which turns companions into friends is not necessarily a noble one. We all know the delicious temptation of a shared hatred or grievance or a secret evil. And when we are among like-minded friends our views and standards seem indisputable to us. Therefore, every real friendship is a kind of rebellion against authority and public opinion, a potential resistance for good or evil.

The second weakness of natural friendship is that every friendship in one way or another ignores the views of outsiders who don't share the enthusiasm of the friends for their special subject—stamp collecting, golf, higher mathematics or whatever it is. This partial indifference to outside opinion, proper and necessary, can grow into a general disdain and deafness for all opinions or pleas of "outsiders." Hence artists who may rightly ignore the art ideas of the common man may also proudly ignore his opinions about honesty, cleanliness and civility.

Here the greatest danger of friendship crops up—corporate pride. It is in our own circle that we are slowest to recognize it. True friendship is four or five people who like one another meeting to do things that they like. Any secrecy is accidental, and exclusiveness is just an unavoidable by-product.[6] But the spirit of exclusiveness is an easy step, and the degrading pleasure of exclusiveness comes next. Soon all that is left is an absurd little self-elected aristocracy basking in mutual admiration.

Another facet of pride in friendship, worst in religious friendships, is the false presumption that we four or five have unique discrimination and good taste to have discerned the inner beauty of each other. In reality, Christ has chosen us for each other. The friendship is not our reward for our cleverness, but God's instrument to open our eyes to his beauty as revealed in these friends.

Scripture rarely uses friendship as a symbol of the highest Love. God is pictured as our Father (parental affection) and Christ is pictured as the Husband (erotic love), because no sane person would take these as physical realities. But friendship is in fact too spiritual to make a good symbol for spiritual truths.

The Greek word *eros* means the kind of love that lovers are "in." Sexual experience is another matter; it can occur without eros. Sexual desire itself simply wants an event within one's own body, but eros wants the beloved.

Some people today consider married sex without eros impure, and any sexual activity prompted by eros automatically right, even if it involves adultery, deception, betrayal and desertion. In contrast, Lewis judges the sex act, like any other act, on the basis of justice, unselfishness, obedience and the keeping of promises. The fulfillment of sexual needs is a good, healthy part of marriage, with or without eros.

Eros sees the beloved one as important far beyond relationship to the lover's needs. Eros is the king of pleasures, but eros regards pleasure as a kind of by-product. When abstinence is necessary, eros somehow makes it easier. And, if necessary, eros would rather be unhappy with the beloved than happy on any other terms. If we were not human beings, we would find eros very hard to imagine. As it is, we find it very hard to explain.

Certain key elements of eros are often overlooked. One is its light side. In our century eros has been solemnized to a ridiculous extent, especially by those who use it for advertising purposes. There is an element of comedy, play and even buffoonery in the body's expression of eros. We can ignore this factor, to our loss, but we can't escape it. The flesh is poetically beautiful at moments, but it also has elements of obstinate and ludicrous un-poetry. We might as well accept the comic aspect of eros and, if possible, enjoy it. It is bad to be unable to take a joke, especially a divine joke.

On the other hand, in the act of love we are not only ourselves. We are in some way representatives of all the masculinity and femininity in the world, taking part in a brief ritual or drama. Nudity emphasizes our common humanity and the universal *he* and *she*, and lovers put on nakedness as a ceremonial robe or as the costume for a playful drama. In this drama, the man is momentarily supremely dominant, like a conqueror, and the woman is responsively, almost abjectly, surrendered. Woman cannot grant such dominance to any human in reality without peril to her soul, nor can man claim it, but the enactment of those roles in the love act is natural and fitting.

As nature crowns man with dominance in the act of love, so Christian law crowns him with headship in the relationship of marriage. This means that he is to love his wife as Christ loved the church *and gave his life for her*. This headship is most fully embodied in the marriage in which the wife, like the church, receives much and gives little. At the time Lewis wrote this, he was married to a woman with cancer. The headship of a husband is seen most clearly, he said, in the sorrows of marriage—in a husband's unwearying care for a good wife who is sick and suffering or his inexhaustible forgiveness for a bad wife. And the husband whose headship is Christlike (the only kind of headship granted) never despairs.

Obviously, erotic love seems divine in its selflessness, reckless devotion and power. Many people in the past have felt that the main spiritual danger in eros was the carnal sensuality of the marriage bed. Lewis points out that the Bible never takes such a view. What Paul warned against in marriage (1 Cor. 7:32–38) was the preoccupation with domesticity and the practical cares of living. In fact, Lewis declares, the great, permanent temptation of marriage is not to sensuality, but to avarice.

Theologians have often feared that lovers might idolize each other. There is a tendency to a preoccupation with the beloved which can interfere with the spiritual life, it is true. But there is certainly no danger of married people idolizing each other; the prose, intimacy and affection of marriage all work against that. If both lovers are thirsting for God, then as friends they can be gloriously helpful to each other. But even in courtship the idea that the beloved could satisfy one's thirst for God, if one has that thirst, is ridiculous.

The real danger is that lovers will idolize eros himself. Of all the loves, he is most godlike. But when he is treated as a god, he becomes a demon. Eros can make temptations speak with the voice of duties. Some lovers will do almost anything for love's sake, sacrificing their conscience and decency upon his altar. Screwtape had quite a bit to say about that useful fact in his letters to Wormwood. Lovers often feel like martyrs. When someone explains, "Love made me do it," there is almost always a touch of boasting, defiance or devotion, rather than regret, in the confession. Refusal to obey eros feels like apostasy, and obedience to him becomes a religious act.

Incredible as it seems to new lovers, eros has his lapses. He sounds eternal, but he is the most mortal of our loves. One doesn't always feel "in love." And those who depend upon mere feeling to do all that is necessary for them, find their marriages endangered and possibly ruined. They blame the results on love or on the beloved. The fact is that it takes humility, charity and God's grace to continue what eros begins. Eros needs help; he needs to be ruled by a higher love. Erotic love is never enough. No natural love or combination of natural loves is enough.

Part Two: God Is Love

When C. S. Lewis began his book *The Four Loves*, he expected to base it upon the saying "God is love." He intended to show that human loves are really love insofar as they resemble the Love that is God. He meant to show that Gift-love is true love and that Need-love is not. But he soon found the reality more complicated than he had supposed.

Most loves can be divided into two categories—those that give and those born of need. The typical ordinary example of Gift-love is a man providing in advance for the well-being of his family after he is gone; the typical example of Need-love is a frightened child running to its mother's arms.

Divine love is, of course, Gift-love. God lacks nothing and gives everything. Human Gift-loves are really godlike, especially if they are boundless and unwearied in giving. Our Gift-loves have joy, energy, patience, readiness to forgive and desire for the good of the beloved that are a splendor to encounter. We can thank God for such love in people. But such human loves can be mistaken for divine, and if we give them unconditional allegiance, they destroy us and themselves. No human Gift-love in itself brings one to God. "No kind of riches is a passport to the Kingdom of Heaven."[7]

No one calls a child selfish when he turns to his mother for comfort, and no one calls an adult selfish when he turns to others for company. Indeed, there is something wrong with the child or adult who does not. Of course there are at times reasons for denying these needs, and needs can be selfishly indulged. But those are different matters. We need other people, and our Need-loves for them are basically good.

Need-love, unfortunately, lasts no longer than the need. That is why so many parents are neglected by their grown children. But moral principles such as gratitude may preserve the relationship, and another kind of love may be grafted on the Need-love and take over.

A man's spiritual health, Christians agree, is measured by his love for God, and man's love for God is very largely or entirely Need-love. It is obvious that we come to God needing forgiveness and support. But actually our whole being is one vast need—empty yet cluttered, unfinished, "crying out for Him who can untie things that are now knotted together and tie up things that are still dangling loose."[8] God encourages us to come to him with Need-love. In the New Testament he says, "Come to me, all who labor and are heavy laden" (Mt. 11:28). And in the Old Testament he says, "Open your mouth wide, and I will fill it" (Ps. 81:10). Neediness is the only permanent thing about us in this life.

We come to his fullness with our need, to his sovereignty with our humility, to his righteousness with our penitence and to his limitless power with our cry for help. That is our highest, healthiest and most realistic spiritual condition— Need-love. And our need of God can never end, even in the next life. But Lewis warned that our awareness of the need can die; and when it does, the love dies, too.

Beyond Gift-love and Need-love there is a higher category of love, the unselfish appreciation of goodness. When we experience this love for people we often call it admiration or hero worship; when we experience it for God we call it worship. We judge and pronounce the object of this love to be very good. We pay attention to this good with thankfulness.

On a lower level, we would not deface a great work of art even if we were dying (and even if we were the last people on earth). So in Appreciative love we celebrate the goodness of what we love and want it to continue being what it is and rejoice that such a wonder exists. The love of Nature that some people experience is a form of Appreciative love.

Appreciative love in itself has no needs and no gifts. But in life Need-love, Gift-love and Appreciative love are always quickly shifting back and forth and blending into each other. Only Need-love can ever stand alone for any length of time.

Living on Charity

Today *charity* usually means gifts to the poor, but originally it meant "love, in the Christian sense." Giving to the poor is one of the most obvious things a person with Christian love does, and so it is easy to see how the new meaning was added to the word.[9]

In 1954 a lady wrote to Lewis and asked him if taking in a poor illegitimate child would be charity, and his answer was, "Of course . . ." He explained to her that the Greek New Testament word for charity is *agape*. It is the kind of love God has for us and is good in all circumstances—in contrast to the three natural loves, storge (family affection), philia (friendship), and eros (sexual love). All are good in their proper place, but every place is proper for agape.

Charity, which is not a feeling, but a state of the will, enables us to love lepers, criminals, enemies, morons and boors. (Natural Gift-love only enabled us to love those who somehow appealed to us.) Paradoxically, divine Gift-love, Love himself working in a man, enables man to have Gift-love toward God himself. Gift-love longs to serve or even to suffer for God. We can serve God by giving our wills and hearts to him, and he has taught us that we can also give to him by feeding and clothing strangers in need.

Strange as it seems, charity also includes a supernatural Need-love of God and of one another. We are in need, and God creates Need-love within us. His grace gives us an almost glad acceptance of our neediness. Without such grace we can hardly acknowledge our own neediness with sincerity. First, we are tempted to think God loves us because we are lovable. Then we think we have magnificently repented. Then we think God will admire our humility. Next we can offer him our clear-sighted and humble recognition that we still lack humility, and so on forever. We cling to some last claim to intrinsic freedom, power or worth until we give it all up and become "jolly beggars," sorry for our sins, but not our needs.

Charity is the love we need from other humans, too, but it is not the love we want. We want to be loved for our good qualities. It is shocking and wounding to be told that we are loved with charity rather than with affection, friendship or eros. As a vivid illustration, Lewis asked the reader to imagine yourself as a newly-wed spouse struck down with an incurable disease which makes you physically useless, helpless and repulsive, mentally impaired and bad-tempered. Imagine your husband or wife faithfully supporting you and caring for you through the years. In such a case, it is clearly harder (and perhaps more blessed) to receive than to give! For such a person to take this sweetly would require a more than natural receptivity of charity from fellow humans; it would require God's grace.

We are all, to a lesser degree, in the invalid's position. All of us who have good parents, spouses or children may be sure that at times we are receiving charity and are loved not because we are lovable but because Love himself is working in those who love us. It is all to the good to realize that. Charity is both a shameless, grateful Need-love and a selfless Gift-love.

Lewis was slow to speak about our natural loves as rivals to the love of God, because most of us are still at a stage of rivalry between love for ourselves and love for others. Lewis didn't want to press upon people the duty of getting beyond earthly love when they had not yet succeeded in getting that far! He believed, moreover, that the most lawless and inordinate loves are closer to God's will than self-protective lovelessness. And lovelessness *is* self-protective, because to love is to be vulnerable. If you love even an animal your heart is sure to be wrung.

Our natural loves can be inordinate, and that means too much in proportion to our love for God. But in that case it is the love for God that needs to be greater, not the other love less. And it doesn't really matter which feeling of love is more intense. The question is which love we put first and serve. It is a matter of will. As Lewis noted in one of his letters to his friend Sheldon Vanauken in the latter's book *A Severe Mercy*, Vanauken was led from US to US AND GOD and needed to continue to the attitude GOD AND US.

Christians should all along make the set of their wills clear to their earthly beloveds, in a thousand subtle ways, so that they will know the earthly love is "under God." A real disagreement about this should make itself felt early enough in a relationship to prevent marriage or serious friendship from coming to be. We must be blind and deaf to our nearest and dearest when they come between us and our obedience to God in a test of conflicting loves.[10]

As in *The Problem of Pain*, *Miracles* and *Letters to Malcolm: Chiefly on Prayer*, Lewis ended *The Four Loves* looking to heaven for the ultimate perspective on his subject. Most of us hope that when our bodies are resurrected, the affections and relationships of our earthly life will be resurrected as well. We expect our natural loves to enter heaven. But only what can become heavenly can enter heaven. Charity is eternal, and it is by the presence of charity in them that our natural loves can enter eternal heaven. They must be converted, and the process must begin here on earth.

It is only through being somehow like God, by reflecting his beauty, loving-kindness, wisdom or goodness, that any human has excited our love in the first place. We have never loved a person too much, but we have not quite understood what we were loving. When we see God's face we shall know that we have always known it, for he has been the mover in all our experiences of innocent love.

In *The Great Divorce* a visitor from hell was being asked to stay in heaven by the shining lady who was his wife. She confessed to him that her love for him on earth had been mainly a Need-love. He asked her, in despair, if she didn't need him any longer.

> "But of course not!" she smiled. "What needs could I have, now that I have all? I am full now, not empty. I am in Love himself, not lonely. Strong, not weak. You shall be the same. Come and see. We shall have no *need* for one another now: we can begin to love truly."[11]

There is one more aspect of love that Lewis barely mentions. It is the highest of all, the third part of charity. It is a supernatural Appreciative love for God. A taste of it makes all other desires, even peace or the end of fear, look like broken toys and faded flowers. Lewis didn't claim to have certainly experienced that love; he admitted he may have only imagined tasting it. God knows. But Lewis knew that it is the true center of all human and angelic life. He dared not write about it.

Perhaps for most of us, he concludes, the best at the present is to become increasingly aware of the absence of awareness of God in our lives, like the man in a story who looked in a mirror and found no face there. For further news of supernatural Appreciative love of God, he tells us to turn to his betters.

C. S. Lewis's humility was the hallmark of his books and poems, and one can take his disclaimers of spiritual advancement in the same way one takes St. Paul's conviction that he was the chief of sinners. As Lewis himself said, "We can easily imagine conditions far higher than any we have really reached."[12] The farther one can see ahead, the less apt one is to feel oneself far advanced.

The Four Loves was published in 1960, and Joy Lewis died that summer. C. S. Lewis had written *The Four Loves* during their brief marriage. His following love poem was never published in his lifetime and is not dated or explained, but it would seem to date and explain itself.

> All this is flashy rhetoric about loving you.
> I never had a selfless thought since I was born.
> I am mercenary and self-seeking through and through:
> I want God, you, all friends, merely to serve my turn.
>
> Peace, re-assurance, pleasure, are the goals I seek,
> I cannot crawl one inch outside my proper skin:
> I talk of love—a scholar's parrot may talk Greek—
> But, self-imprisoned, always end where I begin.
>
> Only that now you have taught me (but how late) my lack.
> I see the chasm. And everything you are was making
> My heart into a bridge by which I might get back
> From exile, and grow man. And now the bridge is breaking.
>
> For this I bless you as the ruin falls. The pains
> You give me are more precious than all other gains.[13]

Further Reading about Love

"It is still possible, even in an age so ferociously anti-romantic as our own, to write fantastic stories for adults: though you will usually need to have made a name in some more fashionable kind of literature before anyone will publish them."[14]

Till We Have Faces by C. S. Lewis is an adventure of contrasting and conflicting loves in an ancient barbaric kingdom. It was judged by Owen Barfield and John Lawlor to be Lewis's finest work. Lewis called it his favorite book and his worst flop.

The Four Loves by C. S. Lewis was published three years before his death. In it he clearly explains family affection, friendship, sexual love and charity. He includes insights into Gift-love, Need-love, love of country and love of Nature.

"The Shoddy Lands" in *Of Other Worlds: Essays and Stories* by C. S. Lewis is a fantasy story about the loveless inner mind of an engaged girl.

"Ministering Angels" in *Of Other Worlds: Essays and Stories* by C. S. Lewis is an ironic science fiction story about sexual desire and religious love in an isolated research camp on Mars.

The Allegory of Love by C. S. Lewis was Lewis's first claim to professional fame. It is his analysis of the role of courtly love in medieval literature.

"The Sermon and the Lunch" in *God in the Dock* by C. S. Lewis is a brutally honest peek into a preacher's household, with Lewis's view on family affection.

That Hideous Strength by C. S. Lewis is Lewis's third science fiction novel. One of its major themes is the marriage relationship of the hero and heroine, who finally receive the fulfillment of erotic love.

A Severe Mercy by Sheldon Vanauken tells a true story of philia and charity and eros in which Lewis played a major part. This book includes eighteen letters from Lewis to Vanauken.

Notes

1. Lewis, *The Four Loves*, p. 139.
2. Lewis, *Till We Have Faces*, pp. 302–3.
3. Lewis, *The Great Divorce*, p. 93.
4. Lewis, *The Four Loves*, p. 67.
5. Ibid., p. 70.
6. Lewis, *Transposition and Other Addresses*, p. 64.

7. Lewis, *The Four Loves*, p. 14.

8. Ibid., p. 11.

9. Lewis, *Mere Christianity*, p. 100.

10. Lewis, *The Four Loves*, pp. 141, 143.

11. Lewis, *The Great Divorce*, p. 116.

12. Lewis, *The Four Loves*, P. 159.

13. Lewis, *Poems*, pp. 109–10. In 1976 this poem became available to the public as the lyrics of a song by Phil Keaggy on his album *Love Broke Thru* on the New Song label.

14. Lewis, "On Criticism," *Of Other Worlds: Essays and Stories*, pp. 27–28.

Chapter 12

Ethics

*"Of all the awkward people in your house or job there
is only one whom you can improve very much."*
"The Trouble with 'X'...," God in the Dock[1]

Part One: Middle-Aged Moralizing

The last writing that C. S. Lewis ever did for publication was an
article about sex for *The Saturday Evening Post*. This is apparently what he was working on when a good friend visited him
one day and asked him how he happened to be writing for a
popular American magazine. Lewis explained that the editors
had got the notion that he was full of paradoxical ideas, and so
they named a subject for him and paid generously. The friend,
Nevill Coghill, asked if Lewis was then busy inventing some
paradoxes.

"Not a bit of it," Lewis replied. "What I do is to recall, as
well as I can, what my mother used to say on the subject, eke it
out with a few similar thoughts of my own, and so produce
what would have been strict orthodoxy in about 1900. And this
seems to them outrageously paradoxical, *avant-garde* stuff."[2]

Lewis entitled his *Saturday Evening Post* article "We Have
No 'Right to Happiness'" and proposed the *avant-garde* idea

that we have no more unqualified right to sexual happiness than we do to any other form of happiness such as wealth, ecstasy, beauty or good luck. Who would excuse an alcoholic because drunkenness made him happy? Or a ruthless tycoon because money made him happy? Yet a seducer, adulterer and family deserter is often "justified" because his motive was his own happiness.

When Lewis was a youngster in the early 1900s he believed the popular words, "Why all this prudery? Let us treat sex just as we treat all other impulses." When he grew up he realized that people who talked that way meant just the opposite—that sex was to be treated as no other impulse is treated in civilized society. Any merciless, treacherous or unjust behavior—breaking vows, hearts and lives—is to be condoned if its goal is "four bare legs in a bed."

It really irritated Lewis when people reacted to his clear-cut ethics by defending the "holiness" of sex. Sex is no more moral or immoral than nutrition, as Lewis saw it. But the sexual behavior of humans is sometimes good and sometimes bad, just like any other kind of behavior. The sexual act, like any other act, is holy when it is done with good faith and charity, to the glory of God.

Sex is nothing to be ashamed of, as people often say. But the state of our sexual instinct today—warped, exploited, and inflamed—*is* something to be ashamed of. Chastity is not the most important of the Christian virtues, but it is surely the most unpopular.

We grow up today surrounded by propaganda in favor of unchastity, largely created by people who want to make money on us. Screwtape told his nephew Wormwood that the value devils have given to the word *Puritanism* is one of the really solid triumphs of the past hundred years. "By it we rescue annually thousands of humans from temperance, chastity, and sobriety of life."[3]

Standards of decency and propriety change. Decent language, clothing and behavior vary from time to time and place to place. But whenever people break the current rules of propriety in order to excite lust, they are offending against chastity. In Lewis's day the striptease act was a most obvious public example.

Lewis invented a famous comparison between a striptease act and a parallel entertainment in a hypothetical country where well-fed people paid to see a covered plate brought out on the stage. The lid was slowly lifted and just before the lights went out everyone caught a glimpse of a mutton chop! There is something wrong with the appetite, Lewis concluded.

Either our sexual appetite or Christianity is wrong, Lewis reasoned, because the demands of Christianity clash so with our instinct. Our instinct must have gone wrong. Christianity teaches "either marriage, with complete faithfulness to your partner, or else total abstinence." As hard as that is, Lewis claims, it is possible with God's help and worth the effort.

Lewis believed that it is better for Christians not to try to legally impose their marriage standards upon others through strict divorce laws. Let the nonbelieving couples have their own civil marriage agreement if they prefer, or none at all. Save the Christian vows for those who mean to keep them. Far greater distinction between Christian marriages and non-Christian marriages would be a healthy thing. We do non-Christians no favor by encouraging them to make church vows they do not intend to keep, adding perjury to unchastity.

Furthermore, Lewis felt that of all the sins in the world, homosexuality is the last one that concerns the government. So long as no innocent party is injured, there is no reason to make it a crime. Lewis felt only bewildered pity for homosexuals, and he felt there is much hypocrisy in the general opinion that this vice is a most intolerable evil. Nauseating, yes, but not intolerable. Cruelty is surely more evil than lust. The furor against homosexuality has, in Lewis's opinion, been neither Christian nor ethical.

"The sins of the flesh are bad," Lewis admitted, "but they are the least bad of all sins."[4] He had lost his own chastity at the age of fourteen and had not felt the slightest guilt about it. It took him as long to acquire inhibitions as it takes other people (according to their claims) to get rid of them. He eventually called himself a converted pagan living with apostate Puritans.

Almost twenty years after Lewis lost his chastity he became a Christian. Ten years later he wrote the chapter "Sexual Morality" in *Mere Christianity*. Another twenty years later (fifty years after his adolescent escapade) he wrote "We Have No 'Right to Happiness.'" There he practically threw out the term "sexual morality." Morality is morality, he insisted. There are no special kinds.

In a day when chastity is unpopular, the chaste person feels on the outside. Lewis suspected that in an age of promiscuity many people toss away their chastity mainly in order to feel included socially. Obviously many people first smoke or get drunk for the same reason. There are worse results, as well, when one's goal is to be included.

Rings and Things

Money and sex are not our only natural motives in life. Once C. S. Lewis introduced himself as a "middle-aged moralist" and gave an entire oration at the University of London warning his student audience of the dangers of "the Inner Ring." The desire to be inside an inner ring is also one of the great permanent mainsprings of human action. There is a terror of being left outside, and one cannot always tell if he is in or out. Inner rings have no formal organization; you gradually discover that the group exists and that you are outside it. Later, perhaps, you discover that you are admitted. What a delicious feeling of acceptance, of secret intimacy. Now you can make it hard for other people to get in. After all, that is a main purpose of the group.

Perhaps you will never get in. But you can be an "inner-ringer" whether you get in or not. You can become one either by passing triumphantly in or by pining outside; either way your life and character are damaged. All kinds of inner rings are around us; contact with them is unavoidable. One can avoid being an inner-ringer only by conscious and continuous effort!

Lewis was in his early teens when he went through a period of vulgarity under the influence of an immature young teacher. What attacked Lewis through that teacher was the world: "the desire for glitter, swagger, distinction, the desire to be in the know."[5] Lewis lost his childlike humility and worked hard for a while, he later observed, to make himself into a fop, a cad and a snob.

One of Wormwood's temptations for his patient in *The Screwtape Letters* was possible friendship with a rich, smart, anti-Christian group of people who fed his vanity. "There is a subtle play of looks and tones and laughs by which a mortal can imply that he is of the same party as those to whom he is speaking," Screwtape explained. "He will assume, at first only by his manner, but presently by his words, all sorts of cynical and sceptical attitudes which are not really his. But if you play him well, they may become his. All mortals tend to turn into the thing they are pretending to be."[6]

Wormwood's trick failed, but Mark Studdock, in *That Hideous Strength,* was already caught at the beginning of the novel. This ordinary man had just moved from the outside to the inside of a circle that called itself "the Progressive Element in College" where he taught. "It had all happened quite suddenly and was still sweet in the mouth."[7] Since this book is a fantasy and in part a horror fantasy, Mark's foolish greed for a secure place in the inner circle, which he didn't really under-

stand at all, gradually plunged him into the clutches of a satanic conspiracy. Easily confused and manipulated, he allowed
himself to be used as a tool for insane treachery before the story
ended.

As Lewis said in his London lecture, the passion for the
inner ring easily makes an ordinary man do very bad things. He
told his audience of college students that at least two or three of
them would become something very like scoundrels before they
died, judging from the size of the group. By scoundrels he
meant unscrupulous, treacherous, ruthless egotists. And he
warned them that in nine cases out of ten they would be drawn
into that kind of life by genial, confidential, delightfully sophis-
ticated new friends whose good opinion seemed valuable at the
time. Step by step, in a jolly friendly spirit, future scoundrels
depart from the rules in order to fit into an inner ring. Whether
it ends in scandal and prison or in wealth and honors, the person's character has been destroyed.

Lewis's advice boils down to this: work diligently and excel-
lently at the main business of your profession and spend your
spare time with true friends—the people you really like. Refuse
the quest of the inner ring.

Lewis began his lecture on the inner ring by reading a passage about the Russian army from the novel *War and Peace*. It
showed how within the army there were circles of power and
prestige apart from the official structures. Lewis knew this to
be true in any army. He admitted that military service includes
the threat of every temporal evil: "pain and death which is what
we fear from sickness; isolation from those we love which is
what we fear from exile; toil under arbitrary masters, injustice,
humiliation, which is what we fear from slavery; hunger, thirst
and exposure which is what we fear from poverty."[8]

Lewis hated war and disliked military service, but he was
never a pacifist. Shortly after World War 1 he sympathized with
his friends Owen Barfield and Nevill Coghill who felt like

being conscientious objectors if another war erupted unless there was something really worth fighting for.[9] He didn't stick to that idea, and it is the closest he ever got to pacifism. To him all killing is not murder any more than all sexual intercourse is adultery. When worse comes to worst, he suggested, if a Christian cannot restrain a person in any other way, he must try to kill him.

Lewis felt that gaiety and wholeheartedness is a more fitting accompaniment of military courage than shame and a long face. He admired and understood the chivalry of medieval knights. The Christian may kill if necessary, but he may not hate and must not enjoy killing. He must basically wish his enemies good in this life or the next, even when slaying them.

Of course no Christian may obey the government if he or she knows that to do so is sin. But the justice or injustice of a given war is usually too complex for an ordinary Christian citizen to judge. Lewis offered his own suggestion for Christian men who are drafted. Let them be "conscientious objectors" in the army instead of in jail at home. Let them serve and bear arms, but let them refuse to murder prisoners or bomb civilians or to obey any other distinctly anti-Christian orders. Such conscientious objectors might get shot for refusing to cooperate, but in their death they might do great good.

War, however, is not the only dilemma a Christian faces. Lewis was asked pointblank once if it is wrong for a Christian to be ambitious and strive for personal success. He said that if ambition means the desire to get ahead of other people it is bad. Wanting to do a thing well is good, but wanting to be more successful than other people is not. In fact, when it comes to making money, the New Testament clearly tells us to work—in order to have something to give to the needy.

Lewis claimed that when he died he would not care how many imposters had bilked him, but he would be tormented if he had refused even one person who was really in need. Charity

is an essential part of Christian living, as Matthew 25 would
seem to indicate in the parable of the sheep and the goats.
Lewis did not talk about percentage giving. He said the only
safe rule is to give more than we can spare. Our charities should
pinch and hamper us. If we live at the same level of affluence
as other people who have our level of income, we are probably
giving away too little. Obstacles to charity include greed for luxurious living, greed for money itself, fear of financial insecurity
and showy pride.

"Nearly all those evils in the world which people put down
to greed or selfishness are really far more the result of Pride."[10]
Why does a rich man push himself and other people in order
to gain more wealth and power? Pride. Pride wants to have
more than anyone else, and pride wants power over other people. Lewis calls pride spiritual cancer and says it eats up every
possibility of love, contentment or common sense. Real pride is
different from honest childlike pleasure at having pleased someone or admiration for someone else expressed by the phrase "I'm
proud of you." The most innocent, humble and shallow kind of
pride is called vanity.

Pride is the anti-God state of mind. Pride led to the devil's
becoming the devil, and it is pride he uses as his ultimate
weapon against humanity. Pride is the utmost evil. It means
enmity from person to person and between a person and God.
No one proud can know God. Therefore, pride in religious people is subtle and deadly. God forbids it because he wants us to
really be in touch with him, not worshiping an imaginary God
of our own. To be in touch with the real God means self-for-
getting, joyful humility. And the first natural step in getting rid
of pride is to admit that we are proud.

Lewis claimed that unchastity, anger, greed, drunkenness
and all those sins are mere fleabites in comparison to pride. But
Lewis was greatly impressed by a basic pair of everyday vices he
observed in men and women. As he saw it, men are more likely

to leave for others what they ought to do themselves, and women are more apt to do for others what they ought to leave alone. Neither sex naturally minds its own business (in opposite senses)! Therefore Lewis pictured purgatory as a confused, upset kitchen with all kinds of emergencies occurring at once. The men are forced to get up and do their part in coping with the mess. The women are forced to sit in their chairs and restrain themselves from getting involved. When both groups had mastered these assignments, Lewis figured, they would be ready to enter heaven.

Lewis's own most obvious bad habit was his addiction to tobacco. When I had tea with Lewis in 1956, he started out by offering me a cigarette. With a touch of embarrassment I thanked him but explained that I didn't smoke. As he lit up, he congratulated me and heartily advised me never to begin. He had begun smoking as a boy, stealing cigarettes from his father's supply. In later years, when he wanted to quit, he found that he *could* exist without smoking, but it was such an effort that he couldn't concentrate on anything else at the same time. Not smoking was a full-time job for him, so he gave it up. Once he was asked if a person surrendered to God should be cantankerous or smoke. He by-passed the given examples and said that you can't judge by the outside. You need to know what kind of raw material Christ is working with.

Long before the medical statistics were available, Lewis admitted that smoking was a bad idea. But he definitely resisted the idea that alcoholic beverages had to be totally avoided by Christians. He especially resented any church making teetotaling a condition of membership. The wine in the Bible, he insisted, was real, fermented alcoholic wine—as the repeated warnings against drunkenness from Genesis to Paul's Epistles illustrate. Islam, not Christianity, demands total abstinence; and Lewis would have greatly resented Muslims imposing their religious scruples upon everyone else. Christianity teaches temperance in drinking and all other things. This means going the right length and no further. Of course this means abstaining from alcohol whenever there is a good reason, as there often is—to save money for the poor, to discourage companions from drinking too much or to keep oneself from getting drunk. Lewis could understand the bitterness of people who have to live with alcoholics. But there are many ways to be intemperate besides drinking. Just because you don't fall down in the middle of the road doesn't mean that in God's eyes you are temperate.

Lewis was also asked about gambling. He felt sure that if it becomes important in a person's life it is evil. And if it becomes a means of large financial transactions without doing any good, it is evil. Similarly, he was outspoken against the manufacture of silly luxuries and gaudy, useless gadgets plus the even sillier advertisements to persuade us to buy them. He felt that materials and human skill and time shouldn't be invested in such rubbish. He also felt that the world is in lunatic condition with everyone living by persuading everyone else to buy things.

Lewis wasn't sure whether small-scale gambling was always bad or not, it was so foreign to him. He called it the only vice which never tempted him. If anyone came to him asking to play bridge for money, he would say, "How much do you hope to win? Take it and go away."[11]

Part Two: The Choice Is Ours

"It is not for me to lay down laws," Lewis admitted, "as I am only a layman, and I don't know much." He believed that a perfect imitation of the life of Christ would mean referring every act, feeling or experience to God. It would mean looking at everything as something from God and asking in every case, "How would He wish me to deal with this?"[12]

Lewis said a serious attempt to practice the Christian virtues for six weeks or more is a most valuable experience. The main thing we learn by trying it is that we fail. This gets rid of the tempting idea that we can be good enough to bargain with God. After a man tries very hard to be good he has a clear idea of how bad he really is.[13]

In a sense Christians are always "dressing up as Christ," especially when they say, "Our Father." There is a kind of pretense which helps people to grow into what they like to pretend to be. Pretending to be like Christ helps us to become more like him. There are many things, especially mental things, which one can't do if he or she is seriously trying to be like Christ. Becoming Christlike is not just a matter of right and wrong acts or a matter of rules. It is more like painting a portrait. This is far harder than obeying a set of rules, but God helps us to do it.[14]

If a Christian schedules his life with a set of strict rules (as the Jews did) it puts him between two dangers. When he fails to follow his set routine, he is defeated. When he succeeds, he has a deceptively good conscience and feels satisfied with himself even in complete absence of all real charity and faith.[15] Real Christian ethics can't be reduced to rule keeping.

"Our emotional reactions to our own behavior are of limited ethical significance," Lewis observed.[16] He had found that the amount of shame and disgust he felt about his own sins was all out of proportion to their comparative gravity. Little sins which happen to be ungentlemanly as well as un-christian, for example, shamed him much more than some really ghastly uncharities.

Lewis advised a lady that her feelings were not herself, but only a thing that happened to her. He advised her to give thanks for them when they were humble, loving and brave, and to pray for their alteration when they were conceited, selfish and cowardly. But she was not to bother much about them, because what really matters is a person's intentions and behavior.[17] He advised this same lady to read a modern translation of the New Testament intelligently, to pray for guidance, and to be as obedient as possible to her conscience in all matters.

Lewis recommended daily prayers, religious reading and church attendance as necessary parts of the Christian life. They continually remind us of what we believe. Because of our changing moods, a belief must be fed in order to remain alive in the mind; otherwise it tends to drift away. When Lewis was an atheist he had moods in which Christianity looked terribly probable, and when he was a Christian he had moods in which Christianity looked very improbable. Moods are bound to change. A man's mood goes most strongly against his Christian belief when he wants a woman or wants to lie or feels very pleased with himself or sees a chance to make some money in a way that is not perfectly fair. Then he has to rely upon will.[18]

No feeling can be relied upon to last at all. Knowledge, principles, and habits can last; but a feeling is only a feeling—influenced by the weather and the state of a person's digestion.[19]

C. S. Lewis described *The Screwtape Letters* as "ethics served with an imaginative seasoning."[20] Early in that book Screwtape is advising Wormwood to get his young Christian to feel disappointed with fellow worshipers in church. Wormwood must never let the young man reason, "If I, being what I am, can consider that I am in some sense a Christian, why should the different vices of those people in the next pew prove that their religion is mere hypocrisy and convention?"[21]

Lewis warned in *Mere Christianity* that the devil always sends errors into the world in pairs of opposites, such as totalitarianism and individualism. The former tries to make all people alike, like cogs in a machine, and the latter tries to divorce people from each other, so that they feel no common bond of responsibility and caring. The devil likes to direct our attention to the error we dislike most so that we will back into the opposite one in reaction.

Screwtape explains this device a little differently to Wormwood. Devils direct the fashionable outcry of each generation against those vices of which it is least in danger, and they popularize whatever virtue is closest to the prevailing vice. Hence a lecherous, unchaste generation is put on guard against Puritanism when Puritanism is a dead issue anyway; at the same time it extols the virtues of healthy honesty and tolerance. An idle, feckless generation is on guard against materialism, and a materialistic generation is on guard against improvidence. The game, Screwtape explains, is to have everyone running about with fire extinguishers whenever there is a flood.

Another of Screwtape's many tricky assaults upon ethical living is to get people to ask about a proposed course of action, "Is it progressive or reactionary? Is this the way that History is going?" instead of "is it righteous? is it prudent? is it possible?"[22]

A Godfather's Advice

C. S. Lewis wrote a much simpler warning about life's decisions to a child once. Lewis was the Christian godfather of a boy who was about to be confirmed. He sent him a gift of money and a playful, warm letter in which he said he supposed he must try to give some advice. Then he warned the boy not to count on or demand special feelings when he took his first communion. If desired religious feelings come, one can thank God. If they don't come, one goes on doing what he is told. Lewis said this was one of the very few subjects he felt he knew something about.

He had one other piece of advice for the boy. It was a checklist for life activities. There are only three kinds of things anyone ever needs to do. First, Lewis pointed to the things we *ought* to do, like working well in school and being nice to other people. Second, Lewis pointed to the things we *have* to do, like dressing and shopping. Third, Lewis pointed to the things we *like* to do, which each person must discover for himself. Unfortunately, some people get off the track and waste much of their time and energy doing things for none of the three good reasons.

Lewis wrote many charming, respectful letters to children, but he did not like all young boys so well as he seemed to like his godchild. In fact, when someone once asked him about the Old Testament story of God sending bears to tear up the boys who were taunting the prophet Elisha, he prefaced his answer by saying that for some boys he had known that would be a good idea.[23]

Lewis didn't get along well with neighborhood boys who stole the nectarines off his trees, came to the door repeatedly each year as "carollers" demanding money, trespassed in his garden, and knowingly disturbed Joy in her serious illness. He had to battle smoldering resentment.

Finally, some of the boys were caught red-handed by the police after breaking into Lewis's little garden building and stealing several unusual items of value. The theft had obviously been planned, and some of the loot was already sold when they were caught. Further, some of the boys had been convicted of similar crimes before. Instead of punishing them, the indulgent judge inflicted a small fine upon their parents and told the boys to give up such "pranks." Lewis felt the incident was characteristic of our confused age. He thoroughly believed in retributive punishment.

An earlier brush Lewis had with the law was, in his own words, tragicomical. A woman named Mrs. Hooker spent part of 1951 and 1952 posing as the wife of C. S. Lewis and running up bad debts in their name. When at last one of her victims learned from Lewis that he didn't even know the woman, both Mrs. Hooker and Lewis, along with the creditors, had to go to court. Lewis had never been to court before and found it repulsive to see a guilty person at bay, even in a kind and fair court. Mrs. Hooker already had twenty-one convictions on her record, and she was what Lewis called a confidence trickster. Nevertheless, Lewis's belief in retribution was balanced by compassion and concern. He prayed for Mrs. Hooker and asked at least one of his friends to pray for her also.

At the time of the Hooker episode, Lewis observed to one of his friends that people who are unwillingly burdened with the psychological disorder of homosexuality and who fail repeatedly in their efforts to lead chaste lives may indeed, in their struggles, manifest a special work of grace that we do not now see. He combined a profound respect for troubled people with an unswerving allegiance to traditional morality.

Lewis ended his final essay, "We Have No 'Right to Happiness,'" with a gloomy warning. If we wholly grant ourselves a "right to happiness" for the sexual impulse, the "right" will spread. This fatal idea of unrestrained self-gratification will sooner or later seep through our lives and every impulse of every person will be his own law. Then "our civilization will have died at heart, and will—one dare not even add 'unfortunately'—be swept away."[24]

Further Reading about Ethics

"No book is really worth reading at the age of ten which is not equally (and often far more) worth reading at the age of fifty—except, of course, books of information."[25]

The Horse and His Boy by C. S. Lewis, the fifth of the Narnian series, deals with cruelty, injustice, power, pride, wealth, danger, freedom and responsibility. It is an adventure full of good and bad deeds, wisely told.

Mere Christianity by C. S. Lewis is written in four parts. Book III, Christian Behavior, deals in clear specifics about morality, virtue and sin in everyday living.

God in the Dock by C. S. Lewis bears the subtitle "Essays on Theology and Ethics." Part III contains nine essays on ethical topics.

"On Ethics" in *Christian Reflections* by C. S. Lewis is a spirited argument against the "new moralities." It is a serious consideration of Christian ethics from a philosophical point of view.

The Abolition of Man by C. S. Lewis is a small book about human values and the universal nature of ethics.

"The Poison of Subjectivism" in *Christian Reflections* by C. S. Lewis calls people to return to belief in objective values before we perish.

The Taste for the Other by Gilbert Meilaender presents a superb survey of Lewis's social and ethical views.

Notes

1. Lewis, *God in the Dock*, p. 154.
2. Nevill Coghill, "The Approach to English," *Light on C. S. Lewis*, p. 64.
3. Lewis, *The Screwtape Letters*, p. 55.
4. Lewis, *Mere Christianity*, p. 80.
5. Lewis, *Surprised by Joy*, p. 68.
6. Lewis, *The Screwtape Letters*, pp. 53-54.
7. Lewis, *That Hideous Strength*, p. 6.
8. Lewis, *Letters of C. S. Lewis*, p. 166.
9. Ibid., p. 86.
10. Lewis, *Mere Christianity*, p. 95.
11. Lewis, *God in the Dock*, p. 60.
12. Ibid., p. 50.
13. Lewis, *Mere Christianity*, pp. 109-10.
14. Ibid., pp. 147-48.
15. Lewis, *Letters to an American Lady*, p. 36.
16. Lewis, *Letters to Malcolm*, p. 99.
17. Lewis, *Letters of C. S. Lewis*, p. 233.
18. Lewis, *Mere Christianity*, pp. 108-9.
19. Ibid., p. 84.
20. Lewis, *Letters of C. S. Lewis*, p. 234.
21. Lewis, *The Screwtape Letters*, p. 18.
22. Ibid., pp. 129-30.
23. Lewis, *Letters of C. S. Lewis*, p. 262.
24. Lewis, *God in the Dock*, p. 322.
25. Lewis, "On Stories," *Of Other Worlds*, p. 15.

Chapter 13

Truth

"If you want a religion to make you feel really comfortable,
I certainly don't recommend Christianity."
"Answers to Questions on Christianity," God in the Dock.[1]

Part One: Finding the Truth

In July of 1928 C. S. Lewis finally got started writing his first book of prose. He had been busy gathering material for it and itching to do the actual writing for some time. Many delightful sentences had popped into his head before he was ready to start writing, but once he started he found that half of them couldn't be used after all because, having learned more about the subject, he found that they weren't true. "That's the worst of facts," he told his father in a letter, "they do cramp a fellow's style."[2]

This book ended up as *The Allegory of Love*, Lewis's great scholarly success that was finished and published eight years later. What an eight years! In that time Lewis would lose his father, come to belief in God, move to his permanent home at the Kilns, become a confessing Christian, and bring out *The Pilgrim's Regress*.

The fact that Lewis became a Christian long before he finished the book changed the book along with much else in his life. His test of music, religion and even visions (if one has them) was the question of whether they made one more obedient, more God-centered and neighbor-centered and *less self-centered*. That is exactly what Christian belief did for Lewis—it was one more thing that did "cramp a fellow's style."

How did Lewis come to believe that Christianity is true? He said it was the usual combination of authority, reason and experience. All of our knowledge depends upon those three elements. In this case Lewis decided to accept the authority of many wise people in different times and places who taught the reality of the spiritual world. His honest logic eventually discovered that materialism is more far-fetched than belief in spiritual reality.[3] (For the details of Lewis's reasoning on this, read Book One of *Mere Christianity*.) The results of his limited experience in the spiritual life seemed to bear it all out; it was not at all like the results of an illusion.[4]

Emotional religious experience comes and goes, Lewis says; especially goes. We cannot depend upon it to uphold our belief. The purpose of faith is to retain our hold upon the truth that seems irresistible and obvious during times of special grace, but which seems more or less unclear at ordinary times. Faith means the power of continuing to believe what we once honestly thought to be true, until really good reasons for a change of mind come along. Feelings alone are inadequate reasons to accept or reject truth.[5]

Screwtape had plenty of tricks besides the use of feelings to deflect humans from Christ. One was the game of having humans decide to believe something, not because it is true, but for some other reason. If it is for personal advancement, so much the better. Since God refuses to be used as a convenience, Satan is delighted when people decide to revive belief in God in order to achieve something— even something otherwise good. As much as the devils hate the idea of allowing Christianity to flow over into political life ("the establishment of anything like a really just society would be a major disaster")[6] they neverthe-less encourage people to treat Christianity as a means to social justice. The idea is to value Christianity not because it is true, but because it may produce something more important.

In *The Great Divorce* an unbelieving resident of hell exclaimed that surely no one would ever be penalized for his honest opinions. The fact was that his own self-serving, sloppy opinions had never been intellectually honest at all; sins of the intellect are really sins. There have also been people so absorbed in proving God's existence that they came to care nothing for God himself. There have been people so occupied in spreading Christianity that they thought nothing of Christ. This is the subtlest of snares.[7]

Rational as he was, Lewis thoroughly believed in the mysti-cal experience, a way to go out of this world before death. Mysticism is the temporary shattering of our ordinary spatial and temporal consciousness and our rational intellect, and it is not just an illusion. Some Christian saints have experienced it, but Lewis felt we are not all to expect that type of experience. He did not. He knew that for him to pursue it out of curiosity and lust for spiritual adventure would be wrong.

Since mystics from all kinds of religions have much the same mystical experience, it might seem that what they share in com-mon is the real religious truth, stripped of all mistaken or incidental doctrines or creeds. This is the view of mysticism that Lewis could not buy. He likened mystical experiences to a sea voyage; all people who leave the port of ordinary consciousness are bound to find the same things at first. But the important question is where the voyage ends. Where does the trip take the voyager? The lawfulness, safety and utility of the voyage depend upon the motives, skill and constancy of the voyager and on the grace of God.

Another English author of Lewis's generation, Aldous Huxley, experimented with drugs in his search for truth. He hoped that drugs would prove an inexpensive shortcut to spiritual wisdom and religious perception for ordinary people. Ironically, both Huxley and Lewis were called permanently "out of this world" on the same day, November 22, 1963. Lewis did not mention any names, but he said his faith would not be at all disturbed if drugs or even diabolical activity produced mysticism that seemed identical to experiences of the great Christian mystics. He flatly stated that mysticism does not validate any religion in which it happens to occur, and practicing mysticism does not in itself prove any person's sanctity. The true religion gives value to its own mysticism, not vice versa.

One Pentecost Sunday Lewis preached a sermon that began with his view of *glossolalia*. He admitted that the idea of gibberish had often been a stumbling block for him, and he saw it as an embarrassing phenomenon. In fact, he felt that in many instances it is a kind of hysteria or nervous excitement rather than an operation of the Holy Spirit. A non-Christian could thereby explain away all instances. Likewise, the erotic language and imagery often used by great Christian mystics could be used by non-Christians to explain religious mysticism as merely an unusual erotic phenomenon. But Lewis preached a very long sermon to show wonderful ways in which the Supernatural really does enter into our natural lives, flooding our limited senses and feelings with new meaning. Like it or not, we cannot shelve the story of Pentecost; it is at the center of the birth-story of the church. It is the very event which Christ told the church to wait for in almost his last words before the Ascension. Scripture tells us so.

Rebunking Scripture

Lewis coined the word "rebunker" once to describe his friend Charles Williams. It means one who shows the value of something that other people have debunked. Lewis, in contrast to most intellectuals of his day, valued the Bible as our first source of truth. As an example, he once dismissed some ideas of Pascal by simply saying that in cases where Pascal contradicted Scripture he must be wrong.[8]

Although C. S. Lewis believed wholeheartedly in the authority and authenticity of the Bible, he once wrote a letter to Dr. Clyde Kilby in which he ruled out the idea that every statement in Scripture must be *historical* truth. Almost everyone agrees that the parables are not historical truth, for example. Lewis also felt that apparently conflicting accounts about details of Judas's death in Matthew 27:5 and Acts 1:18-19 ruled out their both being exact historical truth. Furthermore, although Lewis never doubted the historicity of an account because the account was miraculous, he believed that Jonah's whale, Noah's ark and Job's boils were probably inspired stories rather than factual history.

Lewis believed that the entire Bible is inspired, but he disbelieved that inspiration is present throughout the Bible in the same mode and degree. The most obvious evidence for this is Paul's testimony in 1 Corinthians 7. There he said, "To the married I give this ruling, which is not mine but the Lord's. . . ." His very next sentence began, "To the rest I say this, as my own word, not as the Lord's. . . ." (NEB). Paul here seemed to claim a difference in degree of inspiration.

Another interesting contrast can be found between Luke's introduction to his Gospel, in which he claims to have researched and planned his account, and the prophetic words of Caiaphas, the evil high priest, as recorded in John 11:49-52. We are clearly told that Caiaphas was inspired without knowing it and spoke divine truth he did not intend or comprehend. Luke and Caiaphas seemed to experience different modes of inspiration.

Lewis believed that God guided all the writers and preservers of the Bible so that the finished work carries the Word of God. We are to steep ourselves in its tone or temper and so learn its overall message. The readers, as well as the writers, of Scripture need God's guidance.

Of course some people will read Scripture as merely human literature, Lewis said. Some will read the life of our Lord as nothing but a human life, and some will read human life itself as only an animal life of unusual complexity. They will always be coming up with new evidence to prove that point of view. We have to expect that. In the same way, someone who can not read at all might "prove" to other illiterates that a poem was nothing but black marks on white paper; no matter how carefully he analyzed the paper and ink chemically, he would find no poem in them.

At the end of the book *Miracles*, Lewis asked people to read the New Testament for themselves and to beware of modern scholars. Likening himself to a sheep, Lewis once gave a long intense talk about the validity of the Bible to students at a theological college.[9] He asked the young "shepherds" to listen carefully to his "bleating." His complaint was that modern New Testament criticism has asked us to give up the huge mass of orthodox beliefs shared by the early church, the church fathers, the Middle Ages, the Reformers and even the last century. Then for a dozen pages he demolished the unassailable arguments of the New Testament critics with wit and fervor—pointing out some of their errors with the gusto of a Christian who is also a literary historian.

"A sacred book rejected is like a king dethroned," Lewis observed.[10] Some who disbelieve the Bible courteously want it to remain a beloved work of literature. Lewis thought that impossible. It will either return as a sacred book or enter the ghost life of a museum piece—except among the believing minority who read it to be instructed. And for them a modern version is usually more practical. "The only kind of sanctity which Scripture can lose . . . by being modernized is an accidental kind which it never had for its writers or its earliest readers," Lewis said in his warm introduction to J. B. Phillips's translation *Letters to Young Churches*.

Once, in a letter to T. S. Eliot, Lewis said, "Odd, the way the less the Bible is read the more it is translated."[11] He and Eliot were both literary advisors for a revision of Psalms.

In the psalms there are some difficult passages that seem to express evil attitudes. Lewis admitted this in his book *Reflections on the Psalms*. He tackled the problem areas in the psalms because all holy Scripture is in some sense the Word of God, and so there is use to be made of it all. He once warned a woman not to condemn any Scripture passages that would seem to show God in some way evil. There is surely some great truth about the goodness of God in such a passage if we could see it. Perhaps such baffling passages were included for the great sages and mystics, not for us. "Would not a revelation which contained nothing that you and I did not understand, be for that reason rather suspect?"[12]

Even a person devoted to finding truth must realize that many questions, some very interesting questions indeed, simply can't be answered. One of Lewis's main efforts as a teacher was to train people to say those (apparently difficult) words, "We don't know."[13] He often wondered how different the content of our faith will look when we see it in the total context. "Not one jot of Revelation will be proved false; but so many new truths might be added."[14]

Part Two: Sharing the Truth

When C. S. Lewis was in his middle teens, he sent a letter to his best friend, Arthur, imploring him to tell the absolute truth. The two boys were sharing their creative writing, and Lewis was afraid that Arthur was not candid enough with him.[15] Lewis wanted to become a great poet then. By his midtwenties he was giving up that favorite ambition, but he still devoted some time every day to writing poetry. "My prose style is really abominable," he wrote in his journal, "and between poetry and work, I suppose I shall never learn to improve it."[16]

By work, Lewis here meant household tasks. "Domestic drudgery is excellent as an alternative to idleness or hateful thoughts—which is perhaps poor Mrs. Moore's reason for piling it on all the time; as an alternative to the work one is longing and able to do . . . it is maddening."[17] Over twenty years later "poor Mrs. Moore" was an extremely demanding elderly woman and Lewis couldn't even be absent for an afternoon without carefully planning ahead. He was swamped and understandably resentful.

Lewis confessed to his good friend Owen Barfield that we make the error of resenting as interruptions to our chosen lifework the obligations that are actually set for us. It seems as if Lewis was often set to the humble task of helping individuals who hurt. His chosen lifework was teaching and writing about things he felt and believed.

"All I am doing is to ask people to face the facts," Lewis said, "to understand the questions which Christianity claims to answer. And they are very terrifying facts. I wish it was possible to say something more agreeable. But I must say what I think true."[18]

The basic facts that Lewis taught are the universal moral law and the failure of humanity to live up to it. God is the mind at the back of the moral law, and also a Person whom we have offended. As we are now, we both hate and love goodness. God himself became a man to save us from the disapproval of God. "Not only do we need to recognize that we are sinners; we need to believe in a Saviour who takes away sin."[19] The basic message comes through again and again in Lewis's writing. He said himself, "Most of my books are evangelistic."[20]

We are surely to seek the salvation of others, but when we do so we must remember that God has his own way with each soul. It is wrong to demand that everyone conform to the same pattern. We must also remember that what we do, rather than what we say, contributes most to other people's conversion.[21]

"Woe to you if you do not evangelize," Lewis warned some theological students once.[22] A century ago the main task of the church in England was to nurture those who had been brought up in the faith. Today its chief task is to convert and instruct infidels.

As Lewis saw it, there are two lines of attack: emotional and intellectual. If Lewis had been given the gifts necessary for emotional evangelism, he would have used them; he felt that it has an important place today. But his gifts were all in the area of intellectual evangelism.

One of the great difficulties in such evangelism is to keep the audience's attention upon the question of truth. The speaker or writer must make it clear that he is not just saying things he likes. The listeners have to be forced back repeatedly to the issue of truth and falsity. Listeners always think the speaker is recommending Christianity not because it is *true*, but because it is *good.* Then they like to get off onto all kinds of subjects related to good or evil. By forcing them to consider the truth of Christianity the Christian can undermine both their belief that some religion is good in moderation and their disbelief in the doctrine of obtaining eternal salvation only by the name of Christ.

As C. S. Lewis first saw it many years ago, most English were not reached either by highly emotional revivalism or by the unintelligible language of highly cultured clergymen. What they needed was a translator. Lewis took upon himself the task of turning Christian doctrine into language that unscholarly people would attend to and understand.

When he responded to one bitter attack upon his work five years before he died, Lewis admitted that he may have made theological errors and that his manners may have been defective. With typical modesty, Lewis said he was ready to learn to do better if he received constructive suggestions. Then with typical combative spirit he challenged his critic to divulge what methods *he* employed when *he* tried to convert the great mass of storekeepers, lawyers, realtors, morticians and police in his own city—and with what success. "One thing at least is sure," Lewis concluded. "If the real theologians had tackled this laborious work of translation about a hundred years ago, when they began to lose touch with the people (for whom Christ died), there would have been no place for me."[23]

Lewis decided that translating a passage of standard theology into the simple vernacular should be a compulsory part of every ordination examination before a student could enter the ministry. A missionary to the Bantus learns Bantu; a missionary to the English should speak plain English. It would be a hard test. For one thing, ordinary speech requires about ten times as many words as learned language rightly used.[24] Translating is not only essential for communicating with common people, but it tests whether one knows what one means or not. If you cannot translate your thoughts into uneducated language, your ideas are not yet really clear in your own mind.[25]

Our responsibility is to present the unchanging message of the gospel in the particular modern language of our own age. Ironically, some ministers do just the opposite, taking current ideas and dressing them up in old traditional religious language.[26] We also need to be on guard against the fashionable words of our own circle.[27] Such words seem warm and full of implications to us when they are in vogue, but they are likely to be unintelligible to outsiders. Furthermore, highly popular words often serve more as emotional signals than as a source of firm intellectual understanding between insiders themselves.

Lewis gave out plenty of pointers on how to become a better writer, but his most succinct advice for developing good style was to know exactly what you want to say and to be sure you are saying exactly that.[28]

He once confided to another outstanding Christian writer, Dorothy Sayers, that for him apologetic work was dangerous to his faith. "A doctrine never seems dimmer to me than when I have just successfully defended it."[29] Furthermore, he confided to his friend Sister Penelope once that he often got the feeling when he woke up in the morning that there was nothing he *disliked* so much as religion—that it went against his grain! He sincerely believed that we cannot always take for ourselves the advice that we successfully give to others and that "truth is more effective through any lips other than our own."[30]

Modernism's Mistakes

C. S. Lewis did not always find that truth through the lips of the clergy. He spoke out repeatedly against the presence of unbelieving priests in the Church of England, warning that this may soon destroy the Church. Once lay people tried to hide the fact that they believed so much less than their minister; now they try to hide the fact that they believe so much more. Some priests have become so "broad" or "liberal" or "modern" that they discard any real supernaturalism and thus cease to be Christian at all.

Lewis granted any person the right to discard and change his belief, but he insisted that a priest who discards his belief is obligated to change his profession. Lewis considered it a form of prostitution when a man appears in print claiming to disbelieve everything that his vocation presupposes. No wonder such a man gets quoted in the papers for agreeing with the opposition; it is as if a film star came out against cosmetics.

As early as *The Screwtape Letters*, Lewis pictured the devil praising a vicar who had been watering down the faith so long for a supposedly incredulous and hardheaded congregation that he now shocked them with his unbelief and undermined many a soul's Christianity.[31] As late as the last chapter of *Letters to Malcolm*, Lewis was analyzing why liberal Christians were so negative toward him. They sincerely believe, as he saw it, that the world will abandon all pretense of Christianity rather than accept the Supernatural. They are trying to free Christianity from the scandal of supernaturalism in order to save some vestige of the faith. Accommodating preachers and unbelieving members act as if Jesus told us to go into all the world and tell the world it is quite right![32]

As Lewis saw it, the great division in Christianity is not between branches or denominations, but "between religion with a real supernaturalism and salvationism on the one hand, and all watered-down and modernist versions on the other."[33] "By the way," Lewis asked Malcolm, "did you ever meet, or hear of, anyone who was converted from skepticism to a 'liberal' or 'demythologized' Christianity? I think that when unbelievers come in at all, they come in a good deal further."[34]

In *The Great Divorce* Lewis introduced an apostate bishop who had once found himself in contact with a current of liberal ideas and plunged in because it seemed modern and successful. Soon he didn't *want* crude salvationism or real spiritual fears and hopes to be true. He was afraid of unpopular ideas or ridicule, and he drifted, unresisting and unpraying, into utter disbelief. His reward in this life was popularity and sales for his books, and he ended up in the next life giving theological lectures in hell.

When this apostate bishop took a tour to the edge of heaven, a Bright Person met him and urged him to repent and believe and come along to the mountains of heaven. "I will bring you to the land not of questions but of answers, and you shall see the face of God."[35] The ghost thought that sounded stifling. The shining spirit assured the ghost that in heaven one experiences truth in new ways. "I will bring you where you can taste it like honey and be embraced by it as by a bridegroom. Your thirst shall be quenched.... I will bring you to Eternal Fact, the Father of all other facthood."[36]

C. S. Lewis had said once that if a person looks for truth he may find comfort in the end, but if he looks for comfort he will not get either comfort or truth—only wishful thinking which ends in despair.[37]

Further Reading about Truth

"The imaginary histories written about my books are by no means always offensive. Sometimes they are even complimentary. There is nothing against them except that they're not true, and would be rather irrelevant if they were."[38]

A Mind Awake edited by Clyde Kilby and *The Quotable Lewis* by Wayne Martindale and Jerry Root are anthologies of quotations by C. S. Lewis.

C. S. Lewis on Scripture by Michael J. Christensen sets forth Lewis's thoughts on the nature of biblical inspiration and the role of revelation, and Lewis's relevance to the inerrancy controversy troubling evangelicals fifteen years after Lewis's death.

"Modern Theology and Biblical Criticism" in *Christian Reflections* by C. S. Lewis attacks the authority of New Testament critics and defends the truth of the Bible.

"Historicism" in *Christian Reflections* by C. S. Lewis attacks the practice of misusing and misinterpreting history in order to wrest metaphysical or theological conclusions from it.

"Religion: Reality or Substitute?" in *Christian Reflections* by C. S. Lewis frankly explores faith, doubt, reason and honesty.

"Meditation in a Toolshed" in *God in the Dock* by C. S. Lewis contrasts the two possible ways of viewing everything we experience.

"Christian Apologetics" in *God in the Dock* by C. S. Lewis brings together almost all of Lewis's beliefs and concerns about leading people to Christ.

Notes

1. Lewis, *God in the Dock*, p. 58.
2. Lewis, *Letters of C. S. Lewis*, p. 127.
3. Lewis, "Book I," *Mere Christianity*.
4. Lewis, *Christian Reflections*, p. 41.
5. Ibid., p. 42.
6. Lewis, *The Screwtape Letters*, p. 119.
7. Lewis, *The Great Divorce*, pp. 32, 68.
8. Lewis, *Letters of C. S. Lewis*, p. 242.
9. Lewis, *Christian Reflections*, p. 152.
10. C. S. Lewis, *The Literary Impact of the Authorized Version* (London: Univ. of London, 1950), pp. 25–26.
11. Lewis, *Letters of C. S. Lewis*, p. 304.
12. Ibid., p. 253.
13. Ibid., p. 295.
14. Ibid., p. 267.
15. Ibid., p. 28.
16. Lewis, *Selected Literary Essays*, p. ix.
17. Lewis, *Letters of C. S. Lewis*, p. 92.
18. Lewis, *Mere Christianity*, p. 25.
19. Lewis, *God in the Dock*, p. 260.
20. Ibid., p. 181.
21. Lewis, *Letters of C. S. Lewis*, p. 261.
22. Lewis, *Christian Reflections*, p. 152.
23. Lewis, *God in the Dock*, p. 183.
24. Ibid., p. 256.
25. Ibid., pp. 98–99.
26. Ibid., p. 93.
27. Ibid., p. 257.
28. Ibid., p. 263.
29. Lewis, *Letters of C. S. Lewis*, p. 209.
30. Ibid., p. 195.
31. Lewis, *The Screwtape Letters*, p. 82.
32. Lewis, *God in the Dock*, p. 265.
33. Lewis, *Letters of C. S. Lewis*, p. 170.
34. Lewis, *Letters to Malcolm*, p. 119.
35. Lewis, *The Great Divorce*, p. 36.
36. Ibid., pp. 37–38.
37. Lewis, *Mere Christianity*, p. 25.
38. Lewis, *Of Other Worlds*, p. 50.

Culture:
What Is Our
Worldview?

Chapter 14

Sciences

*"In science we have been reading only the notes to
a poem; in Christianity, we find the poem itself."*
Miracles[1]

Part One: Hard Science and Soft Heads

"Lewis knew nothing about science except that he hated it."[2]
This offhand remark by a Princeton professor of English in the
New York Times Book Review in 1979 seems to represent a very
popular, if uninformed, point of view. Lewis's purported ignorance of science can serve two possible purposes. First, it can
counter the tendency for naive people to believe that Lewis
knew all about everything—in case there is such a tendency.
Second, it can be used to discredit Lewis as a literary critic, religious thinker and observer of the human scene. Faith in science
and belief that Lewis was ignorant of science combine in some
minds as a reason to avoid examining Lewis's ideas about the
meaning of life.

Lewis has rankled scientists as well as English professors.
His personal physician and good friend R. E. Havard, who considered himself somewhat of a scientist, once heard a group of
scientists discussing Lewis. One of Lewis's own faculty

colleagues said, "He is a dangerous man." Havard asked, "Dangerous to whom?" and the man quickly shifted ground, if Havard's account is accurate. The man apparently considered Lewis dangerous to his kind of scientific agnosticism about life.[3] There was friction between Lewis and certain kinds of scientists, and it continues today.

Once when Lewis was telling his brother about a series of moderately popular science classics he was reading, he recalled Samuel Butler's remark that a priest is a person who disseminates little lies in defense of a great truth, and a scientist is a person who disseminates little truths in defense of a great lie.[4] The great lie that Lewis was always combating was materialism.

Lewis's own stepson and financial heir David Gresham commented publicly on his stepfather for the first time in 1979 in Chad Walsh's book *The Literary Legacy of C. S. Lewis*: "He was incredibly ignorant of such things as biology; he thought that a slug was a reptile."[5] (This comment is bound to remind readers of Lewis's letters that during their brief life together, when David was a teenager, Lewis found him an intellectual prig and not very pleasant company.) Gresham does not hint at what "such things as biology" are, but he probably meant the various biological sciences. It is true that for all his acute observation of the organic, Lewis never studied biological sciences and had no interest in physiology. But the idea that Lewis thought slugs have bones or else that snakes don't is out of bounds. One can almost imagine Lewis referring to a dragon or lizard as a worm (an archaic literary term he used) and being misunderstood by the American boy. Whatever Lewis said to Gresham once about a slug, if Lewis's ignorance of biology was "incredible" it was no doubt incredible only in contrast to his immense education in other fields.

Slugs were also involved in a far earlier attack on Lewis's knowledge of science. In 1946 J. B. S. Haldane, a noted British professor of biology and physiology who wrote several books, vehemently criticized Lewis's ideas and incidentally likened his fictional characters to slugs in a cage who seek cabbage rather than electric shocks. (Ironically, Lewis was fanatically opposed to conditioned behavior.) Haldane's specialty was human genetics, but his special commitment was to Communism. He accused Lewis of writing wrong science in his fiction, of insulting scientists, and, most importantly, of opposing scientific social planning.[6]

Lewis retorted that of course he wrote wrong science; his science fiction trilogy was strictly imaginative romance. He didn't think there was any accurate science in it and didn't expect anyone else to either. He pointed out, however, that his own science in fiction was about as accurate as Haldane's erroneous statements about history in nonfiction.[7]

In response to the charge that he vilified scientists in his fiction, Lewis almost whooped. In his opinion Weston, "a buffoon-villain," was a gas-bag who seemed incapable of inventing a mousetrap, much less the spaceship Lewis attributed to him as part of the plot. (In a personal letter Lewis once told Owen Barfield that Weston and several other villains in his fiction were all portraits of Barfield; he joshed Barfield unmercifully in letters.[8]) In *That Hideous Strength* Lewis was attacking public bureaucrats and certain philosophers, not scientists. To make that very clear he included a true scientist named Hingest who was murdered by the scoundrels at N.I.C.E. when he left there because he discovered that the group didn't really care about science after all. In that book the hero, Ransom, says clearly that sciences are good and innocent in themselves.

In 1977 a "lost manuscript" was published for the first time. It was presented as an aborted science fiction novel that C. S. Lewis wrote in 1938, shortly after he wrote *Out of the Silent Planet*. The author-narrator refers to himself as C. S. Lewis, and he includes characters from C. S. Lewis's other novels.

(Needless to say, if someone were inventing an apocryphal Lewis novel, that would be the way to make it seem obviously by Lewis.)

If it had been written in 1938, this novel would show Lewis a bit ahead of his time in science fiction ideas. But if written after Lewis's death, as many believe, *The Dark Tower* was derivative as well as a literary spoof. Thirty years make an immense difference.

The critics have roundly condemned *The Dark Tower* as unworthy of C. S. Lewis in every way[9] (plot, pacing, literary style, moral tone, characterization, and a sense of purpose), but it draws upon an interesting idea about time. The author refers to *An Experiment with Time* by J. W. Dunne, a book which Dorothy Sayers had mentioned. *The Dark Tower* plays with Dunne's idea of serial time (as J. B. Priestly did quite differently in his play *Time and the Conways*). The last eight pages of this unfinished story are evidently a fragment that Lewis really wrote. He hatched the idea that another race has specialized in the knowledge of time as ours has specialized in the knowledge of space.[10]

In *The Discarded Image,* about twenty-five years later, he remarked, "Without a parable modern physics speaks not to the multitudes." Long before Fritjof Capra's popular *The Tao of Physics* (1976) and other books on the topic, Lewis observed that the language of mathematics is the purest expression of modern physics and that attempts to illustrate the arcane truths of post-Newtonian physics by suggestive terms other than mathematics is resorting to the kind of expression used by mystics. "The curvature of space," he claimed, "is strictly comparable to the old definition of God as a circle whose center is everywhere and whose circumference is nowhere."[11] This was not at all a disparaging remark.

The Nature of Things

Anyone who doubts Lewis's informed interest in the large issues of scientific theory should read at least the epilogue of *The Discarded Image*. It proves that he was neither indifferent nor hostile to science, but grappling with it from the historical and philosophical perspective that was his mindset. He probably had little interest in the phylum, class, order, family, genus and species of slugs, even as a boy. The big, general questions interested him more than the specific ones.

Astronomy was one of Lewis's earliest loves, and he had a telescope which he occasionally used when he was older. Once as a middle-aged professor he was saying goodnight to some friends at college and pointed out to them the extremely rare conjunction of five planets "all brilliantly visible in a circle in the sky at once."[12]

By the time Lewis had reached the midpoint of his life, however, he found that astronomy had become disappointing to him. The material universe would arouse in him very intense, impatient interest for a short time which left him uncomfortable. He suspected that this was caused by the fact that all the really interesting things about the material universe can't be found out. He likened astronomy to learning a little bit about a curtain when he was longing for news of what lies behind it.[13] Lewis fully respected the work of astronomers, chemists and other scientists. But his own heart was increasingly drawn beyond the facade of the material universe, beyond its reduction to atoms and mathematical formulas, to the reality of philosophical and religious truth. People with this kind of temperament are sometimes said to be intuitive in a special sense of the word. Lewis's was a minority attitude, but not a rare one.

Lewis believed that the reasons why the universe exists and whether or not there is anything different behind the things that science observes is not in the domain of science at all. Even if science learned all about everything in the universe, it could not answer questions about its meaning. This is the domain of philosophy and theology, as Reason told John in *The Pilgrim's Regress.*

Lewis never considered real science a threat to religion at all. (Of course, popularized science may be a threat to the religion of people who are easily taken in.[14]) Lewis saw serious "scientific" materialism not only as a threat to religion but also as a threat to itself. His Christian theology could embrace all that science learns about the universe; but materialism, which arbitrarily rules out the Supernatural, accidentally rules out itself as well as religion. Lewis often made the point that if man is an organic accident in a meaningless universe, he has no way to know it because his own thoughts are only organic accidents. Lewis was frustrating to materialists on this score. He reduced that position to the status of an opinion rather than a scientific conclusion.

Another favorite target of Lewis's that offends many people loyal to modern science is what he considered technology gone wild. It did not matter to Lewis that his own grandfather had gradually risen from Welsh peasantry to Belfast affluence as half of "MacIlwaine and Lewis: Boiler Makers, Engineers, and Iron Ship Builders." (This grandfather was the son of a Welsh preacher-farmer and was himself a Christian concerned with the welfare of laborers.) The successful machinery business had allowed Lewis's father to train as a lawyer, which allowed Lewis himself to become a comfortable scholar who disliked excess technology. Lewis looked upon machinery in general as more of a burden and waste than a blessing. (Presumably, he did not include the printing press in that opinion.)

In *The Abolition of Man* Lewis told the story of an Irishman who found a certain kind of stove that cut his fuel bill in half. He bought two of the stoves in order to heat his house with no fuel at all. That is how our society has gone overboard on industrialization. Lewis believed that the triumphs of the modern scientific movement may have been too rapid and purchased at too high a price. He wondered if reconsideration and something like repentance may be required. That was his concern in 1947; he was often ahead of his time.

Lewis's attack on automobiles and other labor-saving machinery in *The Pilgrim's Regress* was heavy-handed, but his deft jab at the same target a decade later has gone almost unnoticed. He was basically defending great old books and the study of history when he had the devil Screwtape declare, with exaggeration befitting his reputation as a liar, "great scholars are now as little nourished by the past as the most ignorant mechanic who holds that 'history is bunk.'" Here Lewis had Screwtape quoting the actual words of Henry Ford.

Lewis complained some about the internal combustion engine and made sure that it never got to Narnia, but he made use of it in this world. And he loved trains, especially slow trains, from babyhood to his last year. He commented upon an American correspondent's ability to use a typewriter by saying that he could no more do that than he could drive a locomotive.[15] He added that he would prefer to drive a locomotive.

The advance of applied science includes much that is beneficial, such as typewriters and trains. But Lewis brings to our attention that what we call man's power over Nature usually turns out to be a power exercised by some people over other people with Nature as its instrument. He once referred to "barbarism made strong and luxurious by mechanical power."[16]

Loren Eiseley, American anthropologist and author (1907-1977), published an essay called "The Lethal Factor" the year Lewis died. He referred to Lewis's science fiction as profound morality plays and pondered Lewis's idea that good is getting better and bad is getting worse. "He sees the finest intellects, which in the previous century concerned themselves with electric light and telephonic communication, devote themselves as wholeheartedly to missiles and supersonic bombers."[17] According to

Eiseley, Lewis felt that once only barbarians would have attacked helpless civilian populations from the air, but now our civilization has accepted the inevitability of such barbarism.

Lewis had the lofty idea that unperverted science was the search for truth, not a sop for greed and tool for destruction.

Part Two: Soft Sciences and Hard Heads

"He was against democracy, coeducation, taxation, and nuclear disarmament,"[18] Princeton professor Samuel Hynes remarked in 1979 in the *New York Times Book Review*. He did not say where he got those impressions of Lewis; perhaps from the Narnian Chronicles, in which there was a joyful oligarchy, an unpleasant coeducational school called Experiment House, freedom from oppressive taxation, and a devastating *word* in the world of Charn that destroyed every living creature. That version of nuclear armament was unleashed by Jadis, the beautiful and cruel queen of Charn in spite of Lewis's claim as author that he disapproved.

As a word-watcher, Lewis noted the public's apparent taste for using the words *dash, initiative, magnetism* and *personality* to describe its leaders (Jadis had those in abundance). He contrasted this with the traditional desire for justice, incorruption, diligence and clemency in rulers.[19] "The first symptom is in language," he warned when contemplating evil social planning. He was horrified by the pseudoscientific word *liquidate* used in place of the frank word *kill*.[20] (In 1979 a book came out that informs us that *summary sentence* has served as a polite euphemism for *liquidation* of large groups of people; here it would seem that a pseudojudicial term is being used in place of a pseudoscientific word in place of the frank word *kill*.) Lewis saw *scientific social planning* as the guise in which any major social manipulation was apt to appear in his time because of the public awe of scientists in his day. The manipulation would not necessarily be for the worse, but Lewis felt that the trend of our time is generally to make things worse.

In *The Screwtape Letters* devils prefer to keep their victims away from the study of real science because it sometimes clears people's minds and opens the way for Christianity. Lewis proposed that mathematicians, astronomers and physicists are often religious and even mystical; biologists much less often; and economists and psychologists very seldom indeed. He thought that as their subject matter comes nearer to man himself their antireligious bias hardens.[21] Lewis also felt that jargon, "mere syntax masquerading as meaning," is especially common among politicians, journalists, psychologists and economists.[22]

In *That Hideous Strength* the journalist and "scientific popularizer," Mark Studdock, lacked a sound scientific education as well as a historical perspective. To him statistics about agricultural workers were real, but a real farmer was only a shadow of reality. He liked to write about vocational groups, elements, classes and populations rather than about men and women, because he believed as firmly as any mystic (but very differently) in the superior reality of the unseen. Therefore, Mark was easily misled by a group of political gangsters who were really in the service of demonic forces. In real life Lewis believed that almost all political revolts do more harm than good (because they create fresh oppression) and that no person or group is virtuous enough to hold uncontrolled power over others. The higher the pretentions of power, the more dangerous power is. (Lewis stated repeatedly that he was a thorough democrat.[23])

The danger of power with high pretentions is the reason for Lewis's distrust of the humanitarian theory of punishment, a theory extremely popular in his day. The theory was that criminals should be cured, whether they like it or not, rather than receiving retribution for their crimes. This medical model of criminality in our century leaves out the fact of evil. The punishment, if there is any at all (Lewis complained, "Criminal law increasingly protects the criminal and ceases to protect his victim"), is only therapeutic. The old idea of just deserts is thereby discarded, and with it goes the rights of the person presumed to need therapy. Lewis pointed out vividly that when rulers are foolish or wicked the humanitarian theory of punishment becomes an intensely cruel kind of therapy. Anyone can become an object of enforced therapy.[24]

Without naming Freud, Lewis pointed out that Freudians consider religion a neurosis. In an illustration that must have seemed almost paranoid to some of his readers, he suggested that a government with that view of religion could decide to cure religious citizens whether they wish it or not, with torture if necessary. He simply did not trust government in the role of therapist. Thirty years after Lewis stated his conviction, other writers have joined him, noting that in a day when dangerous murderers "for their own good" are turned loose without punishment, the next step is for people who have done no harm to be imprisoned "for their own good." So baldly put, the proposition sounds like alarmist rhetoric. But the fact is that writers concerned about juvenile justice claim that many youngsters who are uncared for but innocent have been imprisoned for their own "protection."[25]

It is likely that Lewis would have high regard for the efforts of Charles Colson, whose turn to the faith came about in response to *Mere Christianity*. Colson has actively sought to make prisons less destructive and dehumanizing and has become an advocate of the concept of restitution, where criminals (from big-time embezzlers to drunk drivers) would repay their victims. This is the direction in which Lewis's thoughts about penology seemed to lead.

Values and Mysteries

Lewis was indeed grateful for any social reforms, but he was not a utopian. He considered faith in the wisdom and goodness of people in power to be "eggs in moonshine." Accordingly, he considered theocracy, or any other rule that forbids wholesome doubt and sanctions its leaders the worst possible government. Lewis insisted that no one knows enough about the present and future to make a political program that is more than "probably right" at best. This political conviction of Lewis's was one of his reasons for arguing with Haldane against Communism and also arguing against non-Communist scientism, which he saw as a serious threat to freedom.

Scientism, according to Lewis, is the belief that the survival of our species is the highest of all goals and that this has to be pursued (probably scientifically) even if it strips humanity of all those values which give it dignity—compassion, happiness and freedom.[26] Twenty-five years after Lewis defined scientism, B. F. Skinner advocated it in his popular book *Beyond Freedom and Dignity*, in which he attacked Lewis twice. Using Lewis's own book title *The Abolition of Man*, Skinner said that man's abolition is long overdue, and good riddance. He advocated scientific behavior control in order to prolong the future of the human species. Lewis gave scientists credit for holding this view less frequently than their readers.

B. F. Skinner, who apparently meant well, urged the scientific community, or some part of it, to manipulate human beings and determine their behavior, thus supposedly altering the course of human history toward the type of survival that is our best end. In *Beyond Freedom and Dignity* Skinner wrote that rational man should discard his belief in the Supernatural, especially God and miracles, and his personal claims to freedom and dignity. Skinner, speaking as what he considered a highly intelligent but thoroughly conditioned human animal, claimed to have figured out rationally, in spite of his conditioning, what is true and good for the rest of the human species. He called his conclusions "the scientific conception of man" and dismissed resistance to his ideas as merely emotional responses.

Lewis's position, of course, is that there is nothing trivial about an appropriate emotional response. It is one of the highest human functions. Lewis's own response to scientism was, "I care far more how humanity lives than how long."[27]

In fact, it was Lewis's discovery that a pupil of his in the 1930s found hope and meaning for life in the idea of interplanetary colonization that started him writing his science fiction. He felt that a "scientific" hope of defeating death through improving and perpetuating the human species was a rival to Christianity that should be met head on.

In 1932 Lewis mentioned in a letter to his brother that he had taken dinner with a poor lonely old partially deaf man, to bring him some cheer. Lewis entertained him for about an hour with chit-chat about life on other planets, education, Einstein and similar things. Suddenly the old man exclaimed, "Ah, I see you know all about this universe business!" Lewis was immensely amused.[28]

Another favorite target of Lewis's was evolution as popularly imagined. He did not try to refute Darwin's theorem in biology, although he suggested that it may have flaws. He said that what Darwin really accounted for was perhaps not the origin, but the elimination of species and that time and research may somewhat discredit Darwin. In his books *The Ghost in the Machine* and *The Case of the Midwife Toad*, Arthur Koestler discusses reasons for the growing discontent among contemporary biologists who now believe that Darwin's theory reflects only part of the picture. That was not Lewis's real concern. His concern was the popularity of "evolutionism," the anti-Christian myth of progress.

Lewis made three points in attacking evolutionism. First, he said, the myth of biological and social progress began before Darwin's theory existed. Second, Darwinism does not support the belief that natural selection working through chance variations usually produces improvement. There is no proven law of progress in biology. Third, there is also no historical evidence of good progress in ethics, culture and health of society.[29] "In science, Evolution is a theory about *changes*; in the Myth it is a fact about *improvements*."[30]

Lewis grew up believing the myth of progress and always felt it had a noble grandeur. Not even the Greeks or Norsemen ever invented a better story, he admitted. The gradual glimmerings of sentience and rationality, the struggle through eons for today's supremacy, the present glory doomed to ultimate extinction—it makes a grand, tragic epic. But it is not at all true.

In response to both scientism and evolutionism, Lewis claimed that if things can improve, there has to be some absolute standard of good above and outside the cosmic process. Otherwise "becoming better" means simply "what we are becoming," and there is no sense in talking about it. That would be like congratulating yourself for being wherever you are when you congratulate yourself. "Mellontalatry, or the worship of the future, is a *fuddled* religion."[31]

Lewis fell away from his boyhood Darwinism and tentative Freudianism ("I am sometimes tempted to wonder whether Freudianism is not a great school of prudery and hypocrisy"[32]), but he did not entirely discredit biological change and psychiatry. He obviously found Carl Jung interesting although not entirely sound, and even proposed the droll idea that Jung's theory of archetypes was itself an archetype. He claimed that the mystery of primordial images is much more mysterious than Jung realized. Lewis's knack for practical psychological insights was completely independent of technical background but obviously not without profound respect for theoretical aspects of the subject of which he was ignorant. He warned people to avoid anti-Christian psychologists who would try to cure them of their faith, but he had a great belief in the complexity of our inner selves.

Once Lewis likened one's ordinary self to the material universe, in that he called them similar facades. He cared about what is behind the facade. He told readers that, from his self-observation, what you usually call your *self* is only a thin film on the surface of an unsounded and dangerous sea. But, he added, in that sea there are radiant things, delights and inspirations as well as snarling resentments and nagging lusts. Both psychologists and theologians use symbols when they try to probe the depth beneath the surface of a person.

In Lewis's opinion, physicists and psychologists are always making progress as they probe the surface of reality. When other people wrongly use the discoveries of the physicists and psychologists, that is not the fault of the physicists and psychologists. Lewis respected their work. He felt that physics and psychology were perhaps closely related.

"The point, however," he concluded, "is that every fresh discovery, far from dissipating, deepens the mystery."[33]

Further Reading about Science

"Look: the question is not whether we should bring God into our work or not. We certainly should and must. As MacDonald says 'All that is not God is death.'"[34]

The Discarded Image by C. S. Lewis is an explanation of the medieval model of the universe which helps to comprehend the nature and limitiations of the contemporary model more accurately.

Of Other Worlds by C. S. Lewis contains some of Lewis's views about science and science fiction as well as his comments on fantasy.

The Restitution of Man by Michael D. Aeschliman examines C. S. Lewis's case against materialistic scientism.

"Religion and Rocketry" and "The World's Last Night" in *The World's Last Night* by C. S. Lewis are essays which in part attack space exploration and evolutionism.

"The Laws of Nature" and "Religion and Science" in *God in the Dock* by C. S. Lewis are two brief essays that show how science has *not* knocked the bottom out of the Christian view of the universe.

"Religion without Dogma?" in *God in the Dock* by C. S. Lewis was Lewis's reply to a Professor Price who had maintained that science has discredited Christian teaching and that psychical research is our only hope for future belief in God and immortality.

"Two Lectures," "Behind the Scenes" and "Bulverism" in *God in the Dock* by C. S. Lewis show facets of Lewis's demanding approach to facts and meaning.

"Funeral of a Great Myth" and "De Futilitate" in *Christian Reflections* by C. S. Lewis announce our "cosmic futility" and some comic fatuity as well.

"Psycho-Analysis and Literary Criticism" in *Selected Literary Essays* by C. S. Lewis sets forth some of Lewis's responses to the psychiatric theories of Freud and Jung.

Notes

1. Lewis, *Miracles*, p. 157.
2. Samuel Hynes, "Guardian of the Old Ways," *New York Times Book Review* (8 July 1979), p. 26.
3. R. E. Havard, "Philia: Jack at Ease," *C. S. Lewis at the Breakfast Table*, ed. James Corno (New York: Macmillan, 1979), p. 225.
4. Unpublished letter from C. S. Lewis to his brother W. H. Lewis dated April 8, 1932; available in the Wade Collection.
5. Chad Walsh, *The Literary Legacy of C. S. Lewis* (New York: Harcourt Brace Jovanovich, 1979), p. 15.
6. J. B. S. Haldane, "Auld Hornie, F. R. S.," *Modern Quarterly* (Autumn 1946).
7. Lewis, "A Reply to Professor Haldane," *Of Other Worlds*, p. 177.
8. Lewis, *Letters of C. S. Lewis*, p. 217.
9. Walsh, *Literary Legacy* pp. 96–97.
10. C. S. Lewis, *The Dark Tower* (London: Collins, 1977), p. 84.
11. C. S. Lewis, *The Discarded Image* (Cambridge: Cambridge Univ. Press,

1964), p. 218.

12. Derek Brewer, "The Tutor, A Portrait," *C. S. Lewis at the Breakfast Table*, p. 48.

13. C. S. Lewis, *They Stand Together* (London: Collins, 1979), p. 405. This is an observation expressed to Arthur Greeves in a letter dated February 1, 1931.

14. Lewis, "Dogma and the Universe," *God in the Dock*, pp. 38–47.

15. This remark appears in a letter to Joan Lancaster in the Wade Collection.

16. C. S. Lewis, *A Preface to Paradise Lost* (London: Oxford Univ. Press, 1942), p. 132.

17. Quoted in *CSL: Bulletin of the New York C. S. Lewis Society* (November 1978), p. 5.

18. Hynes, "Guardian" p. 3.

19. Lewis, "De Descriptione Temporum," *They Asked for a Paper*, p. 18.

20. Lewis, "A Reply to Professor Haldane," *Of Other Worlds*, p. 81.

21. Lewis, "Religion without Dogma," *God in the Dock*, p. 135.

22. C. S. Lewis, "Bluspells and Flalanspheres," *Rehabilitations and Other Essays* (London: Oxford Univ. Press, 1939), p. 150. Also available in *Selected Literary Essays*, p. 264.

23. Lewis, "A Reply to Professor Haldane," *Of Other Worlds*, p. 81.

24. Lewis, "The Humanitarian Theory of Punishment," *God in the Dock*, p. 293.

25. Howard James, *Children in Trouble* (New York: D. McKay, 1970).

26. Lewis, "A Reply to Professor Haldane," *Of Other Worlds*, p. 77.

27. Lewis, "Is Progress Possible?" *God in the Dock*, p. 311.

28. Unpublished letter from C. S. Lewis to his brother W. H. Lewis dated April 8, 1932; available in the Wade Collection.

29. Lewis, "The World's Last Night," *The World's Last Night*, pp. 101–3.

30. Lewis, "The Funeral of a Great Myth," *Christian Reflections*, p. 85.

31. Lewis, "Evil and God," *God in the Dock*, p. 21.

32. Lewis, "Psycho-Analysis and Literary Criticism," *They Asked for a Paper*, p. 129.

33. Lewis, "The Seeing Eye," *Christian Reflections*, pp. 169–70.

34. Sheldon Vanauken, *A Severe Mercy* (San Francisco: Harper & Row, 1977), p. 106.

Chapter 15

The Arts

"Hang it all, the very fairy-tales embody the truth."
Letter to Sheldon Vanauken[1]

Part One: The Arts in Life

"If I should give you just one piece of advice, it is this," C. S. Lewis told me. I was twenty-one and he was fifty-seven. We were sitting on a couch together having tea and cakes. It was an informal, merry conversation from beginning to end, but at this point I turned on my memory full force.

"Read books for *pleasure!*" he urged. Avoid reading for the purpose of impressing other people. Don't think of reading as a duty. Don't read just to get ahead or to be in style. Read what you really enjoy.

There was some serious philosophy behind Lewis's light-hearted but sincere advice to me. He was opposed to cultish devotion to literature, although he lived and breathed literature all his life. He meant it when he called books a main ingredient in his well-being. He cherished early memories of fairy tales from his Irish nurse, and before he could read or write he was dictating stories to his father. His intense love for books lasted from very early childhood to his deathbed, and he wrote book after book about other people's books—but he refused to make literature or any other art the meaning of life. And he did not try to impress people with his love for the arts.

That may be the reason why Lewis's stepson could say in print, "Music meant little to him."[2] That contradicts what Lewis wrote about himself. His excitement about music was first expressed repeatedly in his letters to Arthur Greeves. Lewis's youthful exposure to great music was through inferior phonographs produced early in this century, and he was amazed and rather confused when he first heard it live, which sounded so different. He had to learn to like the real thing better than the copy. He realized how absurd that was, and he told about it at least twenty years later in his essay "Religion: Reality or Substitute."

As a young man Lewis considered music immensely important and thrilling, whether recorded or live. To him music produced a kind of madness. He found Chopin's Preludes almost unbearably emotional, even when played in an inferior way. In those days literature was not so stirring to Lewis as music.

During one period at the Kilns the family had a recorded symphony every Sunday evening, listening to all the Beethoven symphonies in turn. "This is one of the best hours of the week," Lewis said at the time, and he compared and analyzed the symphonies. Late in 1934 Lewis attended a concert at Oxford conducted by Sir Thomas Beecham and described it as the best he had ever heard. He said the London Philharmonic was marvelous, and he happened to like every one of the pieces on the program, even the Elgar selection which he did not fully understand. Beethoven's Fifth Symphony was included, and Lewis said that Beecham brought things out of it of which Lewis had never dreamed. "Apart from this, very little has happened to me," he remarked to Arthur Greeves concerning late 1934. He mentioned, as if they were of little importance to him compared to the Beecham concert, some lectures he had given that would probably advance his career.[3]

After Lewis's death his "foster-sister's" husband, Leonard Blake, a music teacher, reminisced about Lewis. He said that they did not often discuss music, but that when they did Lewis was as penetrating and thought provoking as on most other subjects. "Frankly, I was only too glad to hear him talk about anything, for whether one agreed with him or not, what an education that was!"[4] It seems that in his later years Lewis did not take much time for his love of music, putting other things first. But he made it clear that he was especially fond of Wagner and had a particular dislike for the organ and church hymns. To the end of his life, he said, he found bagpipes so emotionally intoxicating that he couldn't tell one piece from another or a good piper from a poor one. He never got over the feeling that some tunes are so vile that they are hopeless, but he wondered if he was not sufficiently musical to perceive possibilities in them. He left it to true musicians to decide if even a tune so odious as "Home Sweet Home" could be successfully put to good use by a great composer.

In the church, Lewis advised, let choirs sing well or not at all, in order not to offend unbelievers. He thought that unbelievers have a bad enough impression of Christianity without our adding to it with bad music.

Lewis's stepson David Gresham says that he had even less interest in painting and sculpture than in music and seldom attended movies or the theater. It is true that although Lewis was not ignorant of art history, he paid far more attention to the beauties of nature than to manmade visual beauty. He recalled in his chapter "How the Few and the Many Use Pictures and Music" that where he grew up the only good pictures were book illustrations by Beatrix Potter and Arthur Rackham. Much later he learned to respond "receptively with obedient imaginative activity" to works such as Tintoretto's

Three Graces or Botticelli's *Birth of Venus*.[5] He clearly considered himself a lover of art as well as music, although he devoted little attention to either in later years. He was notorious for never arranging and furnishing his rooms pleasantly at home or at college, so there was no evidence that he cared about visual arts in everyday life.

In the last years of his life Lewis took a warm interest in dramatic productions at Cambridge, according to his closest friend there, Richard W. Ladborough.[6] But it is a fact that Lewis never considered himself a theater lover. In his journal he once described an evening wasted on a performance of *King Lear* at Oxford: "It was all that sort of acting which fills one first with embarrassment and pity, finally with an unreasoning personal hatred of the actors. 'Why should that damned man keep on bellowing at me?' They nearly all shouted hoarsely and inarticulately."[7]

Lewis generally disliked Walt Disney's animations, and he once described part of what was right and wrong about Disney's *Snow White*.[8] What he liked best was the accurate and traditional portrayal of the witch as beautiful as well as cruel. Apparently those who supervised production of the animated version of *The Lion, the Witch and the Wardrobe* didn't know his convictions about cartoon witches or else disagreed. They changed his own beautiful White Witch into a very ugly creature and caused her to shout a great deal. Lewis was scathing about aesthetic mistakes like that without judging people for their taste.

The Matter of Taste

Lewis combined an easy acceptance of the fact that good people are apt to have bad taste in the arts with absolute confidence that good art is vastly better than bad art. He readily admitted that literary people include no small percentage of the ignorant, the caddish, the stunted, the warped and the truculent.

Nevertheless, literary people will read a great work ten, twenty or thirty times while unliterary people will not. Unliterary people miss a great good.

Of course literary people disagree about what is great and why. Lewis said we read great critics because they are very good reading even when we don't fully agree with them. It is right for us to enjoy finding out how a first-class mind responds to a great work. (Along the line of negative criticism, Lewis himself claimed jokingly of Wordsworth's "Excursions" and Byron's "Don Juan" that however much you have read, you've already read the best, because they both keep getting worse.) According to author John Wain, a student and friend of Lewis's, he disliked much literature from about 1914 onward because it reflected modern life. But he devoted his critical energies to supporting works he admired rather than attacking specific works he disliked. He once wrote to me that he considered Orwell's *1984* far inferior to his *Animal Farm*, which received less attention, but he did not elaborate on either.

One of Lewis's earliest books was a cordial debate with the distinguished literary critic E. M. W. Tillyard over the proper nature of poetry. Lewis wanted less emphasis on the poet's life and personality in the study of poetry—especially when it leads away from poetry and into gossip. (The brief book *A Personal Heresy* is so lively that it was still selling about sixty years later.) Here, as elsewhere, Lewis claimed to see a growing "poetolatry," a kind of cult in which dead authors achieve the status of saints, relics from their personal lives are bought and sold, and students act out forms of devotion in the guise of studying literature. Lewis particularly disliked tributes in which authors such as Shakespeare are ranked with Christ.

It is worth noting that in the same year that *A Personal Heresy* was published Lewis wrote to his brother Warren that without firsthand experience it would be hard to understand how a dead man out of a book can be almost a member of one's family. He said this in relation to Samuel Johnson. Then he exclaimed about the possibility of their someday meeting Johnson, now that they, like Johnson, were Christians.

Many people disagree with Lewis about the danger of poet-olatry. Furthermore, it was Lewis himself who defended the British monarchy by claiming that if people don't have royalty to revere, they will lavish their interest on less worthy people.

Veneration of great dead authors has not in fact become a besetting heresy of modern society. But Lewis's position serves especially well now that he himself is dead and widely venerated. No one can accuse him of welcoming "Lewisolatry." He was an extrovert, but he cherished privacy. He felt that his books, like everyone else's, should stand or fall on their merit alone.

Part Two: Life in the Arts

"Forget art, forget history and withdraw into Christianity with Lewis as your guide." The Princeton English professor who made this facetious recommendation in the *New York Times Book Review* claimed to find anti-intellectual know-nothingism among Lewis admirers and believed that a streak of this kind of irresponsibility in Lewis incited the attitude in his "covens of disciples"—who would have been better off without him.[9]

It is not clear how the author of the seven-hundred-page book *English Literature in the Sixteenth Century Excluding Drama* (in the Oxford History of English Literature series) could encourage his readers to forget the arts and history. Perhaps Lewis's comment in *Preface to Paradise Lost* applies well to his own books today. As long as you think the corkscrew was meant for opening cans or the cathedral for entertaining tourists you can say nothing to the point about them. Once you know what corkscrews and cathedrals are intended to do and how, you are ready to judge their utility and the good or bad they accomplish. Then one can venture to judge if we would be better off without them.

Lewis said flat-out in 1939 that Christians will take literature a little less seriously than cultured pagans and may thus
appear shallow or flippant to those who make a kind of religion
of aesthetic experience. To a Christian the salvation of a single
soul is more important than the world's best art. Lewis likened
a poet's personality to the position of a window in a room. "But
windows are not put there that you may study windows; rather
that you may forget windows." In Lewis's opinion if the glass
distracts you from the landscape, there is something wrong with
the window or your eye.[10]

Furthermore, Lewis scoffed at the notion that the public has
a duty to the artist but that the artist has no duty at all. In previous centuries the business of the artist was to delight and
instruct the public. In this century some artists demand recognition without paying attention to the public's tastes, interests or
habits. Lewis felt that this has come about because of the
decline of quality work in highly industrialized societies with
their planned obsolescence of products and useless busy-work.
We have a duty to feed the hungry, even if they do poor work
or none; but we have no duty to "appreciate" people who are
hungry for acclaim as artists. According to Lewis many modern
novels, poems and pictures are not *work* at all, but mere pud-
dles of spilled sensibility or reflection. This adds to the
alienation that the public and some groups of writers and critics experience—an alienation akin to mutual disdain.[11]

Lewis berated poetic privatism in which the purchasers of a
poem cannot possibly understand it unless they happen to know
the favorite sayings of the poet's aunt's parrot. Lewis hated
needless obscurity and objected when he found unnecessary difficulty in even his favorite authors. It is easy to get published,
Lewis said; the hard part is to get read. That is why he felt the
first duty of an author is to entertain. This entails first writing
about something very interesting and then writing as clearly as
possible. Lewis followed his own advice.

Before Lewis's conversion he had been since boyhood dedicated to a life of intellectual and aesthetic activity—culture. After his conversion culture seemed less important to him, but he continued to spend most of his time on it. He set himself to the task of reconciling the claims of culture with the claim of his Christian faith that his business in life was salvation in Christ and glorification of God. After much thought and research he decided that at the lowest level he was justified in earning his living by serving in the only profession he was suited for—as a provider of culture to his students and readers. He tagged himself a "culture-seller" and decided that it is better for society if some of its "culture-sellers" are Christians, so long as they do what they are paid to do.

Lewis decided that in his own life culture was above all a source of enormous pleasure. These are lawful pleasures for us to enjoy and teach to others. Good taste really is far better than bad taste, although bad taste is not evil. Lewis likened his good taste and pleasure in the arts to having enjoyed his breakfast. He thought that was a good thing, acceptable to God; but he did not think himself a good man for enjoying it.[12]

As committed as he was to the innocent enjoyment of reading, Lewis saw that some literature carries extra value. Referring to their pre-Christian years, he asked his brother once, "How on earth did we manage to enjoy all these books so much as we did in the days when we had really no conception of what was at the centre of them?"[13]

An Enlargement of Our Being

In *The Personal Heresy* Lewis remarked that some poems gave him a new and nameless sensation and enriched him with experience for which nothing in his previous life had prepared him. Some prose did the same. He did not care for the poems and books because they introduced him to their authors, but he

cared for the writing and the authors because they witnessed to
something else.

Lewis went on to comment that a "great poet" may be a person excelling others in knowledge, wisdom and virtue who uses
poetical skill to utter great things. But a great poet may simply
be a person of unusual skill in writing. "A great bore need not be
a great man," he added wryly, "he need only be greatly boring."[14]

Ten years later Lewis went on to say that we can demand of
a great poem some wisdom. We wish to gain some understanding from it. "Wisdom by itself does not make a great poem or
even a poem at all; and the value of a poem is by no means in
direct ratio to its wisdom. But the demand for wisdom
remains."[15]

Near the end of his life Lewis asked his old question, "What
then is the good of—what is the defense for—occupying our
hearts with stories of what never happened and entering vicar-
iously into feelings which we should try to avoid having in our
own person?. . . The nearest I have yet got to an answer is that
we seek an enlargement of our being." Lewis believed that we
want to see with other eyes and feel with other hearts as well as
with our own. Literature is a series of windows, or even doors.
After reading great literature one feels "I have got out"; or even
"I have got in."[16]

Lewis believed that the first impulse in a person is to main-
tain and build up oneself. The corrective impulse is to go out of
the self and heal its loneliness. "In love, in virtue, in the pursuit
of knowledge, and in the reception of the arts, we are doing
this."[17]

All that Lewis valued in this world, except the music of
Wagner, seemed to be threatened by Hitler for several dark
years. Lewis was absolutely enraged about the persecution of
the Jews and declared that Hitler proved himself as contemptible for his stupidity as he was detestable for his cruelty

when he said, "The Jews have made no contribution to human culture and in crushing them I am doing the will of the Lord."

Lewis cried out in reply, "The whole idea of the 'Will of the Lord' is precisely what the world owes to the Jews."[18]

It happens also that the Hebrews were responsible for Lewis's favorite poem, Psalm 19. It ends:

> Let the words of my mouth
> and the meditation of my heart
> be acceptable in thy sight,
> O LORD, my rock and my redeemer.

Lewis tried to live by those words.

Further Reading about the Arts

"In reading great literature I become a thousand men and yet remain myself."[19]

The Personal Heresy by C. S. Lewis and E. M. W. Tillyard contains essays debating matters central to the appreciation of poetry.

A Preface to Paradise Lost by C. S. Lewis searches the meaning of Milton's epic and also expresses many of Lewis's ideas about literature as art.

An Experiment in Criticism by C. S. Lewis is all about books, good reading and the enjoyment of literature.

Poems by C. S. Lewis includes some poems stating Lewis's views about the arts, beginning with "A Confession."

"Christianity and Literature," "Christianity and Culture" and "On Church Music" in *Christian Reflections* by C. S. Lewis contain Lewis's key comments on the arts in Christian perspective.

"Good Work and Good Works" in *The World's Last Night* by C. S. Lewis states briefly Lewis's peppery ideas about quality and responsibility.

Selected Literary Essays by C. S. Lewis contains some essays of
interest to general readers, including "High Brows and Low
Brows" and "The Literary Impact of the Authorized Version."

Notes

1. Sheldon Vanauken, *A Severe Mercy*, p. 92. From a letter written by C.
S. Lewis to Vanauken, December 23, 1950.
2. Walsh, *The Literary Legacy of C. S. Lewis*, p. 15.
3. Lewis, *They Stand Together*, p. 471.
4. *Bulletin of the New York C. S. Lewis Society* (December 1970), p. 6.
5. Lewis, *An Experiment in Criticism* (Cambridge: Cambridge Univ.
Press, 1961), p. 26.
6. Richard W. Ladborough, "In Cambridge," *C. S. Lewis at the Breakfast
Table*, p. 102.
7. Lewis, *Letters of C. S. Lewis*, p. 112. This is an account of February 15,
1927.
8. Lewis, *Preface to Paradise Lost*, p. 56.
9. Hynes, "Gaurdian of the Old Ways" p. 26.
10. Lewis, *The Personal Heresy* (London: Oxford Univ. Press, 1939), p. 26.
11. Lewis, "Good Work and Good Works," *The World's Last Night*, pp.
78–81.
12. Lewis, "Christianity and Culture," *Christian Reflections*, p. 36.
13. Unpublished letter from C. S. Lewis to his brother W. H. Lewis on
December 18, 1939. Available in the Wade Collection.
14. Lewis, *The Personal Heresy*, pp. 114–15.
15. C. S. Lewis, "Williams and the Arthuriad," *Taliessin through Logres* by
Charles Williams and C. S. Lewis (Grand Rapids, Mich.: Eerdmans,
1974), p. 374.
16. Lewis, *An Experiment in Criticism*, pp. 137–38.
17. Ibid.
18. Lewis, *They Stand Together*, p. 468 (letter of November 5, 1933).
19. Lewis, *An Experiment in Criticism*, p. 141.

Chapter 16

Education

"*The task of the modern educator is not to
cut down jungles but to irrigate deserts.*"
The Abolition of Man[1]

Part One: How to Learn and Teach

When C. S. Lewis published his story of suffering after his wife
died, the book was so personal that he used a pseudonym. He
did not go back to his penname, which was Clive (his name)
Hamilton (his mother's family name). Instead, *A Grief Observed*
appeared under the name N. W. Clerk. Lewis had signed many
poems in periodicals "Nat Whilk" or "N. W." (meaning "Who
knows?") for over twenty years. Now he added Clerk (pronounced Clark), which was a word meaning "learned man" in
England in the Middle Ages. That old word is still famous
because of Chaucer's description of a good clerk—"gladly wolde
he lerne and gladly teche." This is what Lewis had in mind
about himself.

Except for his brief duty as a soldier in World War 1, Lewis
was a learner and then a teacher for his entire life until his final
illness. His first teacher was the nurse who told him fairy tales
when he was young. His mother tutored him, and he had gov-

ernesses. When a Miss Harper came to teach, he wrote in his diary (now in the Wade Collection), "She is fairly nice for a governess, but all of them are the same." He had just turned nine. It is highly unlikely that any student of Lewis's ever said, "He is fairly nice for a professor, but all of them are the same."

Lewis's autobiography, *Surprised by Joy*, eloquently describes his painful and blissful educational experiences in various schools, with various kinds of teachers. He was well aware of the evils and abuses in traditional schools as well as the inadequacies of modern experiments in education. Besides the terrible examples of traditional schooling in his own biography, Lewis described a strict, boring school in Narnia where a Miss Prizzle was teaching girls in uncomfortable uniforms a "history" that was duller than true history and less true than exciting stories. Aslan broke in and turned the classroom into a forest glade and chased Miss Prizzle away. At another school in the same story Aslan discovered a tired girl trying to teach arithmetic to a class of piggish boys. Here he carried the teacher away to have some fun and turned the obnoxious boys into real pigs.[2]

In a letter to his brother in 1939 he told about having tea with an ex-student of his who had become a teacher in a school that allowed no punishment of children and expected no obedience, unless the child understood the reason for an order. This teacher had become a mother as well as a teacher and was finding that the idealistic theories did not work. She consulted Lewis about it all, which gave him some satisfaction. In *The Silver Chair* he painted a very caustic picture of modern undisciplined schools by describing Experiment House, showing how children can be neglected and victimized in such places.

One of the most vivid passages in Lewis's own life story expresses his joy when he was done with schools and was able to study alone at the home of his crusty old tutor, Kirkpatrick. Unfortunately, this kind of idyllic learning situation is practically nonexistent. But another educational experience that Lewis enjoyed while he was being taught formally by Kirkpatrick was his own informal correspondence with his young friend Arthur Greeves in Ireland. Over forty years later he reflected to a young friend that he was not willing to have involved discussions with him by mail because when one is writing books all the time it is too fatiguing mentally and physically to put the same kind of work into writing letters. But, he said, in his youth he had conducted long, deep disputations by mail and that was a valuable part of his education. He was surely referring to his intense correspondence with both Greeves and Barfield.[3] His correspondence, of course, was informed by a great amount of reading. Reading and serious letter-writing are two of the most flexible and easily available ways of learning.

According to Major Allan Rook, a Fellow of the Royal Society of Literature, another means of learning from which Lewis profited was his intense discussions with talented undergraduates.[4] Before World War II Lewis repeatedly invited Rook and another student to join him for dessert and an all-night philosophical discussion in his rooms, ending at about 5 A.M. It was stimulating, and the trio came to many conclusions (which Rook has since forgotten). With Rook, Lewis was a purely intellectual, serious, logical and always deep-thinking companion. "He used us as a foil."[5]

Once Lewis said "Rook, you think of me as a Medievalist and a scholar. You're making a mistake. I'm nothing of the sort. I'm a butcher. . . ."[6] In a 1959 letter to ex-student Derek Brewer, Lewis remarked, "Haven't you discovered yet that I'm not a Scholar but only a Learned Man?"[7] And shortly before he died Lewis told the American journalist Sherwood Wirt the same thing—that he was not a scholar of the past, but a lover of it. To Lewis the word *scholar* implied a superb mastery of details he did not have. To Lewis the word *butcher* probably referred to his meat-cleaver style of demolishing arguments. Rook said, "I loved it although I was often on the receiving end."[8] Rook felt no warmth at all from Lewis.

The late Kenneth Tynan, a prominent critic and dramatist, was a student of Lewis's after World War II. Tynan reported that Lewis not only demonstrated prodigious feats of memory and made the past come vividly alive—"As a teacher he was just incomparable"—but that Lewis also took a warm personal interest in him. Tynan enjoyed Lewis's memorable humor and his sympathetic concern as well as his intellectual challenge.[9] Rook and Tynan experienced Lewis the teacher very differently.

A Kind of Love

Lewis once told his old friend Arthur Greeves about a particular student who visited him after graduation. In 1932 Lewis wrote that the ex-student, who had gone into business, came to tell Lewis how much the literature he had studied somewhat reluctantly under Lewis now nurtured him as a delightful recreation. Lewis admitted that this appealed to his vanity and also gave him a sense of professional pleasure. Furthermore, it aroused a kind of love. Lewis suspected that seeing this ex-student follow in his footsteps gave him the pleasure that fathers wish to receive from their sons. To wish for such future pleasure while teaching, Lewis noted, would probably spoil everything.

Readers of Lewis's masterly *Preface to Paradise Lost* will notice that he devotes the fourteenth chapter to developing an idea he attributes to Miss Muriel Bentley, who helped him to better understand Milton. Miss Bentley (later Muriel Jones) was one of his own pupils.

It has sometimes been said that Lewis was impatient with students who were relatively inept or poorly educated. Many have testified otherwise. For example, Patricia Boshell Heidelberger has recalled in a letter to Clyde Kilby how tolerant Lewis was of her and another young girl who had to move into the Kilns in 1940 as war evacuees. Although they were extremely lively, noisy and giggly, he often helped them with their homework and eventually provided secret financial aid to enable them to continue their education as young adults.

Jill Freud, an actress who is married to Clement Freud, a member of Parliament and grandson of Sigmund Freud, has also described living at Lewis's house during World War II. She tells how graciously Lewis motivated her to develop her mind and gave her confidence. She retained a friendship with the Lewis brothers and was expecting to have supper at their house on the very day Lewis died. She called to check, and Warren Lewis told her that his brother had just passed away a half hour before. One of her happier memories is of Lewis's attempt to teach the alphabet to a retarded man during the war:

> For some months we had a young man living at the Kilns. He worked as a house-boy and general help. He was in his twenties. He was probably introduced by the Social Services Department, and he was what we would now call educationally sub-normal. He had the mentality of a child of eight. Every evening Jack Lewis taught him to read. He made drawings and letter cards and he went through the alphabet with him and tried to teach him small words and so on. I don't think he had a great deal of success because the young man found it hard to retain anything. But for more than two months Jack Lewis went through the alphabet with him every evening.[10]

At the same general time that Lewis was making alphabet cards for a retarded man, he was tutoring the daughter of the founder and editor of Penguin Classics, Rosamund Rieu Cowan. Cowan recalls that it was a joy to study with Lewis, that his radio broadcasts were marvelous and his literature lectures wonderful. Not only literature students attended his lectures, but also students of medicine, science and politics. The big hall in Magdalen was so full when Lewis lectured that people even sat on the window sills.

When asked what was so attractive about Lewis's lectures, Cowan answered first that he was extremely well prepared and paced himself so that his listeners could take notes. He made his subject matter live. A student from the 1930s, Mary Rogers, has reflected upon his lectures: "I still remember his brilliant eyes, his devastating wit and penetrating analysis."[11]

It is obvious that Lewis was the epitome of the devoted professional "clerk"—a learner and teacher—never lazy, never bored and never boring. "Gladly wolde he lerne and gladly teche." In my one visit with him in 1956 he tossed off a witty insight that I recognized instantly. I reminded him of its location in one of his books. (It was great fun to hear the familiar sentence in his rich, live voice, of course.) "That's the trouble with publishing books!" he laughed heartily. "Once people read them, your conversation is no longer new!"

Part Two: What to Learn and Teach

"I would say if a man is going to write on chemistry, he learns chemistry. The same is true of Christianity."[12] That was Lewis's answer when Sherwood Wirt asked him how an aspiring young Christian writer might prepare himself. He went on to mention that God is not interested only in Christian writers as such. He is concerned with all kinds of writing.

"In coming to understand anything," Lewis wrote, "we are rejecting the facts as they are for us in favor of the facts as they are."[13] In contrast to a well educated man, Lewis described the gullible Mark Studdock in *That Hideous Strength* as one whose "education had been neither scientific nor classical—merely 'Modern.' The severities of both abstraction and of high human tradition had passed him by. . . . He was . . . a glib examinee in subjects that require no exact knowledge."[14]

Lewis's choice of subject matter in his own life was, of course, "classical"—high human tradition. "To lose what I owe to Plato and Aristotle would be like the amputation of a limb."[15]

He advised people to read an old book after every new one. For people who are not up to that he recommended one old book for every three new ones. "Keep the clean sea breeze of the centuries blowing through your mind." People were no cleverer in the past than now, and they made mistakes. But they made different mistakes from ours.[16]

Lewis believed that people who don't study history are usually caught in the world of the fairly recent past. Historians are not apt to be slaves to either the present or the past. They have perspective.[17]

In reading old books, however, much more than in reading contemporary ones, the reader is apt to need help. Lewis's experience was that whereas a dull reader will not understand an old classic, a highly intelligent and sensitive reader who is not adequately informed will misunderstand—triumphantly and brilliantly. With cleverness and imagination the gifted reader can attribute all kinds of possible meanings—wrong ones—to an obscure passage. "We want to find the sense the author intended."[18] For this we need all the understanding of history and language that we can get.

Lewis credited Owen Barfield with teaching him the foolishness of "chronological snobbery"—the assumption that ideas that have gone out of style must have been proved false. When one realizes that common assumptions of the past have often simply gone out of fashion, one is free to see common assumptions of the present as also eventually going out of style. Then one can judge the truth or falsehood (or suspend judgment) on their merits rather than their placement in history.[19]

Lewis began his profound thesis about values in education, *The Abolition of Man*, by saying, "I doubt whether we are sufficiently attentive to the importance of elementary text-books." He went on to demolish a new 1947 English textbook that, in attempting to help children think more clearly, was actually teaching them that all values are subjective and trivial. The child who is taught that Coleridge was wrong and no waterfall is sublime (the lesson Lewis pounced on) has no notion that ethics, theology and politics are all at stake in such a reduction. The textbook authors may not know that either!

At the end of *The Discarded Image*, published seventeen years after *The Abolition of Man*, Lewis gave the same warning: "Always, century by century, item after item is transferred from the object's side of the account to the subject's."[20] (The waterfall is not sublime; the viewer only feels that it is.) In some extreme cases of behaviorism, Lewis claimed, the person only *thinks* that he thinks (or *feels* that he feels?). Lewis shuddered, "And where we 'go from that' is a dark question."[21]

In contrast to this trend, *The Discarded Image* goes back to the medieval model of the universe, in which everything was linked with everything else in a hierarchical ladder with humans high on the ladder and the celestial bodies permanent and perfectly regular in their movements. (The first nova refuted that belief.) Lewis considered the old model a great and beautiful construction of the imagination, although not true. Contrary to claims made by some Lewis readers, Lewis absolutely does not recommend a return to the medieval model. But he urges us not to accept *any* model as true. Each model reflects the culture's psychology of the age as much as the level of knowledge. We know so little of the whole picture, Lewis concludes, that our minds are like stencils. The design of that stencil determines how much truth will come in and what its pattern will seem to be.

Good and Bad Patterns

As early as 1936 Lewis wrote in a letter to his friend Bede Griffiths that the pagans may have wisely constructed a hierarchical scheme of man, with reason ruling passion and soul ruling body. But in Christ, Lewis concluded, there is neither male nor female, bond nor free. The whole person is offered to

God, and there is no superiority of one faculty over another. That view is reflected in his poem "Reason and Imagination." As much as Lewis enjoyed and emphasized the stately ancient patterns of hierarchy (and in spite of his occasional sexist attitudes), he settled in reality on dynamic, dancing tensions. Lewis greatly enjoyed Dante's story about Pope Gregory learning when he got to heaven that his laborious theory of hierarchies was wrong. Gregory thought that news was the funniest thing he'd ever heard. Lewis liked that open spirit.

To Lewis the great divide in education comes between those who know the *Tao* (as described in *The Abolition of Man*) and those who do not. Those who know the *Tao* believe that certain attitudes are true and others false to the nature of the universe and the nature of ourselves. There is objective value. Teachers who are in the *Tao* automatically seek what Aristotle considered a teacher's aim—to make a pupil like and dislike what he ought. Teachers who are not in the *Tao* would either debunk "ought" or else try to condition students to an "ought" that is a fiction for the advantage of current leaders and their plans for using the people. Lewis's attack on such a perverted education is ferocious indeed.

Lewis's view was that we need both vocational training and education. The former allows us to preserve and propagate life so that the latter can provide us, in our leisure, with materials of thought, art, literature and conversation—the richest part of natural human life in contrast to animal life.

Lewis's idea of the function of a university was not to provide vocational training or even an education, which young adults should have already, but to be a place where those who are thirsty for knowledge can pursue learning. All people desire knowledge, he assumed, but some desire it more fervently and will sacrifice more for it. One student may want to know what happened a million years ago; another, what happens a million light years away; and another, what is happening on the microscopic level. The proper question for a freshman is not "What will do me the most good?" but "What do I most want to know?" Lewis's ideal for a university student was to forget all about self-improvement for three or four years and to absorb himself in some limited part of reality.[22]

Lewis agreed with Hegel that a perfect study of anything requires knowledge of everything, but because time is short we must be selective. In speaking to literature students he expressed his opinion that university study of modern literature is absurd: "The student who wants a tutor's assistance in reading the works of his own contemporaries might as well ask for a nurse's assistance in blowing his own nose."[23] He also held very general courses of study in some disdain; he thought that delving narrowly and deeply was better than getting a broad surface sampling. Needless to say, the fact that Lewis was extraordinarily brilliant and had private schooling for about twenty years at his father's expense, never once holding a job until he completed his extensive academic training to be an Oxford professor, opens him to charges of having an elitist point of view not very practical for less fortunate people. He said he expected university students to be making themselves into philosophers, scientists, scholars, critics or historians.

The most moving and inspiring words Lewis ever wrote about learning were in a sermon he gave in Oxford early in World War II, "Learning in War-Time." How is it right, he asked, for us to spend our time on such comparative trivialities as literature or art, mathematics or biology? This is a question that war presses upon people, but it is a question that is always present for Christians in the light of possibly imminent death and the realities of eternity. Are the activities of a scholar legitimate in a world where human souls are in the balance?

Of course, Lewis answers. Christianity does not exclude any normal human activities. We are told to do what we do to the glory of God. The pursuit of knowledge or beauty can be a kind of service to God if the motive is pure. If pride and conceit overwhelm a scholar, the vocation should be abandoned. But surely for some the learned life is a duty.

Lewis warned of three enemies that keep us from learning in wartime and in peace. The first is excitement of all kinds that distracts us from our work. The answer is to go ahead with work in spite of the distractions. They never end.

The second enemy to learning is frustration about lack of enough time to reach one's future goals. Lewis points out that work is done best by the person who works from moment to moment and takes long-term plans rather lightly. "It is only our *daily* bread that we are encouraged to ask for."[24]

The third enemy of learning is fear of death. War cannot increase the percentage of death; that is 100 per cent. War only causes some deaths to come sooner. "All the animal life in us, all schemes of happiness that centered in this world, were always doomed to a final frustration."[25] But it may be true that a life of learning humbly offered to God is for some souls an appointed approach to the divine reality and beauty in the next life.

All in all, in Lewis's opinion, the only people who achieve much learning are those who want knowledge so badly that they seek it while conditions are still unfavorable, because favorable conditions never come. "We must do the best we can."[26]

Lewis had a stern warning for teachers and students. We must avoid the idea that scholars and poets are intrinsically more pleasing to God than scavengers and bootblacks. Lewis stressed that the work of a Beethoven and the work of a char-woman or a man who is growing turnips become spiritual on precisely the same condition, that of being offered to God and done humbly for the Lord. "We are members of one body, but differentiated members, each with his own vocation."[27]

Lewis's vocation was education, offered to God and done humbly for the Lord.

Further Reading about Education

"I have lived nearly sixty years with myself and my own century and am not so enamoured of either as to desire no glimpse of a world beyond them."[28]

The Abolition of Man by C. S. Lewis is his timely warning about the undermining of essential human values in education today.

"Membership," "Learning in War-Time" and "The Inner Ring" are lectures in *The Weight of Glory* by C. S. Lewis that are addressed primarily to university students although they apply to all people.

"The Idea of an English School" and "Our English Syllabus" in *Rehabilitations* by C. S. Lewis are about subject matter and the approach to learning that Lewis championed.

"On the Reading of Old Books" in *God in the Dock* by C. S. Lewis can most appropriately be read for what it is, an introduction to *On the Incarnation* by St. Athanasius. That classic work is now available in paperback from St. Vladimir's Seminary Press.

C. S. Lewis, Speaker and Teacher edited by Carolyn Keefe is made up of seven essays about special aspects of Lewis as an oral communicator.

Notes

1. Lewis, *The Abolition of Man*, p. 9.
2. Lewis, *Prince Caspian*, pp. 167–69.
3. An unpublished letter from C. S. Lewis to his friend Father Milward on Christmas Day, 1959. In his usual chatty way, Lewis assured Milward that finding meaning in a book (Lewis's, in this case) which the author was not aware of is not unusual. Then he went on to request Milward's prayer for Mrs. Lewis, who was suffering a relapse of cancer. He concluded with the thought that Lazarus was sacrificed by having to die twice. Lewis's letters to Milward are available in the Wade Collection. The final one was written just before his death.
4. Stephen Schofield, "The Butcher," *Church Times* (28 December 1979), p. 7. This article appeared first in the October 1979 issue of *The Canadian C. S. Lewis Journal.*

5. *The Search for C. S. Lewis*, ed. by Stephen Schofield (South Plainfield, New Jersey: Bridge Publishing Inc., 1983) p. 12

6. Ibid., p. 13

7. *C. S. Lewis at the Breakfast Table*, ed. by James Como (New York, New York: Macmillan, 1979) p. 62

8. *The Search for C. S. Lewis*, p. 13

9. Kenneth Tynan, with Stephen Schofield, "My Tutor, C. S. Lewis," *The Canadian C. S. Lewis Journal* (August 1979), pp. 6–7.

10. Jill Freud, "Lewis Teaches the Retarded," *The Canadian C. S. Lewis Journal* (April 1980), pp. 3–5.

11. *Chronicle* of the Portland C. S. Lewis Society (January-March 1979), p. 11.

12. Lewis,"Cross-Examination," *God in the Dock*, p. 258.

13. Lewis, *An Experiment in Criticism*, p. 138.

14. Lewis, *That Hideous Strength*, p. 212.

15. Lewis,"The Idea of an 'English School,'" *Rehabilitations*, p. 64.

16. Lewis,"On the Reading of Old Books," *God in the Dock*, p. 202.

17. Lewis,"De Descriptione Temporum," *They Asked for a Paper*, p. 23.

18. C. S. Lewis, *Studies in Words* (London: Cambridge Univ. Press, 1960), pp. 4–5.

19. Lewis, *Surprised by Joy*, p. 196.

20. Lewis, The Discarded Image (London:Cambridge University Press, 1964) p. 215

21. Ibid, p. 215

22. Lewis, "Our English Syllabus," *Rehabilitations*, p. 87.

23. Ibid., p. 91.

24. Lewis, "Learning in War-Time," *The Weight of Glory*, p. 18.

25. Ibid., p. 52.

26. Ibid.

27. Ibid., p. 49.

28. Lewis, *Studies in Words*, p. 3.

Appendix 1

The Years of the Life of C. S. Lewis

Nine Years of Irish Childhood

1898 Born at Belfast, November 29
1899 Infancy
1900 "Talking like anything," his mother said
1901 Told riddles with brother Warren
1902 Chose the name Jacksie for life
1903 Began learning chess
1904 Unusual rain kept boys indoors more than usual
1905 Family moved to new house, "Little Lea"
1906 First trip to London; enjoyed mice at the zoo most
1907 Vacation at beach in France; began diary

Twenty-three Years of Serious Academic Pursuits

1908 Mother died; boys sent to England for schooling
1909 Suffered at terrible boarding school
1910 Entered Campbell school in Belfast; dropped out ill
1911 Entered Cherbourg school; lost childhood faith
1912 Discovered Wagner and "Northerness"

1913 Won scholarship to Malvern College
1914 Met Arthur Greeves and W. T. Kirkpatrick
1915 Discovered writings of George MacDonald
1916 Was accepted at Oxford University
1917 Entered the army and the Moore family
1918 Was wounded in France; returned to England
1919 Published *Spirits in Bondage* (early poems)
1920 Academic success in philosophy
1921 Visited William Butler Yeats
1922 Academic success in the classics
1923 Academic success in English literature
1924 First employment, at University College, Oxford
1925 Permanent position at Magdalen College, Oxford
1926 Published book-length poem, *Dymer*
1927 Began first novel ("The Most Substantial People")
1928 Began writing *The Allegory of Love*
1929 Regained belief in God; father died
1930 Moved into permanent home, the Kilns

Twenty-three Christian Years of Increasing Accomplishments

1931 Accepted Christianity
1932 Wrote *The Pilgrim's Regress*
1933 Published *The Pilgrim's Regress*
1934 Visited Scotland and Ireland with Warren
1935 Completed *The Allegory of Love* for publication
1936 Discovered writings of Charles Williams
1937 Wrote *The Personal Heresy* with Tillyard
1938 Published *Out of the Silent Planet*
1939 End of his annual walking tours
1940 Published *The Problem of Pain*
1941 Began series of twenty-five wartime radio broadcasts
1942 Published *The Screwtape Letters*
1943 Published *The Abolition of Man* and *Perelandra*

1944 Published *Beyond Personality*
1945 Published *The Great Divorce* and *That Hideous Strength*
1946 Honorary Doctor of Divinity, St. Andrews University
1947 Published *Miracles*
1948 Published *Arthurian Torso*
1949 Published two collections of essays
1950 Published first of the Chronicles of Narnia
1951 "Foster mother," Mrs. Moore, died
1952 Honorary Doctor of Literature, Laval University
1953 Friendship with Joy Davidman grew

Nine Years of Greatest Joys and Losses

1954 Promoted to post at Cambridge University
1955 Published autobiography, *Surprised by Joy*
1956 Published *Till We Have Faces*, his favorite
1957 Married Joy Davidman in her hospital room
1958 Published *Reflections on the Psalms*
1959 Wife Joy suffered cancer relapse
1960 Published *The Four Loves*; his wife died
1961 Published *A Grief Observed* on his bereavement
1962 Began *Letters to Malcolm: Chiefly on Prayer*
1963 Died on November 22, just before sixty-fifth birthday

Appendix 2

Key Places in the Life of C. S. Lewis

1. Wales: Birthplace of Lewis's paternal grandfather, who moved to Belfast.
2. Belfast: Birthplace and childhood home of C. S. Lewis (1898-1908), which he often visited later.
3. Boat crossing between Belfast and Liverpool which Lewis made repeatedly after 1908 (see *Surprised by Joy*, p. 149, and *Letters to an American Lady*, p. 118).
4. Watford, Hertfordshire: Town where Lewis attended his very cruel first boarding school (1908-10).
5. Malvern, Worcestershire: Town where Lewis attended preparatory school and college (1911-14).
6. Great Bookham, Surrey: Rural area where Lewis studied under private tutor Kirkpatrick (1914-17).
7. Oxford: Where Lewis attended university and taught (1917, 1919-54). His home until he died.
8. France: Where Lewis served and was wounded in World War 1 (1917-18).
9. London: Where Lewis recuperated from war wounds; occasionally visited there from childhood to old age.

10. Cambridge: University where Lewis was honored with a
    chair in 1954. He commuted there until 1963.

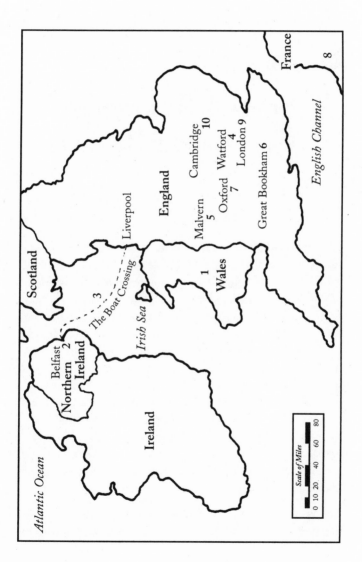

Appendix 3

Special Resources for C. S. Lewis Readers

Organizations and Publications

The Mythopoeic Society was founded by Glen GoodKnight in Los Angeles in 1967 for the study, discussion and enjoyment of myth, fantasy and imaginative literature—particularly the works of J. R. R. Tolkien, C. S. Lewis and Charles Williams. Society activities include an annual convention called *Mythcon* that has been held in California, England, and points between. Proceedings of past conventions are published and available; featured guests have included speakers prominent in Lewis studies. At its height, the Society claimed almost fourteen hundred members in sixteen nations. Membership dues include a subscription to the impressive quarterly journal *Mythlore*. (In 1996 issue 80 of *Mythlore* was published.) Back copies, a newsletter called *Mythprint*, mythopoeic stationery and art are available. Inquiries should be addressed to The Mythopoeic Society, p.o. Box 6707, Altadena, California 91003.

The New York C. S. Lewis Society was founded at the end of 1969 in response to a call by Henry Noel. Since then its membership has grown from the small group attending monthly meetings to about five hundred far-flung subscribers to the 16-page newsletter *C. S. L.: Bulletin of the New York C. S. Lewis Society.* (In 1996 issue 317 of *C. S. L.* was published.) Inquiries should be addressed to corresponding secretary Clara Sarocco, 84–23 77th Ave., Glendale, New York 11385.

The Southern California C. S. Lewis Society was founded in 1974 in response to the vision of Paul F. Ford, who was then of St. Andrew's Benedictine Priory at Valyermo, California. Meetings are held the third Wednesday evening of the month, September–November, January–May on the campus of Fuller Theological Seminary in Pasadena. In the summer this society usually offers a one-week Lewis workshop with a guest teacher at St. Andrew's Benedictine Priory in the high desert east of Los Angeles. The society's newsletter titled *The Lamp-Post,* launched in 1975 by Paul Ford and Kathryn Lindskoog, eventually developed into a handsome 40-page quarterly journal. (In 1996 Vol. 20, No. 1 of *The Lamp-Post* was published.) Inquiries should be addressed to secretary Edie Dougherty, 1212 W. 162nd St., Gardena, California 90247.

In January 1979 the first issue of *The Canadian C. S. Lewis Journal* appeared. This was not the outgrowth of another Lewis society, but the work of Stephen Schofield—a Canadian journalist who had moved to England years earlier. His journal differed from the older ones in its informality and spontaneity and the fact that its editor had met Lewis. After Schofield's demise in 1993, his publication developed into a handsome 72-page biannual journal. (In 1996 issue 89 of *The Canadian C. S. Lewis Journal* was published.) Inquiries should be addressed to editor Roger Stronstad, Western Pentecostal Bible College, Box 1700, Abbotsford, B. C., Canada v2s7e7 or Box 70, Sumas, Washington 98295.

In 1980 a new Anglo-American literary review was launched by Clyde S. Kilby, Barbara Reynolds and Beatrice Batson. Entitled *Seven*, it is an annual scholarly appraisal of seven authors: C. S. Lewis, George MacDonald, G. K. Chesterton, J. R. R. Tolkien, Charles Williams, Dorothy L. Sayers and Owen Barfield. (In 1995 issue 12 was published.) Inquiries should be addressed to The Marion E. Wade Center, Wheaton College, Wheaton, Illinois 60187-5593.

At the beginning of 1989 Kathryn Lindskoog launched *The Lewis Legacy,* which developed into a quarterly 20-page newsletter that combines a wide range of Lewis news, analysis and discoveries with an ongoing exploration of fraud and forgery. (In 1996 issue 69 was published.) Inquiries should be addressed to 1344 E. Mayfair Ave., Orange, California 92867.

Libraries

The Personal Library of C. S. Lewis must have included over three thousand books. At the time of Lewis's death, Major W. H. Lewis retained what he wanted and then turned the rest over to Blackwell's, a large bookstore on Broad Street in Oxford. There some of them were sold individually, and finally Wroxton College in Oxfordshire (a branch of Farleigh Dickinson University of New Jersey) bought the 2,710 that remained. Margaret Anne Rogers catalogued the purchase and described it in her thesis "C. S. Lewis: A Living Library." In 1985 the collection was puchased by the Marion E. Wade Center in Illinois and moved to the United States.

The Marion E. Wade Center at Wheaton College in Wheaton, Illinois, was founded as the C. S. Lewis Collection in 1965 by professor Clyde S. Kilby. He began by donating his own letters from C. S. Lewis, and under his leadership the collection grew to include books and papers of six other authors associated with Lewis: Owen Barfield, G. K. Chesterton, George MacDonald,

Dorothy L. Sayers, J. R. R. Tolkien and Charles Williams. People journey from all over the United States and other countries to make free use of this extremely rich and varied collection. In 1979 its Lewis holdings alone came to 861 holographs; 1008 original Lewis letters; 23 volumes of Warren Lewis's lifetime diaries; more than 650 original letters of Warren Lewis; eleven typed volumes of the Lewis family papers from 1850 to 1930; Lewis's boyhood "Boxen" stories that he wrote and illustrated; letters to and about Lewis; artwork, including the Pauline Baynes map of Narnia and over seventy of her drawings; and a vast storehouse of writing about Lewis as well as memorabilia including Lewis's dining table, Lewis's personal desk and a handcarved wardrobe passed down through the Lewis family.

The Bodleian Library at the University of Oxford has one of the world's greatest collections of English books and rare manuscripts. Revived and enriched by Sir Thomas Bodley shortly after 1600, it is said to be the oldest public library in the world that has continuously served readers to this day. There C. S. Lewis researchers can locate his lively contributions to the minutes of the Martlets literary society, 576 pages of Lewis holographs, 476 original Lewis letters, and many other valuable and interesting materials concerning Lewis, including the original little sketch of Narnia that he gave to Pauline Baynes.

Audio Recordings

C. S. Lewis's recorded voice is available on cassette tapes from the Episcopal Radio-TV Foundation of Atlanta, Georgia. His voice was so rich and expressive that it is well worth hearing. Available for purchase are "Four Talks on Love," "The Great Divide," "Pilgrim's Progress," "Charles Williams," and "The Introduction to *The Great Divorce*." These are all very short, except for the "Four Talks on Love," a set of ten lectures in 1957 for American radio. The others were all recorded for BBC Radio.

In 1976 a six-cassette reading of *The Screwtape Letters* was issued by Walter Hooper and Bob O'Donnell. Their editing changed the story somewhat, detracting from its value. In 1988 Audio Literature released *The Screwtape Letters* as Lewis wrote it, read by John Cleese. Because Cleese's reading is only on two cassettes, four of the thirty-one chapters are omitted.

The Episcopal Guild for the Blind has cassette recordings of Lewis books available for lending, free of charge. They are not for sale. The collection includes the seven Narnian books, *Miracles, Out of the Silent Planet, That Hideous Strength, Mere Christianity, The Abolition of Man*, and *The Problem of Pain*. Lewis's recording of "Four Talks on Love" is also included.

In the 1970s Caedmon Records produced a series of seven readings of the Narnian Chronicles (slightly abridged) by prominent actors like Claire Bloom and Ian Richardson.

In 1980 a highly respected Christian Trio called The Second Chapter of Acts chose Narnia as the theme of their fourth album, titled *The Roar of Love*. Words and music of thirteen of the fourteen songs are by Anne Herring.

The Phil Keaggy album *Love Broke Through* includes a beautiful arrangement of the Lewis poem "As the Ruin Falls."

Dramatizations

The British Broadcasting Corporation first produced Lance Sieveking's radio adaptation of *The Lion, the Witch and the Wardrobe* in 1959, when Lewis was alive. The series consisted of six weekly episodes and was repeated in 1960. Lewis had been consulted about such adaptations in 1954 by an American named Jane Douglass and had expressed his vehement disapproval of an adaptation of this book on television or film, but had agreed to her trying to write an adaptation for radio. Unfortunately for Douglass, he did not like what she submitted to him, and so she gave up the project. Apparently Sieveking won Lewis's approval or at least a reluctant assent.

British composer Donald Swann, who set seven of J. R. R. Tolkien's poems to music, collaborated with David Marsh on an operatic version of *Perelandra*. They went over it with Lewis before his death, and it was performed in concert form in Oxford, London and Cambridge seven months later. A year after Lewis's death, there was a full production of the opera by music students at Haverford College in Pennsylvania. The score has not been published, but it may be borrowed from Galaxy Music Publishers in New York. An operatic version of *The Lion, the Witch and the Wardrobe* by Gerald Larner is available from Novello & Co., Ltd., 27 Soho Sq., London W1, England.

In 1967 *The Lion, the Witch and the Wardrobe* was serialized on television by one of the commercial companies in the United Kingdom. At that time Warren Lewis, who was more tolerant of television than his brother had been, wrote to me, "Last Sunday evening I watched the first installment of C. S. L.'s *The Lion, the Witch and the Wardrobe* on television and it seemed to me that they have made a very good job of it; but I don't know whether it is being shown in your country or not." It was not.

In the 1970s Tom Key, a professional actor and playwright, began presenting his one-man show *An Evening with C. S. Lewis* at churches and colleges across the United States, paying royalties to the Lewis estate. Inquiries about engagements can be addressed to Tom Key at 910 Highland Terrace, Atlanta, GA 30306.

In 1979 the Episcopal Church, which had paid the estate of C. S. Lewis $100,000 for all dramatic rights to the Narnian Chronicles, presented a cartoon version of *The Lion, The Witch and the Wardrobe* on American television. Although it was a faithful condensation of the plot, some of the art work would probably have bothered Lewis. It is now available on videotape.

In 1979 Walter Hooper and Bob O'Donnell (Lord and King Associates of West Chicago) released a three-part rental film about the life and works of C. S. Lewis entitled *Through Joy and Beyond*, featuring Walter Hooper. An abbreviated version of the first two parts is now available on videotape.

A British stage portrayal of C. S. Lewis called *Song of the Lion* was launched by Aldersgate Productions Limited, 12 Palace Street. London SW1E5JF; but it had the misfortune of preceeding the transatlantic groundswell of public interest that began in the 1980s.

In 1986 BBC-TV, Episcopal Radio-TV Foundation and Gateway Films presented their prize-winning drama *Shadowlands,* based on C. S. Lewis's poignant marriage story. This eighty-minute film starring Joss Ackland and Claire Bloom is not completely factual, but it had broad audience appeal and increased public interest in Lewis. It is available on videocassette.

In 1988 WonderWorks broadcast three 165-minute television dramatizations of the Chronicles, including *The Lion, the Witch and the Wardrobe, Prince Caspian and the Voyage of the "Dawn Treader"*, and *The Silver Chair*. They are available on videocassettes.

In 1989 the stage version of *Shadowlands* was immensely successful on three continents.

In 1990 the BBC Audio Collection released *The Tales of Narnia*, a seven-part radio dramatization of the Chronicles by Brian Sibley available on fourteen audiocassettes.

In 1993 the major motion picture version of *Shadowlands* was released, starring Anthony Hopkins and Debra Winger. Although this third version of *Shadowlands* greatly misrepresents Lewis's personality, looks, and way of life, it caused his book sales to skyrocket. It was soon available for purchase on videocassette.

As of 1996, three new dramatizations of Lewis's fiction may soon be filmed. Lewis's stepson Douglas Gresham has plans for a major film of *The Lion, the Witch, and the Wardrobe*. A future film of *The Great Divorce* has been announced by the Episcopal Radio-TV Foundation. And film rights to *The Screwtape Letters* reportedly belong to a hopeful California producer.

Many nonprofit plays and musicals based on Lewis's stories have been created and sometimes presented locally, but their creators usually discover that the managers of the Lewis estate routinely refuse permission for these noncommercial projects to be performed under any circumstances.

Appendix 4

Annotated Chronological Listing of C. S. Lewis's Books

*"What we want is not more little books about Christianity
but more little books by Christians on other subjects—
with their Christianity latent."*
Christian Apologetics, God in the Dock

1. ***Spirits in Bondage*** (London: Heinemann, 1919; San Diego: Harcourt, 1984). A collection of early poems published under the pseudonym Clive Hamilton.
2. ***Dymer*** (London: Dent, 1926; New York: Dutton, New York: Macmillan). One long narrative poem published under the pseudonym Clive Hamilton. It is out of print as a single volume, but was included in the 1969 collection *Narrative Poems*.
3. ***The Pilgrim's Regress*** (London: Dent, 1933; Sheed and Ward; London: Bles; Grand Rapids: Eerdmans). Semi-autobiographical fantasy tracing Lewis's return to Christianity. It is his first book in prose, first foray into Christian apologetics and

the seedbed of most of his later writing.

4. *The Allegory of Love* (Oxford: Clarendon Press, 1936; London: Oxford University Press). Outstanding study of medieval literature and the tradition of courtly love.

5. *Out of the Silent Planet* (Oxford: John Lane, 1938; New York: Macmillan; London: Pan Books). First volume of Lewis's science fiction trilogy.

6. *Rehabilitations and Other Essays* (London: Oxford University Press, 1939; Clair Shores, Michigan: Scholarly Press). Essays on literature and education. Also available from University Microfilms, Ann Arbor, in Xerographic edition. Contents: "Shelley, Dryden, and Mr. Eliot," "William Morris," "The Idea of an 'English School'" "Our English Syllabus," "High and Low Brows," "The Alliterative Metre," "Bluspels and Flalanspheres: A Semantic Nightmare," "Variations in Shakespeare and Others," "Christianity and Literature."

7. *The Personal Heresy* (London: Oxford University Press, 1939). A written debate with E. M. W. Tillyard about the correct theory of poetry.

8. *The Problem of Pain* (London: Centenary Press, 1940; London: Fontana; New York: Macmillan). An attempt to reconcile the fact of suffering with the fact of a good God.

9. *The Screwtape Letters* (London: Bles, 1942; New York: Macmillan; New York: Touchstone). Christian ethics presented from the devil's point of view. The Time Reading Plan edition of 1963 by Time, Inc. includes "Screwtape Proposes a Toast" and an introduction by Phyllis McGinley. It is a handsome, hard-to-find edition. Some later editions add a posthumous preface to "Screwtape Proposes a Toast" which should not be attributed to Lewis.

10. *A Preface to Paradise Lost* (London: Oxford University Press, 1942). A scholarly introduction to Milton's masterpiece.

11. *Broadcast Talks* (London: Bles, 1942; New York: Macmillan). The first part of Lewis's wartime radio series.

Entitled *The Case for Christianity* by Macmillan.

12. ***Christian Behavior*** (London: Bles, 1943; New York: Macmillan). The second part of Lewis's wartime radio series.

13. ***Perelandra*** (London: John Lane, 1943; New York: Macmillan). Second (and most celebrated) of Lewis's science fiction trilogy. Published as *Voyage to Venus* (London: Pan Books) in 1953.

14. ***The Abolition of Man*** (London: Oxford University Press, 1943; London: Bles; New York: Macmillan). An attack on false worldviews and affirmation of true values.

15. ***Beyond Personality*** (London: Bles, 1944; New York: Macmillan). The third part of Lewis's wartime radio series.

16. ***That Hideous Strength*** (London: John Lane, 1945; New York: Macmillan). Third of Lewis's science fiction trilogy. Published as *The Tortured Planet* (New York: Avon Books) in 1946.

17. ***The Great Divorce*** (London: Bles, 1945; New York: Macmillan). A fantasy visit to hell and heaven. Of his own books, this was one of Lewis's favorites.

18. ***Miracles: A Preliminary Study*** (London: Bles, 1947; London: Fontana; New York: Macmillan). An explanation and defense of miracles. The Fontana edition includes Lewis's expansion of chapter three.

19. ***Transposition and Other Addresses*** (London: Bles, 1949; New York: Macmillan; Grand Rapids: Eerdmans). Published in the U.S. as *The Weight of Glory and Other Addresses*. Three sermons and two Christian addresses. Contents: "Transposition," "The Weight of Glory," "Membership," "Learning in War-Time," "The Inner Ring." The 1980 edition adds four more essays ("Why I Am Not a Pacifist," "Is Theology Poetry," "On Forgiveness," and "A Slip of the Tongue") and a partially misleading introduction by Walter Hooper.

20. ***The Lion, the Witch and the Wardrobe*** (London: Bles, 1950; London: Penguin; New York: Macmillan; london: Collins; New

York: HarperCollins) The first of the seven-volume Narnian series for children.

21. *Prince Caspian* (London: Bles, 1951; London: Penguin; New York: Macmillan; London: Collins; New York: HarperCollins) Second of the seven volume Narnian series for children.

22. *Mere Christianity* (London: Bles, 1952; London: Fontana; New York: Macmillian) A volume combining *The Case for Christianity*, *Christian Behavior* and *Beyond Personality* with a new introduction.

23. *The Voyage of "The Dawn Treader"* (London: Bles, 1952; London: Penguin; New York: Macmillan; London: Collins; New York: HarperCollins). Third of the seven volume Narnian series for children.

24. *The Silver Chair* (London: Bles, 1952; London: Penguin; New York: Macmillan; London: Collins; New York: HarperCollins). Fourth of the seven volume Narnian series for children.

25. *The Horse and His Boy* (London: Bles, 1954; London: Penguin; New York: Macmillan; London: Collins; New York: HarperCollins). Fifth of the seven volume Narnian series for children.

26. *English Literature in the Sixteenth Century* (Oxford: The Clarendon Press, 1954). Volume 3 of the Oxford History of English Literature series.

27. *The Magician's Nephew* (London: The Bodley Head, 1954; London: Penguin; New York: Macmillan; London: Collins; New York: HarperCollins) Sixth of the seven volume Narnian series for children. This was the first of the series available in inexpensive hardback from Longman Group, Ltd., in London.

28. *Surprised by Joy* (London: Bles, 1955; Fontana; New York: Harcourt). Lewis's spiritual autobiography takes the reader to the point of his conversion.

29. *The Last Battle* (London: The Bodley Head, 1956; London: Penguin; New York: Macmillan; London: Collins; New York:

HarperCollins). Seventh of the seven-volume Narnian series for children.

30. *Till We Have Faces* (London: Bles, 1956; New York: Harcourt). A difficult but rewarding novel; according to Owen Barfield, Lewis considered it his best work in the sphere of imaginative literature. The Time Reading Plan edition (1966) included a perceptive introduction by T. S. Matthews.

31. *Reflections on the Psalms* (London: Bles, 1958; London: Fontana; New York: Harcourt). Comments on the book of Psalms.

32. *The Four Loves* (London: Bles, 1960; London: Fontana; New York: Harcourt). Analysis of the four human loves and divine Love.

33. *Studies in Words* (Cambridge: Cambridge University Press, 1960). A scholarly study of seven words: nature, sad, wit, free, sense, simple, and conscience.

34. *The World's Last Night and Other Essays* (New York: Harcourt, 1960). A collection of seven essays about Christianity and values. Contents: "The Efficacy of Prayer," "On Obstinacy in Belief," "Lilies That Fester," "Screwtape Proposes a Toast," "Good Work and Good Works," "Religion and Rocketry," "The World's Last Night."

35. *A Grief Observed* (London: Faber and Faber, 1961; Greenwich, Connecticut: Seabury; New York: Bantam; New York: Harper & Row). An account of Lewis's bereavement originally published under the pseudonym N. W. Clerk. The Bantam edition includes an informative afterword by Chad Walsh, and the Harper & Row gift edition includes a warm foreword by Madeleine L'Engle.

36. *An Experiment in Criticism* (Cambridge: Cambridge University Press, 1961). An exploration into the subject of literary criticism and good reading.

37. *They Asked for a Paper* (London: Bles, 1962). A dozen literary and Christian addresses that Lewis gave over a twenty-year

period. Contents: "De Descriptione Temporum," "The Literary Impact of the Authorized Version," "Hamlet: The Prince or the Poem?" "Kipling's World," "Sir Walter Scott," "Lilies That Fester," "Psycho-Analysis and Literary Criticism," "The Inner Ring," "Is Theology Poetry?" "Transposition," "On Obstinacy in Belief," "The Weight of Glory."

38. *Letters to Malcolm: Chiefly on Prayer* (London: Bles, 1964; London: Fontana; New York: Harcourt). Letters about prayer and the Christian life written to a fictitious friend. The first of Lewis's books to be published after his death.

39. *The Discarded Image* (Cambridge: Cambridge University Press, 1964). An introduction to medieval and renaissance literature.

40. *Poems* (London: Bles, 1964; New York: Harcourt). Over a hundred poems written throughout Lewis's life, edited by Walter Hooper. Many of those that Lewis published during his lifetime were inexplicably altered (for the worse) for this posthumous collection.

41. *Screwtape Proposes a Toast and Other Pieces* (London: Fontana, 1965). Eight sermons and lectures, all on religious themes. Contents: "Screwtape Proposes a Toast," "The Inner Ring," "Is Theology Poetry?" "On Obstinacy in Belief," "Transposition," "The Weight of Glory," "Good Work and Good Works," "A Slip of the Tongue."

42. *Of Other Worlds* (London: Bles, 1966; New York: Harcourt). Stories and essays about Story—fiction and fantasy—edited by Walter Hooper. Essays: "On Stories," "On Three Ways of Writing for Children," "Sometimes Fairy Stories May Say Best What's to Be Said," "On Juvenile Tastes", "It All Began With a Picture . . ." "On Criticism," "On Science Fiction," "A Reply to Professor Haldane," "Unreal Estates". Stories: "The Shoddy Lands," "Ministering Angels," "Forms of Things Unknown," "After Ten Years." (Evidence has surfaced that "Forms of Things Unknown" is not by Lewis after all.)

43. *Letters of C. S. Lewis* (London: Bles, 1966; New York: Harcourt; London: Fount Paperbacks). Private letters from 1915 to 1963, collected and edited by W. H. Lewis. A memoir and pictures included. Knowledgable readers discount the attack upon Warren Lewis in Walter Hooper's introduction to the 1988 Fount edition.

44. *Studies in Medieval and Renaissance Literature* (Cambridge: Cambridge University Press, 1966). Seven previously unpublished studies and seven more that were hard to obtain, edited by Walter Hooper. Contents: "De Audiendis Poetis," "The Genesis of a Medieval Book," "Imagination and Thought in the Middle Ages," "Dante's Similes," "Imagery in the Last Eleven Cantos of Dante's Comedy," "Dante's Statius," "The Morte D'Arthur," "Tasso," "Edmund Spenser, 1552-99," "On Reading *The Fairie Queene*," "Neoplatonism in the Poetry of Spenser," "Spenser's Cruel Cupid," "Genius and Genius," "A Note on *Comus*."

45. *Christian Reflections* (London: Bles, 1967; Grand Rapids: Eerdmans). A collection of fourteen papers about or relating to Christianity from the last twenty years of Lewis's life, edited by Walter Hooper. Contents: "Christianity and Culture," "Christianity and Literature," "Religion: Reality or Substitute?" "On Ethics," "De Futilitate," "The Poison of Subjectivism," "The Funeral of a Great Myth," "On Church Music," "Historicism," "The Psalms," "The Language of Religion," "Petitionary Prayer: A Problem Without an Answer," "Modern Theology and Biblical Criticism," "The Seeing Eye."

46. *Spenser's Images of Life* (Cambridge: Cambridge University Press, 1969). Lewis meant to turn his notes from a course he taught on Spenser into a book, but he died before he had the chance. Dr. Alastair Fowler constructed this book from the notes.

47. *Letters to an American Lady* (Grand Rapids: Eerdmans, 1967; New York: Pyramid; London: Hodder and Stoughton). A

collection of personal letters Lewis wrote to a troubled widow
in the southern United States, edited by Clyde Kilby.

48. *A Mind Awake* (London: Bles, 1969; New York: Harcourt).
Clyde Kilby's anthology of brief quotations from the whole
spectrum of Lewis's writing.

49. *Selected Literary Essays* (Cambridge: Cambridge University
Press, 1969). A collection of twenty-two literary essays, edited
and with an introduction by Walter Hooper. Contents: "De
Descriptione Temporum," "The Alliterative Metre," "What
Chaucer Really Did to *Il Filostrato*," "The Fifteenth-Century
Heroic Line," "Hero and Leander," "Variation in Shakespeare
and Others," "Hamlet: The Prince or the Poem?" "Donne and
Love Poetry in the Seventeenth Century," "The Literary Impact
of the Authorized Version," "The Vision of John Bunyan,"
"Addison," "Four-Letter Words," "A Note on Jane Austen,"
"Shelley, Dryden, and Mr. Eliot," "Sir Walter Scott," "William
Morris," "Kipling's World," "Bluspels and Flalanspheres: A
Semantic Nightmare," "High and Low Brows," "Metre,"
"Psycho-Analysis and Literary Criticism," "The
Anthropological Approach."

50. *Narrative Poems* (London: Bles, 1969; New York:
Harcourt). Four long story-poems edited by Walter Hooper.
Contents: "Dymer," "Launcelot," "The Nameless Isle," "The
Queen of Drum."

51. *God in the Dock* (Grand Rapids: Eerdmans, 1970; London:
Bles). Published in England as *Undeceptions*. Forty-eight essays
and a dozen published letters on theology and ethics not before
available to most readers, collected and edited, with an intro-
duction, by Walter Hooper. Contents: "Evil and God,"
"Miracles," "Dogma and the Universe," "Answers to Questions
on Christianity," "Myth Became Fact," "Horrid Red Things,"
"Religion and Science," "The Laws of Nature," "The Grand
Miracle," "Christian Apologetics," "Work and Prayer," "Man or
Rabbit?" "On the Transmission of Christianity," "Miserable

Offenders," "The Founding of the Oxford Socratic Club," "Religion without Dogma?" "Some Thoughts," "The Trouble with 'X' . . . ," "What Are We to Make of Jesus Christ?" "The Pains of Animals," "Is Theism Important?" "Rejoinder to Dr. Pittenger," "Must Our Image of God Go?" "Dangers of National Repentance," "Two Ways with the Self," "Meditation on the Third Commandment," "On the Reading of Old Books," "Two Lectures," "Meditation in a Toolshed," "Scraps," "The Decline of Religion," "Vivisection," "Modern Translations of the Bible," "Priestesses in the Church?" "God in the Dock," "Behind the Scenes," "Revival or Decay?" "Before We Can Communicate," "Cross-Examination," "Bulverism," "First and Second Things," "The Sermon and the Lunch," "The Humanitarian Theory of Punishment," "Xmas and Christmas," "What Christmas Means to Me," "Delinquents in the Snow," "Is Progress Possible?" "We Have No 'Right to Happiness.'"

52. *Fern-seed and Elephants* (Glasgow: Fontana/Collins, 1975). Eight essays on Christianity edited by Walter Hooper, including one never published before about forgiveness. Contents: "Membership," "Learning in War-Time," "On Forgiveness," "Historicism," "The World's Last Night," "Religion and Rocketry," "The Efficacy of Prayer," "Fern-seed and Elephants."

53. *The Dark Tower* (London: Collins, 1977; New York: Harcourt). Four stories and two fragments of novels, edited by Walter Hooper. One of the stories and the title fragment were not previously available. Contents: "The Dark Tower," "The Man Born Blind," "The Shoddy Lands," "Ministering Angels," "Forms of Things Unknown," "After Ten Years." Three of these six items have turned out not to be by Lewis after all: "The Dark Tower," "The Man Born Blind," and "Forms of Things Unknown."

54. *The Joyful Christian* (New York: Macmillan, 1977). Readings from the work of C. S. Lewis selected and produced by Henry William Griffin.

55. *They Stand Together* (London: Collins, 1979; New York: Macmillan). Over three hundred letters, mostly from C. S. Lewis to Arthur Greeves, edited by Walter Hooper. The letters span Lewis's life from 1914 to 1963. Knowledgable readers dismiss the attack upon Warren Lewis's character that comprises most of the ten-page preface.

56. *The Visionary Christian* (New York: Macmillan, 1981). Readings from the work of C. S. Lewis edited by Chad Walsh.

57. *On Stories, and Other Essays on Literature* (New York: Harcourt, 1982). Twenty essays, not all available before. "On Stories," "The Novels of Charles Williams," "A Tribute to E. R. Eddison," "On Three Ways of Writing for Children," "Sometimes Fairy Stories May Say Best What's To Be Said," "On Juvenile Tastes," "It All Began with a Picture," "On Science Fiction," "A Reply to Professor Haldane," "The Hobbit," "Tolkien's *The Lord of the Rings*," "A Panegyric for Dorothy L. Sayers," "The Mythopoeic Gift of Rider Haggard," "George Orwell," "The Death of Words," "The Parthenon and the Optative," "Period Criticism," "Different Tastes in Literature," "On Criticism," "Unreal Estates."

58. *The Grand Miracle, and Other Selected Essays on Theology and Ethics* (New York: Ballantine, 1982). Twenty-six items from *God in the Dock*. "Miracles," "Dogma and the Universe," "Answers to Questions on Christianity," "Myth Became Fact," "Horrid Red Things," "Religion and Science," "The Laws of Nature," "The Grand Miracle," "Christian Apologetics," "Work and Prayer," "Man or Rabbit?" "Religion without Dogma," "Some Thoughts," " The Trouble with X," "What Are We To Make of Jesus Christ?" "The Dangers of National Repentance," "Two Ways with the Self," "On the Reading of Old Books," "Scraps," "The Decline of Religion," "Vivisection," "Modern Translations of the Bible," "God in the Dock," "Cross Examination," "The Sermon and the Lunch," "What Christmas Means to Me."

59. *The Business of Heaven* (London: Collins, 1984; San Diego: Harcourt). Daily readings edited by Walter Hooper.

60. *Boxen: The Imaginary World of the Young C. S. Lewis* (London: Collins, 1985; San Diego: Harcourt). Bona fide Lewis juvenilia, burdened by questionable additions. (Illustrations for "The King's Ring" were by an adult, not by five-year-old Lewis, whose one authentic illustration for the play was omitted. "History of Animal Land" has faulty provenance, and the adult essay "Encyclopedia Boxonia" is evidently not by Lewis.)

61. *Letters to Children* (New York: Macmillan, 1985; London: Collins). All of C. S. Lewis's available surviving letters to children, edited by Lyle W. Dorsett and Majorie Lamp Mead.

62. *Present Concerns* (London: Collins Fount, 1986; San Diego: Harcourt Brace Jovanovich). Nineteen essays, one never before published, edited by Walter Hooper. "The Necessity of Chivalry," "Equality," "Three Kinds of Men," "My First School," "Is English Doomed?" "Democratic Education," "A Dream," "Blimpophobia," "Private Bates," "Hedonics," "After Priggery—What?" "Modern Man and His Categories of Thought," "Talking about Bicycles," "On Living in the Atomic Age," "The Empty Universe," "Prudery and Philology," "Interim Report," "Is History Bunk?" "Sex in Literature." (Parts of "Modern Man and His Categories of Thought" have been questioned.)

63. *First and Second Things: Essays on Theology and Ethics* (London: Collins Fount, 1985). Seventeen previously published essays on a variety of topics, edited by Walter Hooper. "Bulverism," "First and Second Things," "On the Reading of Old Books," "Horrid Red Things," "Work and Prayer," "Two Lectures," "Meditation in a Toolshed," "The Sermon and the Lunch," "On the Transmission of Christianity," "The Decline of Religion," "Vivisection," "Modern Translations of the Bible," "Some Thoughts," "The Humanitarian Theory of Punishment," "Xmas and Christmas," "Revival or Decay?" "Before We Can Communicate."

64. *Timeless at Heart: Essays on Theology* (London: Collins Fount, 1987), Ten previously published selections edited by Walter Hooper. "Christian Apologetics," "Answers to Questions on Christianity," "Why I Am Not a Pacifist," "The Pains of Animals," "The Founding of the Oxford Socratic Club," "Religion without Dogma?" "Is Theism Important?" "Rejoinder to Dr. Pittenger," "Willing Slaves of the Welfare State," "Letters."

65. *Letters, C. S. Lewis, Don Giovanni Calabria: A Study in Friendship* (Ann Arbor, Michigan: Servant Books, 1988). A brief correspondence in Latin between Don Calabria and C. S. Lewis (1947-54), and subsequent Lewis letters to Don Luigi Pedrollo (1954-61), translated into English and edited by Martin Moynihan. This is Lewis's ongoing response to a form letter from a Roman Catholic priest in Italy who had read *Screwtape* in Italian. It is not in Lewis's usual style because of constraints of language and culture. The letters appeared later as *Una Gioia Insolita Lettere tra un prete cattolico e un laico anglicano* (An Uncommon Joy: Letters between a Catholic priest and an Anglican layman.) by G. Calabria and C. S. Lewis (Milan: Editoriale Jaca, 1995). Introduction and notes by Luiciano Squizzato; translation from Latin into Italian by Patrizia Morelli; preface by Walter Hooper.

66. *The Essential C. S. Lewis* (New York: Macmillan, 1988). This 536-page collection of Lewis's previously published writing, edited by Lyle Dorsett, includes three complete books and a comprehensive sampling of briefer items.

67. *The Quotable Lewis* (Wheaton, Illinois: Tyndale House, 1989). An encyclopedic selection of brief quotations from the published works of C. S. Lewis, chosen by Wayne Martindale and Jerry Root.

68. *Christian Reunion and Other Essays* (London: Collins Fount, 1990). A new essay followed by eleven previously published essays, edited by Walter Hooper. "Christian Reunion,"

"Lilies that Fester," "Evil and God," "Dangers of National Repentance," "Two Ways with the Self," "Meditation on the Third Commandment," "Scraps," "Miserable Offenders," "Cross Examination," "Behind the Scenes," "What Christmas Means To Me," "Delinquents in the Snow." Unfortunately, the title essay has faulty provenance and the central 40 percent has been judged an editorial interpolation.

69. *All My Road before Me: The Diary of C. S. Lewis 1922-1927* (London: Collins Fount, 1991; Harcourt Brace Jovanovich). Lewis's off-and-on pre-Christian diary jottings, with a foreword by Owen Barfield; edited by Walter Hooper.

70. *Lewis: Readings for Meditation and Reflection* (London: Collins Fount, 1992; HarperSanFrancisco). First published in England as *Daily Readings with C. S. Lewis.* Eighty-two brief, previously-published passages, edited by Walter Hooper.

71. *The Collected Poems of C. S. Lewis* (London: Collins Fount, 1994). A compilation of *Spirits In Bondage* and *Poems*, with seventeen additional poems, edited by Walter Hooper. Although the introduction states that this single volume includes all Lewis's short poems, a few have been left out. The faulty revisions that first appeared in *Poems* (1964) are not corrected. Most of the penultimate poem, which is one of the longest, is not by Lewis. The belligerent new "Introductory Letter of 1963 by C. S. Lewis" lacks provenance.

Appendix 5

A Year with C. S. Lewis

We have one dozen books of C. S. Lewis's straight explanation and defense of the Christian faith. Here is the one-year reading schedule I propose.

January: Read *Mere Christianity*, the most popular of Lewis's books on theology. This is the book that received publicity for playing a large part in the conversion of Charles Colson.

February: During the month of Valentine's Day, read *The Four Loves*. In 1958 Lewis recorded a set of radio addresses about love for the Episcopal Church in the U. S. Then he added some material and published this book.

Although it is as orthodox as can be, this book was once listed among "Books for Spiritual Growth usually available at Metaphysical Book Shops," along with the autobiography of Paramahansa Yogananda, the teachings of Rosicrucianism, and other esoteric volumes. I say, let's get Lewis on any kind of reading lists we can.

March: For Easter, read *Miracles*. (Lewis says that the Christian story is precisely the story of one grand miracle.) This is a very involved analysis and defense of miracles.

It isn't all easy reading. That is why I was surprised to read that it figured in the conversion of an entertainer named Tommy Sands who used to be the husband of Nancy Sinatra.

April: Tackle *The Abolition of Man*. It was Lewis's favorite of all his books in this category. If you have run into the behavioral psychologist B. F. Skinner and his best seller *Beyond Freedom and Dignity*, you will find in this book a helpful alternative view. This is a profound little volume about human values.

May: Read *The Weight of Glory* —a wonderful collection of sermons and Christian talks that Lewis gave in the 1940s. Some Lewis readers say that the sermon "The Weight of Glory" is their favorite of all his writing.

June: Read the last book that Lewis ever wrote, unless he is writing more now to surprise us in heaven. That book is *Letters to Malcolm: Chiefly on Prayer* —a series of fictitious letters to a close friend in which Lewis shares his personal beliefs about prayer.

July: Read *The Problem of Pain*, which, in 1940, was the first book of straight apologetics that Lewis wrote. He wrote it in answer to a request; we can all be very grateful to the man who made the request!

August: Relax with *Reflections on the Psalms*. Lewis wrote this after helping the Anglican Church with a new translation of the Psalms, which he worked on with T. S. Eliot.

September: Read the seven essays in Lewis's book *The World's Last Night*. As you can guess, the title essay is about the coming return of Christ. If you are interested in eschatology, this essay is for you; if you are not, this essay is for you.

October: Read the fourteen essays in Lewis's book *Christian Reflections*. The last one is a Christian view of space exploration.

November: Give thanks as you read the forty-eight essays and twelve letters in *God in the Dock*. It is a gold mine.

It includes the only two Lewis essays that I have ever heard well argued against—one on the treatment of juvenile delinquents and one on the ordination of women to the priesthood.

It is in this collection that Lewis writes against the commercialization of Christmas and the dreadful busyness of that season.

December: In the last month, you may be too tired or busy to read much. That is the time for Lewis's little collection of essays *Fern-seed and Elephants*.

It includes eight essays, but you will have read seven of them already; the only new one is on forgiveness, and it is easily worth the price of the book.

Then in January you might as well start the cycle again because you will get so much more the second time around!

Appendix 6

C. S. Lewis and Christmas

Our earliest description of Christmas from C. S. Lewis is a bitter one. The year was 1922. As usual, C. S. Lewis and his brother Warren spent the holidays with their widowed father in his big house outside Belfast.

"It was a dark morning with a gale blowing and some very cold rain," Lewis reported in his diary. Their father Albert awakened his two sons, both in their midtwenties, to go to early Communion service. As they walked to church in the dawn light, they started discussing the time of sunrise. Albert irritated his sons by insisting that the sun had already risen or else they would not have any light. He was an illogical and argumentative man.

Saint Mark's Church was intensely cold. Warren wanted to keep his coat on during the service, and his father disapproved. "Well, at least you won't keep it on when you go up to the Table," Albert warned. Warren asked why not and was told that taking Communion with a coat on was "most disrespectful." Warren took his coat off to avoid an argument. Not one of the

First published in *Christianity Today*, 16 December 1983.

three Lewis men had any interest in the meaning of Communion. The two sons hadn't believed in Christianity for years.

"Christmas dinner, a rather deplorable ceremony, at quarter to four," Lewis continued in his diary. After dinner the rain had stopped at last, and Albert urged his two sons to take a walk. They were delighted to get out into the fresh air and head for a pub where they could get a drink. Before they came to the pub, however, some relatives drove by on the way to their house for a visit and gave them an unwelcome ride right back home.

After too much sitting and talking and eating and smoking all day in the stuffy house, Lewis went to bed early, dead tired and headachy. He felt like a flabby, lazy teenager again. It had been another bad Christmas.

In 1929 Albert Lewis suddenly died of cancer. There would be no more coming home for Christmas. Within a couple of years of their father's death, both Warren and C. S. Lewis privately made some major shifts in their ideas about religion. They were separately moving toward Christian faith.

It was 1931. In Shanghai, where he was serving as a British military officer, Warren got up at 6:30 on Christmas morning. There was bright sun, frost on the ground, and what Warren called a faint keen wind. For the first time in many years Warren went to church to take Communion. He was deeply excited about it.

Warren couldn't help thinking about the old days when he had attended Christmas Communion at home in Ireland. "The kafuffle of the early start, the hurried walk in the chill half light, Barton's beautiful voice, the dim lights of Saint Mark's and then the return home to the Gargantuan breakfast—how jolly it all seems in retrospect!" It hadn't seemed jolly at the time. Warren felt great sorrow about the past, but his sorrow was outweighed by gladness and thanks that he was once again a believer in the Christmas story.

On that very day, Christmas of 1931, C. S. Lewis sat down in Oxford to write an eight-page letter to Warren. He began by warning that because of his teaching duties he had done, read, and heard nothing for a long time that could possibly interest Warren. Then he proceded to write one of his usual entertaining letters full of humor and ideas and bits of news. In the middle of the letter he mentioned that it was a foggy afternoon, but that it had seemed springlike early that morning as he went to the Communion service. That is how he admitted the big news that he had taken Communion for the first time in many years.

At that point in the letter, C. S. Lewis recounted a couple of things he had heard in recent sermons. In a sermon on foreign missions the preacher had said, "Many of us have friends who used to live abroad, and had a native Christian cook who was unsatisfactory. Well, after all, there are a great many unsatisfactory Christians in England too. In fact I'm one myself." In a different sermon, that preacher had declared that if early Christians had known they were founding an organization to last for centuries, they would have organized it to death. But because they believed that they were making provisional arrangements for a year or so, they left it free to live. Lewis thought that was an interesting idea.

A neighbor had remarked shortly before Christmas that he objected to the early chapters of Luke, especially the story of the Annunciation, because they were *indelicate*. Such prudery left Lewis gasping.

That Christmas letter from C. S. Lewis found its way to Warren on January 19, 1932, and he wrote in his diary, "A letter . . . today containing the news that he too has once more started to go to Communion, at which I am delighted." Had he not done so, Warren reflected, they would not have been quite so close in the future as in the past.

From 1931 to the end of his life, C. S. Lewis looked at Christmas from a Christian point of view. In 1939 Warren was on duty away from home again, and on Christmas Eve C. S. Lewis wrote that he had been thinking much that week about Christmas cards. Aside from the absurdity of celebrating the nativity at all if you don't believe in the Incarnation, "what in heaven's name is the idea of everyone sending everyone else pictures of stagecoaches, fairies, foxes, dogs, butterflies, kittens, flowers, etc.?"

Warming to his topic, Lewis asked his brother to imagine a Chinese man sitting at a table covered with small pictures. The man explains that he is preparing for the anniversary of Buddha's being protected by the dragons. Not that he personally believes that this is the real anniversary of the event or even that it really happened. He is just keeping up the old custom. Not that he has any pictures of Buddha or of the dragons. He doesn't like that kind. He says, "Here's one of a traction engine for Hu Flung Dung, and I'm sending this study of a napkin-ring to Lo Hung Git, and these jolly ones of bluebottles are for the children."

Aside from thinking about Christmas cards, Lewis had enjoyed himself in two ways that week. He was back at work on his book *The Problem of Pain*, and he was able to enjoy good winter walks. The pond on his property had a thin skin of ice. The beautiful frozen days had been of two kinds: "those with bright yellow suns, turning at sunset to red cannon balls, and those with deep dark-grey fog through which the ridges of the grass loom up white." Near the end of his letter he said, "Well, Brother, (as the troops say) it's a sad business not to have you with me tomorrow morning. . . ." That meant church.

During World War II C. S. Lewis gave a series of talks about Christianity on BBC radio, and later he brought these out as his book *Mere Christianity*. There Lewis summed up Christmas and Christianity in one memorable sentence: "The Son of God became a man to enable men to become the sons of God."

In his 1950 book for children, *The Lion, the Witch and the Wardrobe*, Lewis made it clear that he was all for merry times and good gifts and Christmas pudding. The land of Narnia was under the spell of a wicked white witch who made it always winter and never Christmas. When the great gold lion Aslan brought the thaw that spelled her doom, Father Christmas came at last.

In 1954 Lewis published a very different kind of fantasy about Christmas, "Xmas and Christmas." It is an essay about the strange island called Niatirb (Britain spelled backwards) and the winter festival called Exmas that the Niatirbians observe with great patience and endurance.

One of the customs that fills the marketplace with crowds during the foggiest and rainiest season of the year is the great labor and weariness of sending cards and gifts. Every citizen has to guess the value of the gift that every friend will send him so that he may send one of equal value whether he can afford it or not. Everyone becomes so pale and weary that it looks as if calamity has struck. These days are called the Exmas *Rush*. Exhausted with the *Rush*, most citizens lie in bed until noon on the day of the festival. Later that day they eat far too much and get intoxicated. On the day after Exmas they are very grave because they feel unwell and begin to calculate how much they have spent on Exmas and the *Rush*.

There is also a festival in Niatirb called Crissmas, held on the same day as Exmas. A few people in Niatirb keep Crissmas sacred, but they are greatly distracted by Exmas and the *Rush*.

On December 17, 1955, Lewis wrote to an old friend that he was pleased by the card the man had sent him, a Japanese-style nativity scene. But, he continued, Christmas cards in general and the whole vast commercial drive called "Xmas" was one of his pet abominations. He wished they would die away and leave the Christmas observance alone. He had nothing against secular festivities. But he despised the artificial jollity, the artificial childlikeness, and the attempts to keep up some shallow connection with the birth of Christ.

In 1957 C. S. Lewis published "What Christmas Means to Me." He claimed that three things go by the name of Christmas. First is the religious festival. Second is an occasion for merry-making and hospitality. Third is the commercial racket, a modern invention to boost sales. He listed his reasons for condemning the commercial racket. First, it causes more pain than pleasure. Second, it is a trap made up of obligations. Third, many of the purchases are gaudy rubbish. Fourth, we get exhausted by having to support the commercial racket while carrying on all our regular duties as well. "Can it really be my duty to buy and receive masses of junk every winter . . . ?" Lewis demanded plaintively.

Two years later C. S. Lewis was featured in the Christmas issue of the *Saturday Evening Post*. The issue, dated December 19, 1959, bore on its cover a fifteen-cent price, a picture of a man struggling clumsily to get a package wrapped, and the announcement of a new Screwtape letter by C. S. Lewis. Inside was a life-size, close-up photo of Lewis's face and his essay "Screwtape Proposes a Toast." This was a kind of Christmas gift to the public from the editors.

In 1963 the *Saturday Evening Post* featured C. S. Lewis in its Christmas issue for the second time. This time the price on the cover was twenty cents and the picture on the cover was of a children's choir. Inside was Lewis's article "We Have No 'Right to Happiness'" with the heading "Is happiness—in particular sexual happiness—one of man's inalienable rights? A distinguished author attacks the brutality of this increasingly common notion." In the upper right-hand corner is the announcement, "As this article went to press, its author died at his home in Oxford, England. The article is his last work."

Since Lewis's death on November 22, 1963, a number of his writings from earlier years have become more widely available. A few not published at all in his lifetime have now found their way into print. One of these is his undated poem "The Nativity," available in his book *Poems*. In this brief poem Lewis shows what the nativity scene meant in his own prayer life.

First, Lewis likens himself to a slow, dull ox. Along with the oxen he sees the glory growing in the stable, he says, and he hopes that it will give him, at length, an ox's strength. Second, Lewis likens himself to a stubborn and foolish ass. Along with the asses he sees the Savior in the hay, and he hopes that he will learn the patience of an ass. Third, Lewis likens himself to a strayed and bleating sheep. Along with the sheep in the stable he watches his Lord lying in the manger. From his Lord he hopes to gain some of a sheep's woolly innocence.

One of the earliest photos of C. S. Lewis shows him as a very little boy posed with a Father Christmas doll. The half-smile caught forever on his plump young face seems balanced between anxiety and pleasure. He looks thoughtfully attentive. It is fitting, because he half-smiled at Christmas the rest of his days. We might do well to pause in the "kafuffle" and "Exmas *Rush*" and look into the manger with C. S. Lewis.

Index